Foundation Biology

Dennis Taylor and **Mary Jones**

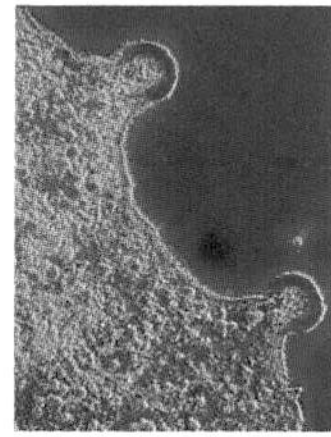

Series editor
Fred Webber

Consultant editors
John Raffan
Michael Reiss

CAMBRIDGE
UNIVERSITY PRESS

Published by the Press Syndicate of the University of Cambridge
The Pitt Building, Trumpington Street, Cambridge CB2 1RP
40 West 20th Street, New York, NY 10011–4211, USA
10 Stamford Road, Oakleigh, Melbourne 3166, Australia

First published 1994

Printed in Great Britain at the University Press, Cambridge

A catalogue record for this book is available from the British Library

ISBN 0 521 421993 paperback

Designed and produced by Gecko Ltd, Bicester, Oxon

This book is one of a series produced to support individual modules within the Cambridge Modular Sciences scheme. Teachers should note that written examinations will be set on the content of each module as defined in the syllabus. This book is the authors' interpretation of the module.

Cover: Transmission electron micrograph of HIV virus budding from the surface of an infected T-lymphocyte. (Institut Pasteur/CNRI/Science Photo Library)

Contents

Introduction

This book is for anyone beginning their study of advanced level biology. It is an essential basis for further studies in biology. When you have completed this module, you should have acquired an understanding of some of the fundamental concepts and facts which you will need throughout the rest of your A or AS level course. You will meet these concepts again and again, so it is very important that you understand them thoroughly, and learn them, right at the beginning of your course.

Chapters 1 and 2 deal with the structure and functions of the basic unit of all living things, the cell.

Chapters 3 and 4 deal with some of the most important molecules which make up living organisms, beginning your study of the branch of biology called biochemistry. You will need a reasonable understanding of chemistry here; if you have a GCSE qualification in science or chemistry, you should have no problems, but be prepared to look up any basic ideas of which you are unsure in a GCSE textbook.

Chapter 5 brings together the topics of cell structure and biochemistry, with a detailed look at cell membranes.

Finally, chapter 6 brings together concepts from all the previous sections of the book – cells, biochemistry (including enzymes) and cell membranes – to give you an introduction to the ways in which cells communicate with one another, and how a complex organism such as a mammal can control its internal environment.

Throughout the book, you will find questions. Most of these need only short answers, and by doing them you can check your understanding of what you have just read. You will find answers to them on pages 89–91. At the end of each chapter there are one or two questions which need longer answers. They often require you to pull together several different ideas covered within the chapter, so are an excellent test of your overall understanding of the topic. You could use these as the basis for discussion or write brief notes on them or full answers.

This book serves as an introduction to any advanced level biology course. In particular it covers the foundation module of the University of Cambridge Local Examinations Syndicate A level modular syllabuses for biology and social biology, and also about one third of the core syllabus for the UCLES linear syllabuses for biology and social biology.

Acknowledgements

1, from *Hooke: Micrographia*, London, 1655, f.p. 115/Wellcome Institute Library, London; 2*b*, 10*cl*, 10*bl*, 11, 13, 16, 17, 18, 19, 24, 26, 28, 39 (background), 39, 47*l*, 69, 70, 76, 83, 85, Biophoto Associates; 6, 8*b*, A. M. Page, Royal Holloway University of London; 7, 49, Claude Nuridsany & Marie Perennou/Science Photo Library; 10*tl*, Ron Boardman/Life Science Images; 10*tr*, Dr Don Fawcett/Science Photo Library; 10*br*, Bill Longcore/Science Photo Library; 11*l*, Dr Gopal Murti/Science Photo Library; 14*b*, 47*r*, David Scharf/Science Photo Library; 15, Philippe Plailly/Science Photo Library; 17*c*, Astrid & Hanns-Frieder Michler/Science Photo Library; 25, M. Hirons/GeoScience Features; 30, James Stevenson/Science Photo Library; 31*t*, Nina Lampen/Science Photo Library; 31*b*, Science Photo Library; 34, Dr Jeremy Burgess/Science Photo Library; 37, CNRI/Science Photo Library; 40*b*, Peter Gould; 41*t*, Robert Erwin/Natural History Photographic Agency; 43, Dr Arthur Lesk/Science Photo Library; 46, Dr Tony Brain/Science Photo Library; 56, JH Robinson/Science Photo Library; 65, Clara Franzini Armstrong/Science Photo Library; 73, St Bartholomew's Hospital/Science Photo Library; 81, GeoScience Features

Cell structure

By the end of this chapter you should be able to:

1 describe and interpret drawings and photographs of typical animal and plant cells as seen under the light microscope;

2 explain the meanings of, and distinguish between, the terms resolution and magnification;

3 describe and interpret drawings and photographs of typical animal and plant cells as seen under the electron microscope, recognising rough and smooth ER, Golgi apparatus, mitochondria, ribosomes, lysosomes, chloroplasts, cell surface membrane, centrioles and the nucleus, including the nuclear envelope and nucleolus;

4 outline the functions of the membrane systems and organelles listed in 3;

5 list the characteristics of a eukaryotic cell;

6 compare and contrast the structure of generalised animal and plant cells;

7 explain, with examples in animals and plants, the meaning of the terms tissue and organ;

8 describe the structure of a prokaryotic cell, and compare and contrast the structure of prokaryotic cells with eukaryotic cells.

The concept of the cell

In the early days of microscopy an English scientist, Robert Hooke, decided to examine thin slices of plant material and chose cork as one of his examples. On looking down the microscope he was struck by the regular appearance of the structure and in 1665 he wrote a book containing the diagram shown in *figure 1.1*.

If you examine the diagram you will see the 'pore-like' regular structures that he called 'cells'. Each cell appeared to be an empty box surrounded by a wall. Hooke had discovered and described, without realising it, the fundamental unit of *all* living things. Although we now know that the cells of cork are dead, further observations of cells in living materials were made by Hooke and other

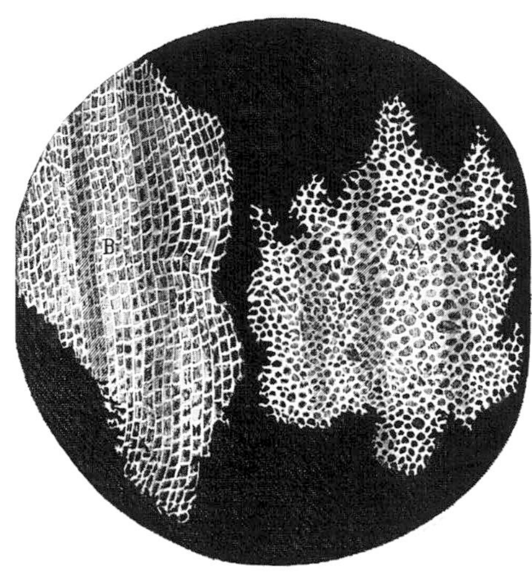

● ***Figure 1.1*** Drawing of cork cells published by Robert Hooke in 1665.

scientists. However, it was not until almost 200 years later that a general cell theory emerged from the work of two German scientists. In 1838 Schleiden, a botanist, suggested that all plants are made of cells, and a year later Schwann, a zoologist, suggested the same for animals.The **cell theory** states that **the basic unit of structure and function of all living organisms is the cell.** Now, over 150 years later, this idea is one of the most familiar and important theories in biology. To it has been added Virchow's theory of 1855 that **all cells arise from pre-existing cells by cell division.**

Why cells?

A cell can be thought of as a bag in which the chemistry of life is allowed to occur, partially separated from the environment outside the cell. The thin membrane which surrounds all cells is essential in controlling exchange between the cell and its environment. It is a very effective barrier, but also allows a controlled traffic of materials across it in both directions. The membrane is therefore described as **partially permeable.** If it were **freely permeable,** life could not exist because the chemicals of the cell would simply mix with the surrounding chemicals by diffusion.

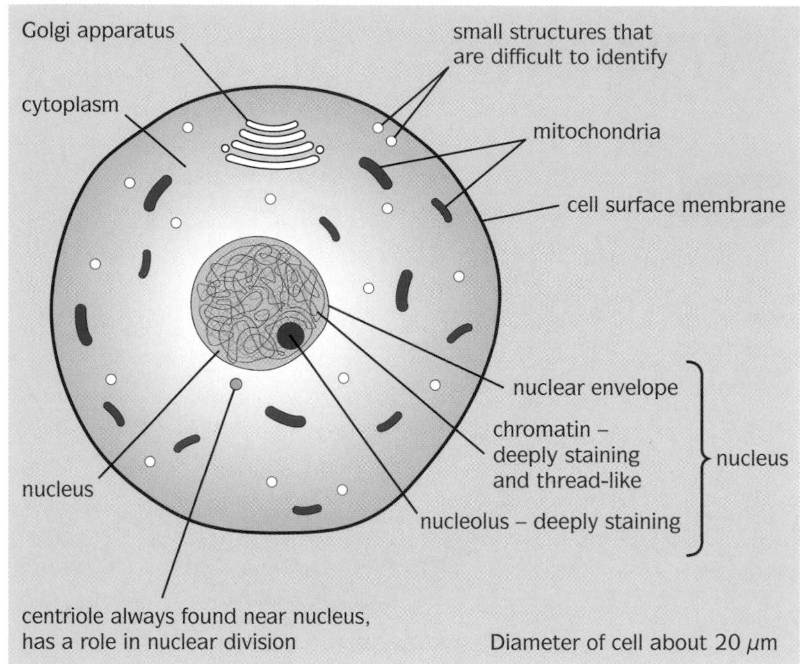

● ***Figure 1.2*** Structure of a generalised animal cell as seen with a very high quality light microscope.

Cell biology and microscopy

The study of cells has given rise to an important branch of biology known as **cell biology**. Cells can now be studied by many different methods, but scientists began simply by looking at them, using various types of microscope.

There are two fundamentally different types of microscope now in use, the light microscope and the electron microscope. Both use a form of radiation in order to create an image of the specimen being examined. The light microscope uses **light** as a source of radiation, while the electron microscope, developed during the 1930s and 1940s, uses **electrons**, for reasons which are discussed later.

Light microscopy

The 'golden age' of light microscopy could be said to be the nineteenth century. Microscopes had been available since the beginning of the seventeenth century, but when dramatic improvements were made in the quality of glass lenses in the early nineteenth century interest among scientists became widespread. The fascination of the microscopic world that opened up in biology inspired rapid progress, both in microscope design and, equally importantly, in preparing material for examination with microscopes. This branch of biology is known as **cytology**. By 1900, all the structures shown in *figures 1.2, 1.3* and *1.4,* except lysosomes, had been discovered.

Figure 1.2 shows the structure of a generalised animal cell and *figure 1.4* the structure of a generalised plant cell as seen with a light microscope. (A generalised cell shows *all* the structures that are typically found in a cell.)

SAQ 1.1

Using *figures 1.2* and *1.4*, which structures do animal and plant cells have in common and which are special only to animal or plant cells?

Animal and plant cells have features in common

In animals and plants each cell is surrounded by a very thin, **cell surface membrane** which is too thin to be seen with a light microscope. Each cell has a **nucleus** which is a relatively large structure that stains intensely with the appropriate stains, and is therefore very conspicuous. The deeply stained material in the nucleus is called **chromatin** and is a mass of loosely coiled threads. This material collects together to form visible separate chromosomes

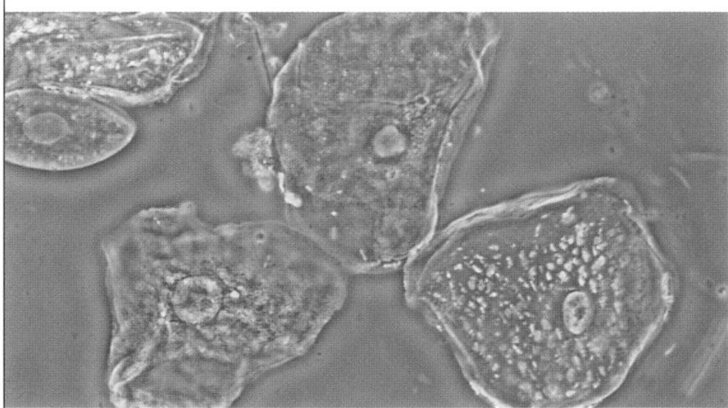

● ***Figure 1.3*** Cells from the lining of the human cheek (×400), showing typical animal cell characteristics: a centrally placed nucleus and many organelles such as mitochondria. The cells are part of a tissue known as squamous (flattened) epithelium.

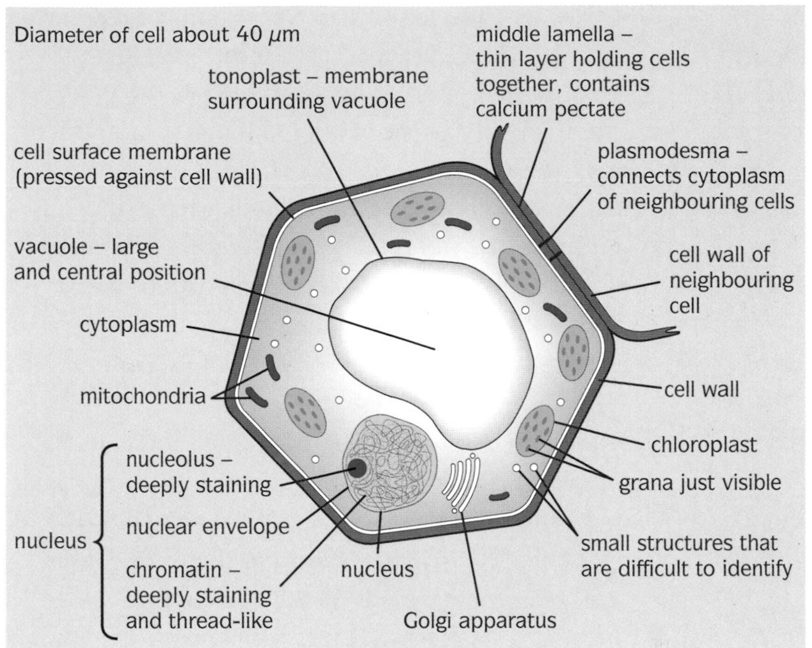

● ***Figure 1.4*** Structure of a generalised plant cell as seen with a very high quality light microscope.

during nuclear division (see page 19). It contains **DNA (deoxyribonucleic acid)**, a molecule which contains the instructions that control the activities of the cell. Within the nucleus an even more deeply staining area is visible, the **nucleolus**, which is made of loops of DNA from several chromosomes.

The material between the nucleus and the cell surface membrane is known as **cytoplasm**. Cytoplasm is an aqueous (watery) material, varying in consistency from fluid to jelly-like. Many small structures can be seen within it. These have been likened to small organs and hence are known as **organelles**. An organelle can be defined as **a functionally and structurally distinct part of a cell.** Organelles are often surrounded by membranes so that their activities can be separated from the surrounding cytoplasm. This is described as **compartmentation.** Having separate compartments is essential for a structure as complex as a cell to work efficiently. Since each type of organelle has its own function, the cell is said to show **division of labour**, a sharing of the work between different specialised organelles.

The most numerous organelles seen with the light microscope are usually **mitochondria** (singular mitochondrion). They are only just visible, but extraordinary films of living cells, taken with the aid of a light microscope, have shown that they can move about, change shape and divide. They are specialised to carry out aerobic respiration.

The use of special stains containing silver enabled the **Golgi apparatus** to be detected for the first time in 1898 by Camillo Golgi. The Golgi apparatus is part of a complex internal sorting and distribution system within the cell.

Differences between animal and plant cells

The only structure commonly found in animal cells which is absent from plant cells is the **centriole**. Under the microscope it appears as a small structure close to the nucleus (*figure 1.2*). It is involved in nuclear division (see page 23).

Individual plant cells are more easily seen with a light microscope than are animal cells because they are usually larger and surrounded by a wall. They possess a number of structures not found in animal cells. For example they are surrounded by a relatively rigid **cell wall** outside the cell surface membrane. The cell wall gives the cell a definite shape. It prevents the cell from bursting when water enters by osmosis, allowing large pressures to develop inside the cell (see page 64). Cell walls may also be reinforced for extra strength. Plant cells are linked to neighbouring cells by means of fine strands of cytoplasm called **plasmodesmata** (singular plasmodesma) which pass through pore-like structures in the walls of these neighbouring cells. Movement through the pores is thought to be controlled by their structure.

Apart from a cell wall, mature plant cells differ from animal cells in often possessing a large **central vacuole** and, if the cell carries out photosynthesis, in containing **chloroplasts**. The vacuole is surrounded by a membrane, the **tonoplast**, which controls exchange between the vacuole and the cytoplasm. The fluid in the vacuole is a solution of mineral salts, sugars, oxygen, carbon dioxide, pigments, enzymes and other organic compounds, including some waste products. Vacuoles help to regulate the osmotic properties of cells as well as having a wide range of other functions. For example, the pigments which colour the petals of certain flowers and parts of some vegetables, such as the red pigment of beetroots, are sometimes located in vacuoles.

Chloroplasts are relatively large organelles which are green in colour due to the presence of chlorophyll. At high magnifications small 'grains', or **grana**, can be seen in them. (The grana, in fact, consist of stacks of membranes.) During the process of photosynthesis light is absorbed by these grana. Starch grains may also be visible within chloroplasts. Chloroplasts are found in the green parts of the plant, mainly in the leaves.

Points to note

- You can think of a plant cell as being very similar to an animal cell but with extra structures.
- Plant cells are often larger than animal cells, although cell size varies enormously.
- Do not confuse the cell *wall* with the cell surface *membrane*. Cell walls are relatively thick and physically strong, whereas cell membranes are very thin. *All* cells have a cell surface membrane.
- Vacuoles are not confined to plant cells; animal cells may have small vacuoles, such as phagocytic vacuoles (page 65), although these are often not permanent.

We return to the differences between animal and plant cells as seen through the electron microscope on page 8.

Units of measurement in cell studies

In order to measure objects in the microscopic world, we need to use very small units of measurement which are unfamiliar to most people. According to international agreement, the International System of Units (SI units) should be used. In this system the basic unit of length is the **metre**, symbol **m**. Additional units can be added in multiples of a thousand, using standard prefixes. For example, the prefix **kilo** means **1000** times. Thus 1 kilometre = 1000 metres. The units of length relevant to cell studies are shown in *table 1.1*.

It is difficult to imagine how small these units are, but it is worth thinking about. Otherwise it is easy to forget, when looking down a microscope and seeing cells clearly, how amazingly small the cells are. *Figure 1.5* shows the sizes of some structures. The smallest structure visible with the human eye is about 50–100 μm in diameter. Your body contains about 60 million million cells, varying in size from about 5–20 μm. Try to imagine structures like mitochondria, which have an average diameter of 1 μm, or bacteria with an average diameter of 0.5 μm. The smallest cell organelles we deal with in this book, ribosomes, are only about 20 nm in diameter! When we consider processes such as diffusion, it is also helpful to have an appreciation of what distances are involved.

Electron microscopes

Earlier in this chapter it was stated that by 1900 almost all the structures shown in *figures 1.2* and *1.4* had been discovered. There followed a time of frustration for microscopists because they realised that no matter how much the design of light microscopes improved, there was a limit to how much could ever be seen using light.

Fraction of a metre	*Length*	*Symbol*
one thousandth = 0.001 = 1/1 000 = 10^{-3}	millimetre	mm
one millionth = 0.000 001 = 1/1 000 000 = 10^{-6}	micrometre	μm*
one thousand millionth = 0.000 000 001 = 1/1 000 000 000 = 10^{-9}	nanometre	nm

* μ is the Greek letter mu

Note: 1 micrometre is a thousandth of a millimetre
1 nanometre is a thousandth of a micrometre

● ***Table 1.1*** Units of measurement relevant to cell studies

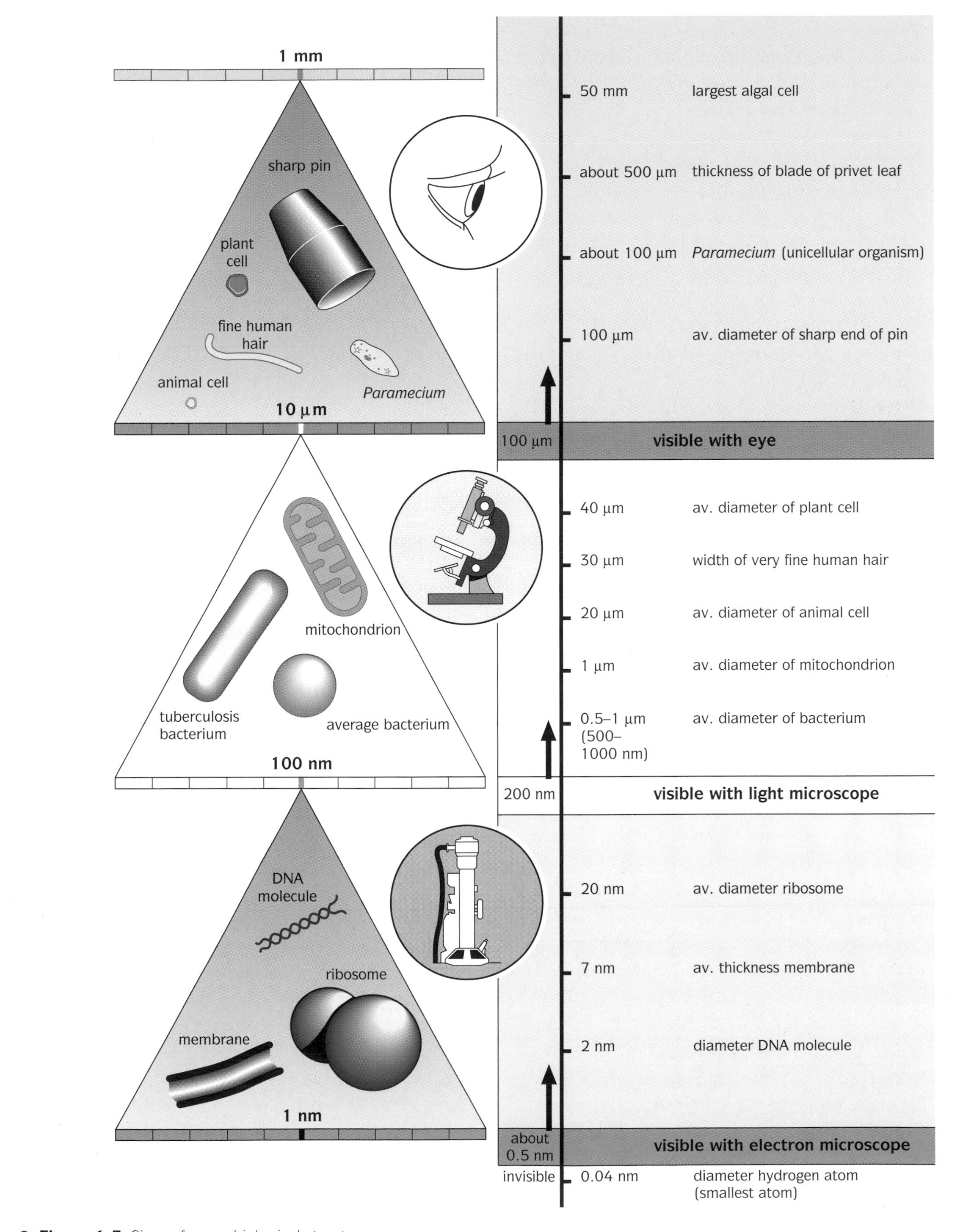

● ***Figure 1.5*** Sizes of some biological structures.

In order to understand the problem, it is necessary to know something about the nature of light itself and to understand the difference between **magnification** and **resolution**.

Magnification and resolution

This difference can be well illustrated by means of photographs. *Figure 1.6* shows two sections from the same plant cell, one viewed with a light microscope, and one with an electron microscope. The important thing to note is that both pictures are shown at the **same magnification**. Look at the pictures. Decide which one you think is clearer and shows more detail.

There is little doubt that the electron micrograph is much clearer. (An electron micrograph is a picture taken with an electron microscope.) This is because it has greater resolution. **Resolution** is defined as the ability to distinguish between two separate points. If the two points cannot be resolved, they will be seen as one point. The maximum resolution of a light microscope is 200 nm. This means that if two points or objects are closer together than 200 nm they cannot be distinguished as separate. A good example of this is provided by centrioles (see page 9).

It is possible to take a photograph such as *figure 1.6a* and to magnify (enlarge) it, but we see no more **detail**; in other words, we do not improve resolution, even though we often enlarge photographs because they are easier to see when larger. Thus an increase in magnification is not necessarily accompanied by an increase in resolution. With a microscope, magnification up to the limit of resolution can reveal further detail, but any further magnification increases blurring as well as the size of the picture.

The electromagnetic spectrum

How is resolution linked with the nature of light? One of the properties of light is that it travels in waves. The length of the waves of visible light varies, ranging from about 400 nm (violet light) to about 700 nm (red light). The human eye can distinguish between these different wavelengths, and in the brain the differences are converted to

a

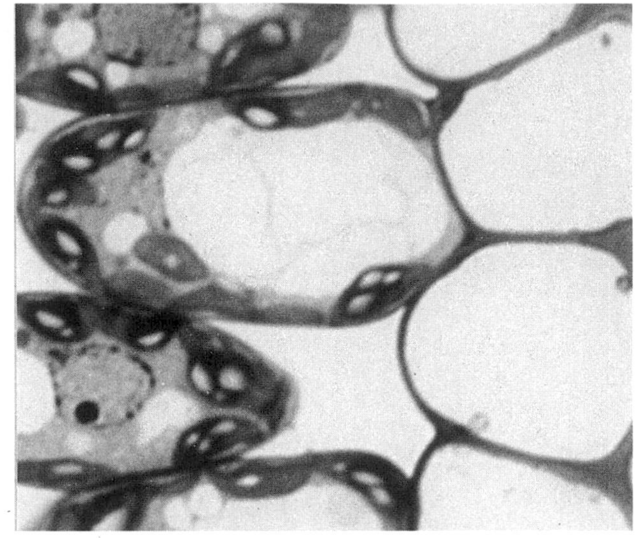

b

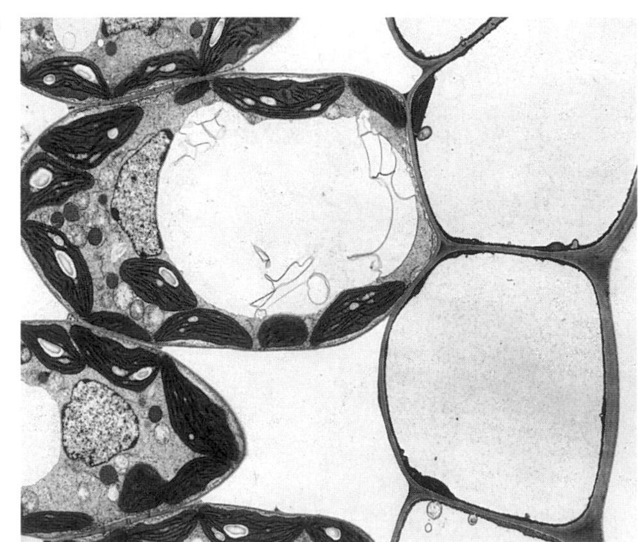

● ***Figure 1.6*** Photographs of the same plant cells seen **a** with a light microscope, **b** with an electron microscope, both shown at a magnification of about ×2500.

colour differences. (Colour is an invention of the brain!) Some animals can see wavelengths that humans cannot. Bees, for example, can see ultraviolet light. Flowers that to us do not appear to have markings often have ultraviolet markings that guide bees to their nectaries *(figure 1.7)*. If you happen to be sharing a dark room with a cobra, the cobra will be able to see *you*, even though you cannot see *it*, because warm bodies give off (radiate) infrared radiation which cobras can see.

The whole range of different wavelengths is called the electromagnetic spectrum. Visible light is only one part of this spectrum, from about 400–700 nm. *Figure 1.8* shows some of the parts of the electromagnetic spectrum. The longer the electromagnetic waves, the lower their frequency (all the waves travel at the same speed, so imagine them passing a post: shorter waves pass at higher frequency).

In theory, there is no limit to how short or how long the waves can be. Wavelength changes with energy: the greater the energy, the shorter the wavelength (rather like squashing a spring!). Now look at *figure 1.9* which shows a mitochondrion, some very small cell organelles called ribosomes (see page 9) and light of 400 nm wavelength, the shortest visible wavelength. The mitochondrion is large enough to interfere with the light waves. However, the ribosomes are far too small to have any effect on the light waves. **The general rule is that the limit of resolution is about one half the wavelength of the radiation used to view the specimen.** In other words, if an object is any smaller than half the wavelength of the radiation used to view it, it cannot be seen separately from nearby objects. This means that the best resolution that can be obtained using a microscope that uses visible light (a light microscope) is 200 nm, since the shortest wavelength of visible light is 400 nm (violet light). In practice, this corresponds to a maximum useful magnification of about 1500 times. Ribosomes can therefore never be seen using light.

If an object is transparent it will allow light waves to pass through it and therefore will still not be visible. This is why many biological structures have to be stained before they can be seen.

● ***Figure 1.7*** In normal light, the nectar guides of the *Potentilla* flower cannot be seen by the human eye. In ultraviolet, they appear as dark patches. The eye of a bee is sensitive to ultraviolet light and can see the guides which lead to the nectaries at the centre of the flower.

The electron microscope

Biologists, faced with the problem that they would never see anything smaller than 200 nm using a light microscope, realised that the only solution would be to use radiation of a shorter wavelength than light. If you study *figure 1.8*, you will see that ultraviolet light, or better still X-rays, look like possible candidates. Both ultraviolet and X-ray

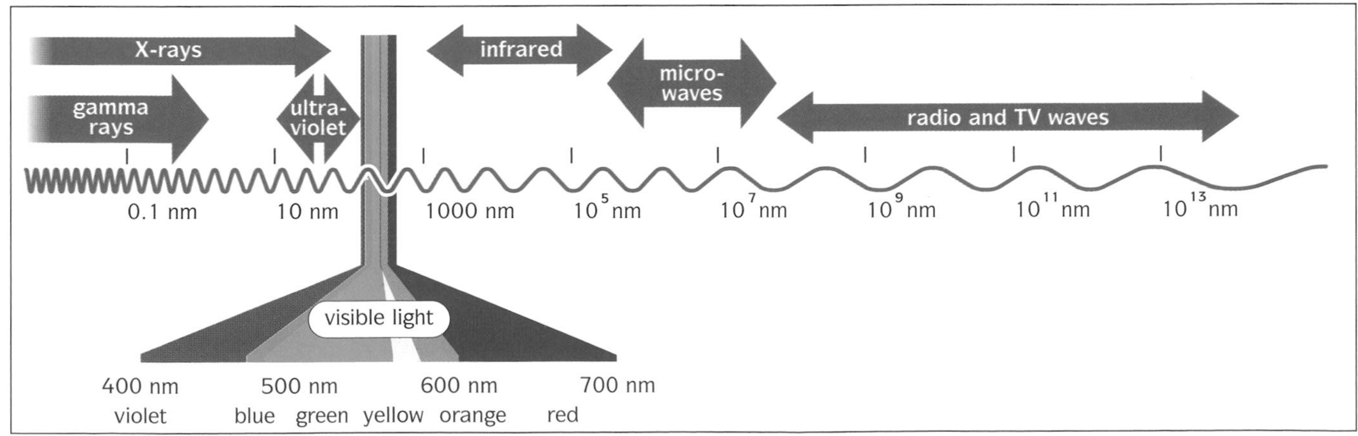

● ***Figure 1.8*** Diagram of the electromagnetic spectrum (NB the waves are not drawn to scale). Light is a form of electromagnetic radiation.

microscopes have been built, the latter with little success partly because of the difficulty of focussing X-rays. A much better solution is to use electrons. **Electrons** are negatively charged particles which orbit the nucleus of an atom. When a metal becomes very hot, some electrons gain so much energy that they escape from their orbits, like a rocket escaping from Earth's gravity. Free electrons behave like electromagnetic radiation. They have a very short wavelength: the greater the energy, the shorter the wavelength. Electrons are a very suitable form of radiation for microscopy for two major reasons. Firstly, their wavelength is extremely short (at least as short as that of X-rays); secondly, because they are negatively charged, they can be focussed easily using electromagnets (the magnet can be made to alter the path of the beam, the equivalent of a glass lens bending light).

Electron microscopes were developed during the 1930s and 1940s but it was not until after the Second World War that techniques improved enough to allow cells to be studied with the electron microscope.

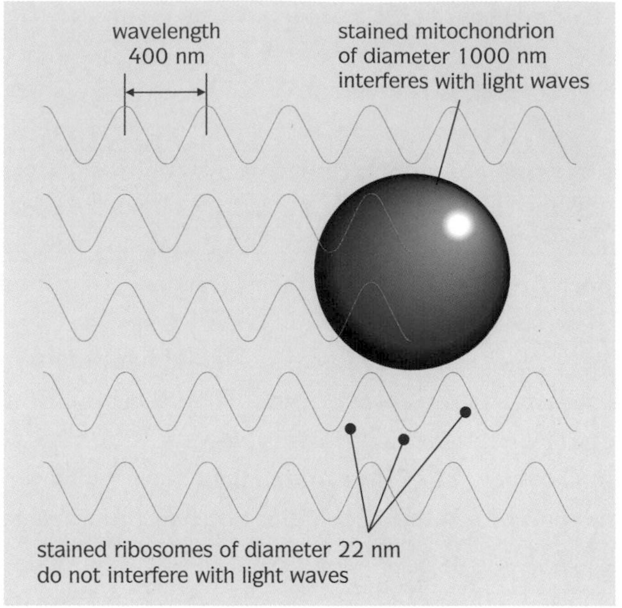

● ***Figure 1.9*** A mitochondrion and some ribosomes in the path of light waves of 400 nm length.

Ultrastructure of an animal cell

The 'fine' structure, or detailed structure, of a cell as revealed by the electron microscope is called its **ultrastructure**. *Figure 1.10* shows the appearance of a typical animal cell as seen with an electron microscope and *figure 1.11* is a diagram based on such a micrograph. The example used is a rat liver cell because liver cells are very active and contain all the common animal cell organelles. They store a lot of glycogen which can be converted to glucose when necessary (page 70).

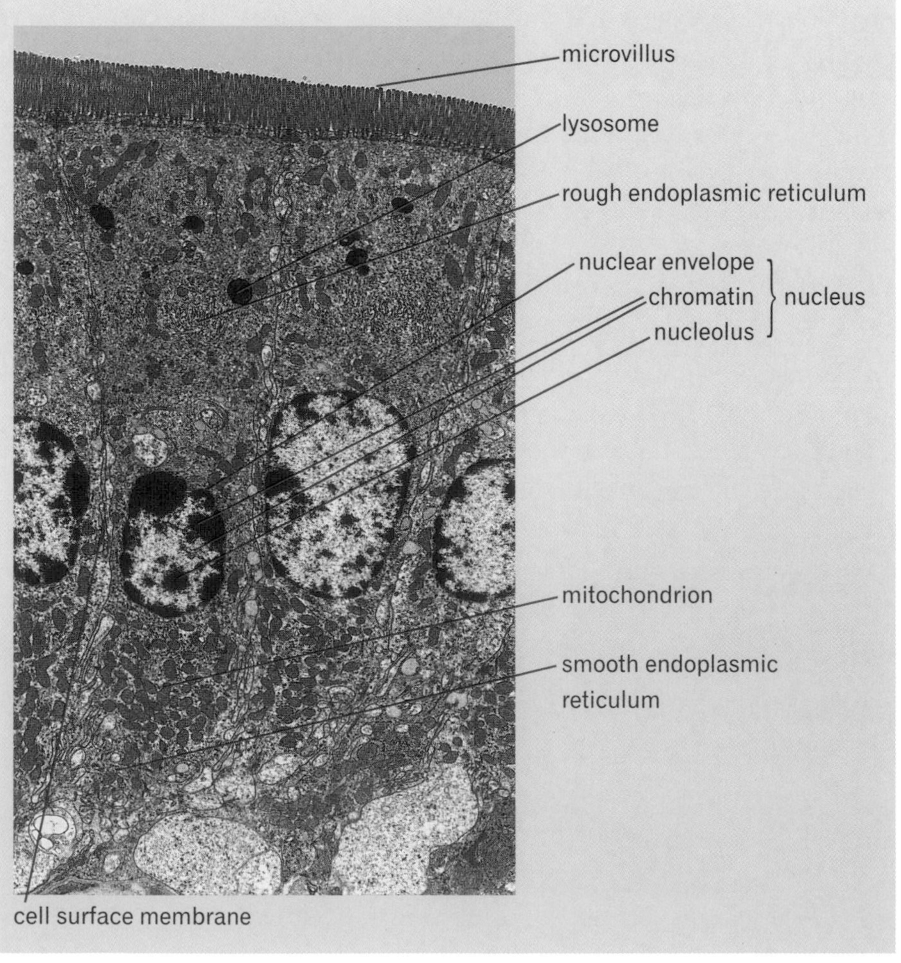

● ***Figure 1.10*** A representative animal cell as seen with an electron microscope. The cell is a small intestine mucosal cell from a mouse (magnification × 10 000).

SAQ 1.2

Compare *figure 1.11* with *1.2*. Which structures can be seen with the electron microscope which could not be seen with the light microscope?

Endoplasmic reticulum and ribosomes

When cells were first seen with the electron microscope, biologists were amazed to see so much detailed structure. The existence of much of this had not been suspected. This was particularly true of an extensive system of membranes running through the cytoplasm which became known as the **endoplasmic reticulum (ER)** *(figure 1.12a)*.

Attached to the surface of much of the ER are many tiny organelles, now known as **ribosomes**. At very high magnifications these can be seen to consist of two parts, a smaller and a larger subunit. In some areas of the cell, the ER lacks ribosomes and appears smooth. This is called **smooth ER** and is now known to have a different function from ribosome-covered ER, which is called **rough ER**. The membranes form a system of flattened sacs, like sheets, which are called **cisternae**. The space inside the sacs forms a compartment separate from the surrounding cytoplasm.

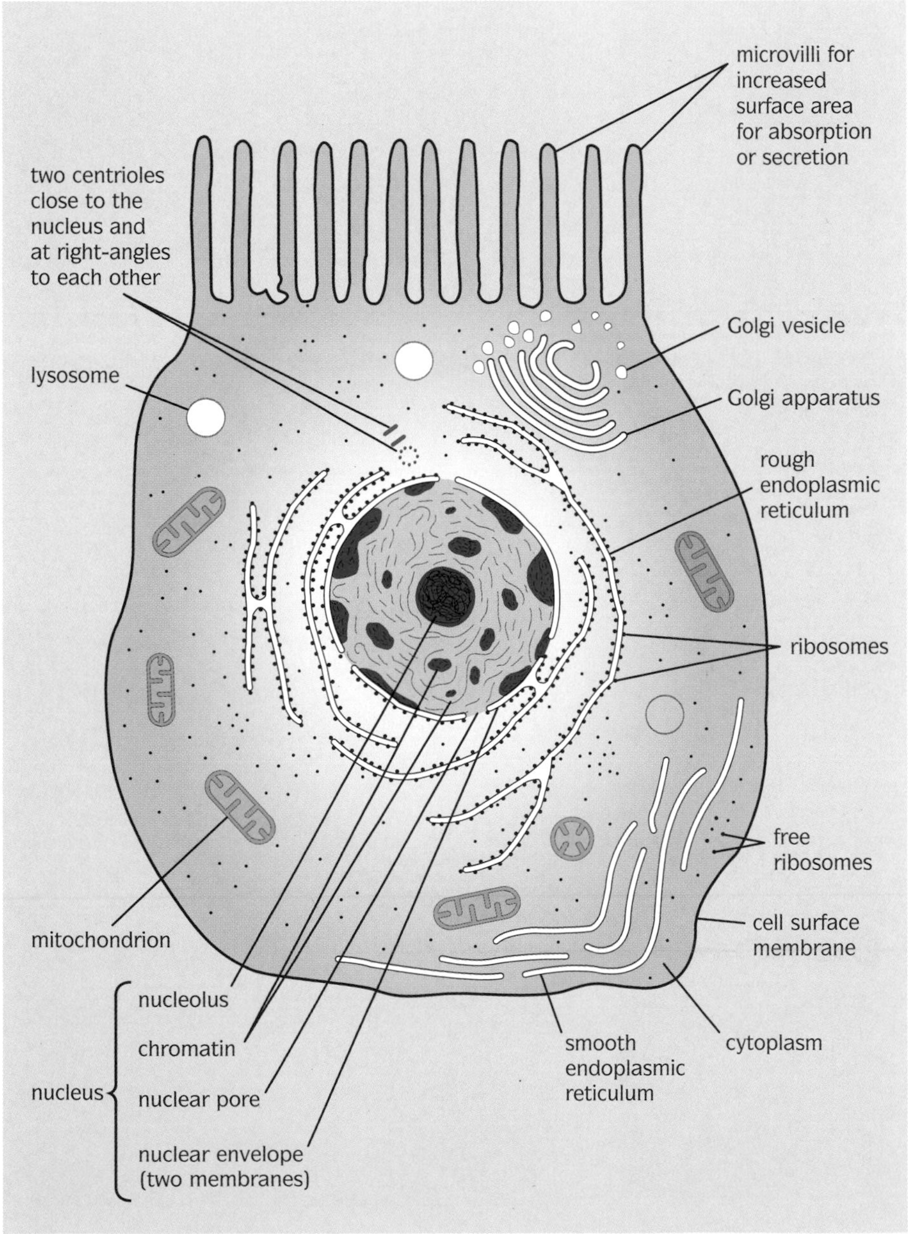

Nucleus and centrioles

The **nucleus** was found to be surrounded by two membranes, not one. This double structure is known as the **nuclear envelope**. The outer membrane of the nuclear envelope is continuous with the ER *(figure 1.11)*. The nuclear envelope is perforated by conspicuous pores, the **nuclear pores** *(figure 1.12b)*. Within the nucleus, the chromosomes are in a loosely coiled state known as chromatin (except during nuclear division, page 19). Just outside the nucleus, the extra resolution of the electron microscope reveals that there are really **two** centrioles, not one as it appears in the light microscope. These lie close together at right-angles to each other *(figure 1.12c)*.

● ***Figure 1.11*** Ultrastructure of a typical animal cell as seen with an electron microscope. NB The ER is more extensive in reality than shown. Free ribosomes may be more extensive. Food granules, e.g. glycogen granules, are sometimes present.

● ***Figure 1.12*** A range of cell organelles as seen with the electron microscope. False colour has been added to highlight structures.

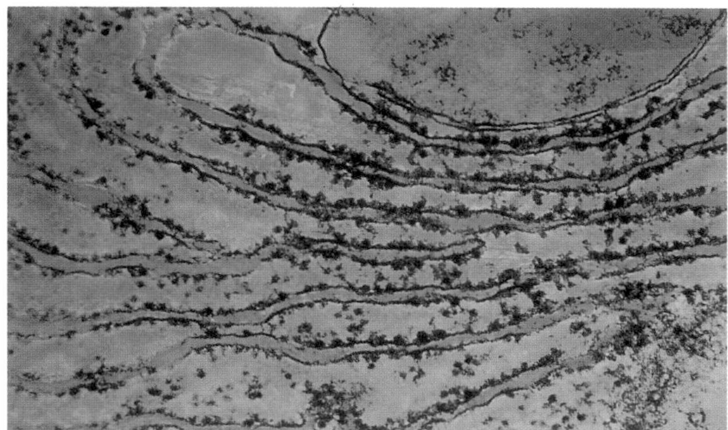

a Rough ER (parallel orange structures) and ribosomes (black particles) (×60 000). The blue structure is part of the nucleus.

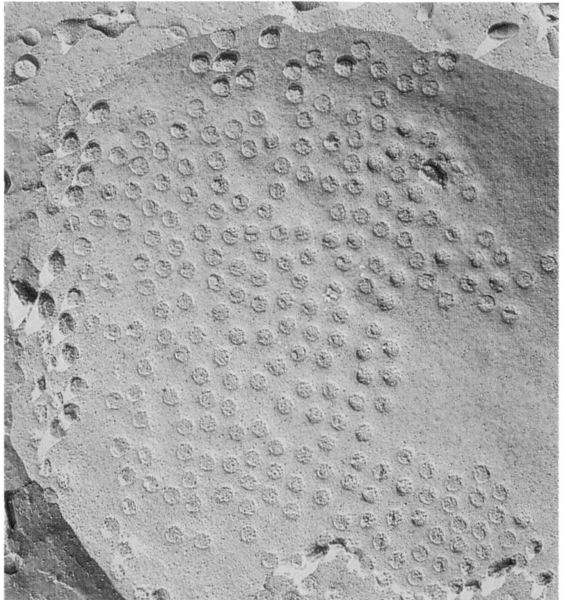

b Nuclear envelope (large oval) with nuclear pores, and part of the surrounding cytoplasm (×16 000). The specimen is freeze-fractured (frozen, then fractured with a sharp knife). The two membranes of the envelope are seen at the bottom where the fracturing between them is incomplete. Pores appear as flat-topped elevations or shallow craters.

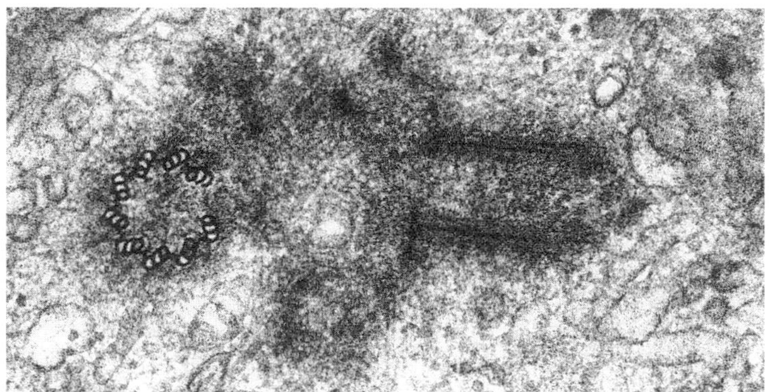

c Centrioles in transverse and longitudinal section (TS and LS) (×40 000). In TS the nine triplets of microtubules which make up the structure can be seen.

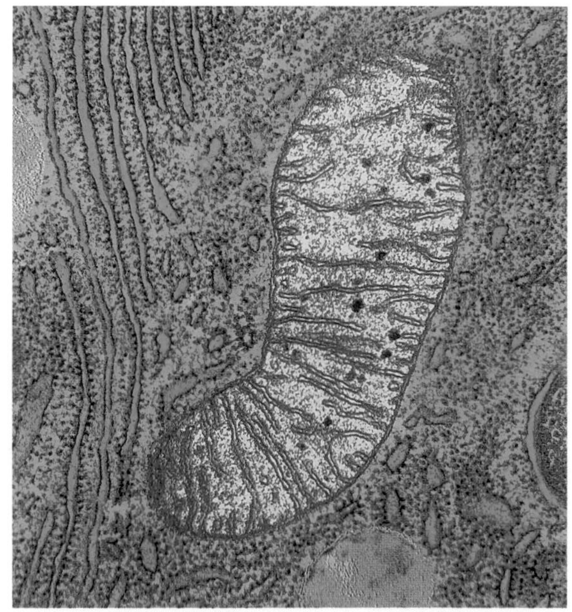

d Mitochondrion (orange) with its double membrane (envelope); the inner membrane is folded to form cristae (×12 000). Mitochondria are the sites of aerobic cell respiration. Note also the rough ER (turquoise).

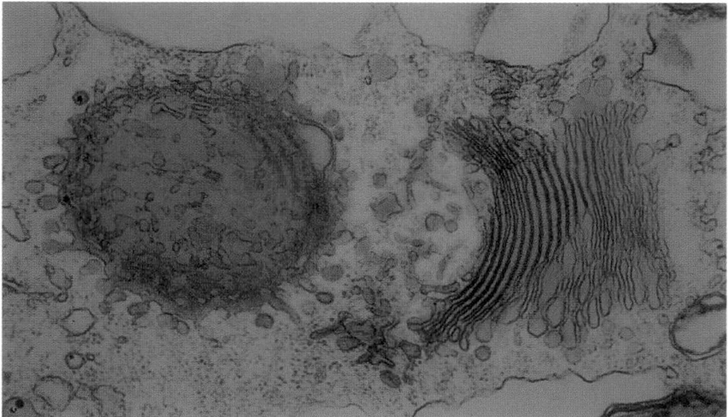

e Golgi apparatus. Two are present, one in TS (left) and one in LS (right). A central stack of saucer-shaped sacs (cisternae) can be seen budding off small Golgi vesicles. These may form secretory vesicles whose contents can be released at the cell surface by a process known as exocytosis (×20 000).

● **Figure 1.12** (cont.)

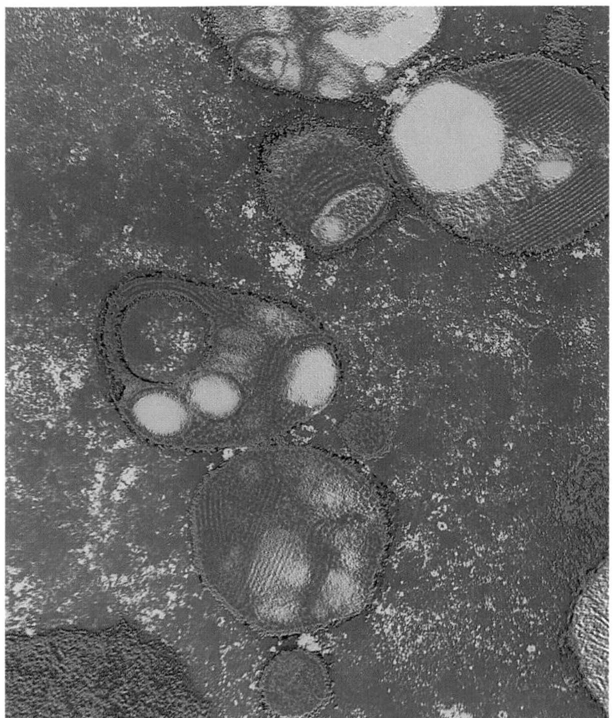

f Lysosomes in a mouse kidney cell. They contain red membrane structures in the process of digestion and green vesicles. Cytoplasm is coloured blue (×40 000).

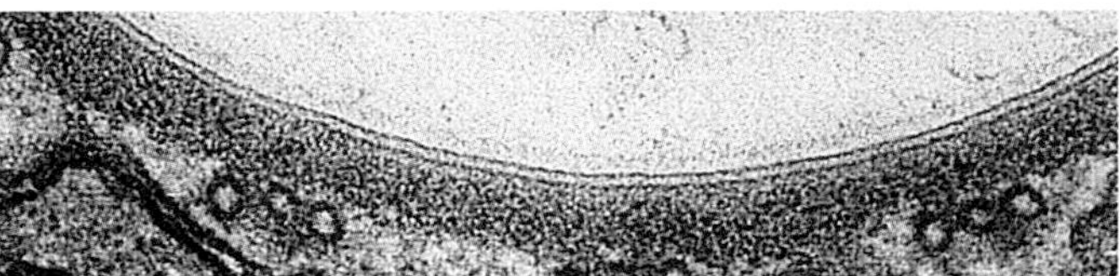

g Cell surface membrane (×100 000). At this magnification the membrane appears as two dark lines at the edge of the cell.

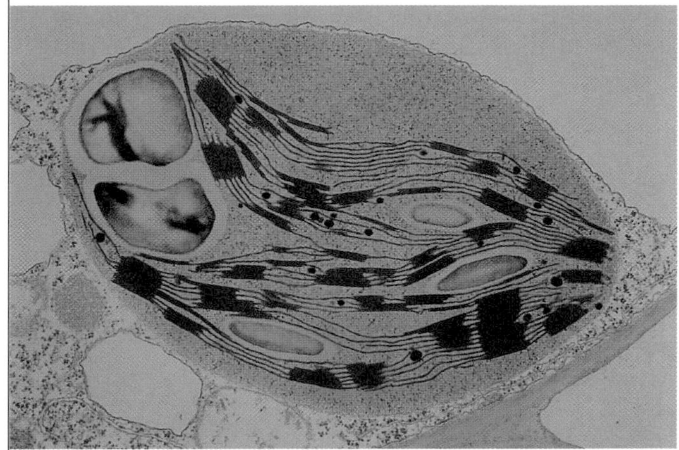

h Chloroplast (×80 000). Five conspicuous starch grains are present. Parallel flattened sacs (thylakoids) run through the stroma and are stacked in places to form grana. Tiny ribosomes (black dots) can be seen in the stroma. Larger black droplets among the thylakoids are lipid droplets.

Outside the nucleus, in the cytoplasm, organelles which can only just be seen with a light microscope can be seen in great detail.

Mitochondria *(figure 1.12d)*

These are seen to be surrounded by two membranes (an envelope). The inner of these is folded to form finger-like **cristae** which project into the interior solution, or **matrix**.

Golgi apparatus *(figure 1.12e)*

This apparatus is a stack of flattened sacs called **cisternae**. The stack is constantly being formed at one end from vesicles which bud off from the ER, and broken down again at the other end to form **Golgi vesicles**, which move to other parts of the cell.

Lysosomes *(figure 1.12f)*

These are surrounded by a single membrane and have no internal structure. They are slightly smaller than mitochondria, commonly 0.1–0.5 μm in diameter.

Cell surface membrane

This is extremely thin (about 7 nm). However, at very high magnifications, at least ×100 000, it can be seen to have three layers (**trilaminar appearance**). This consists of two dark lines (heavily stained) either side of a narrow, pale interior (*figure 1.12g*). Membrane structure is discussed further in chapter 5.

Functions of cell organelles

Compartmentation and division of labour within the cell are even more obvious with an electron microscope than with a light microscope. A summary of the structure of some of the cell components and an outline of their functions is given in *table 1.2*.

Structure	Function
Cell surface membrane Two layers of phospholipid which contain other molecules, particularly proteins (page 60).	Partially permeable membrane controlling exchange between the cell and its environment (page 62).
Nucleus Largest cell organelle. Enclosed by an envelope of two membranes which is perforated by nuclear pores. Contains chromatin and a nucleolus.	The nucleus controls the cell's activities. Division of the nucleus precedes cell division. Chromatin is the loosely coiled form of chromosomes. Chromosomes contain DNA which is organised into functional units called genes. Genes control the activities of the cell and inheritance. The nucleolus manufactures ribosomes, using information in the DNA of which the nucleolus is made. Nuclear pores allow exchange between the nucleus and the cytoplasm, e.g. mRNA and ribosomes leave the nucleus; some hormones and nutrients enter the nucleus.
Endoplasmic reticulum (ER) A system of membrane-bound, flattened sacs forming sheets called cisternae. It is continuous with the outer membrane of the nucleus.	Rough ER has ribosomes on its surface and transports protein, made by the ribosomes, throughout the cell. Rough ER also makes the Golgi apparatus. Smooth ER has no ribosomes and makes lipids (page 39) and steroids, e.g. cholesterol and reproductive hormones.
Ribosomes Very small organelles, only about 22 nm in diameter. They are made of RNA and protein.	Sites of protein synthesis. They are found attached either to ER or free in the cytoplasm.
Mitochondria (singular mitochondrion) Surrounded by two membranes. The inner membrane is folded to form finger-like structures called cristae. The solution inside is called the matrix.	The main function of mitochondria is the later stages of aerobic respiration (oxidation of sugars and fatty acids). As a result of respiration, they make ATP, the universal energy carrier in cells. Also involved in synthesis of lipids.
Golgi apparatus A stack of flattened, membrane-bound sacs called cisternae, continuously being formed from ER at one end and budding off as Golgi vesicles at the other.	Collects, processes and sorts molecules, particularly proteins from the ER, ready for transport in Golgi vesicles to other parts of the cell, or out of the cell (secretion). Golgi vesicles are also used to make lysosomes.
Lysosomes Spherical sacs surrounded by a single membrane. Contain digestive enzymes which must be kept away from the rest of the cell.	Breakdown (digestion) of unwanted structures, e.g. old cell organelles or whole cells, as in mammary glands after lactation; in white blood cells they are used to digest bacteria (see endocytosis, page 65). Enzymes are sometimes released outside the cell, e.g. during replacement of cartilage with bone during development. The head of sperms contains a special lysosome, the acrosome, for digesting a path to the ovum (egg).
Centrioles Small hollow cylinders (about 0.4 μm long) that occur in pairs next to the nucleus in animal cells. Each cylinder contains a ring of microtubules.	Help to form the spindle in nuclear division.The spindle fibres are made of microtubules which grow from the microtubules in the centrioles (page 23).

● ***Table 1.2*** Summary of the structures and outline of the functions of some organelles of an animal cell

Ultrastructure of a plant cell

All the structures described in *table 1.2* are also found in plant cells, except centrioles. The appearance of a plant cell as seen with the electron microscope is shown in *figure 1.13*, with details of the chloroplast in *figure 1.12b*. The relatively thick cell wall and the large central vacuole are obvious, as are the chloroplasts. These structures and their functions have been described on page 4.

A diagram of a typical plant cell as seen with the electron microscope is given in *figure 1.14*.

SAQ 1.3

Compare *figure 1.14* with *figure 1.4*. Which structures can be seen with the electron microscope which could not be seen with the light microscope?

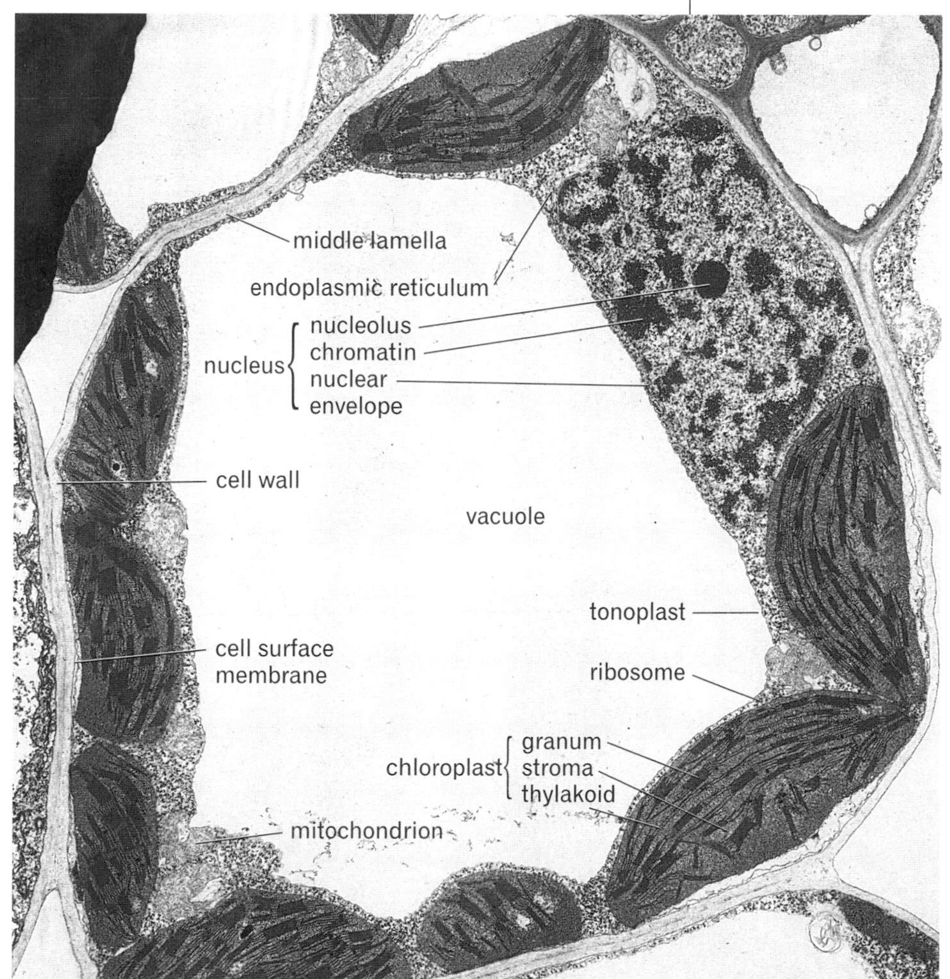

● ***Figure 1.13*** Appearance of a representative plant cell as seen with an electron microscope. The cell is a mesophyll cell from a leaf *(compare figure 1.19)* (×12 000).

Transmission and scanning electron microscopes

Two types of electron microscope are now in common use. The **transmission electron microscope** was the type originally developed. Here the beam of electrons is passed *through* the specimen before being viewed. Only those electrons that are **transmitted** (pass through the specimen) are seen. In the **scanning electron microscope**, on the other hand, the electron beam is used to scan the **surfaces** of structures, and only the **reflected** beam is observed. An example of a scanning electron micrograph is shown in *figure 1.15*. The advantage of this microscope is that surface structures can be seen. Also, great depth of field is obtained so that much of the specimen is in focus at the same time. Such a picture would be impossible to obtain with a light microscope, even using the same magnification and resolution, because you would have to keep focussing up and down with the objective lens to see different parts of the specimen. The disadvantage of the scanning electron microscope is that it cannot achieve the same resolution as a transmission electron microscope which also allows us to see thin sections of specimens, and thus to see inside cells.

Viewing specimens with the electron microscope

It is not possible to see an electron beam, so to make the image visible the electron beam has to be projected on to a fluorescent screen. The areas hit by electrons shine brightly, giving overall a 'black and

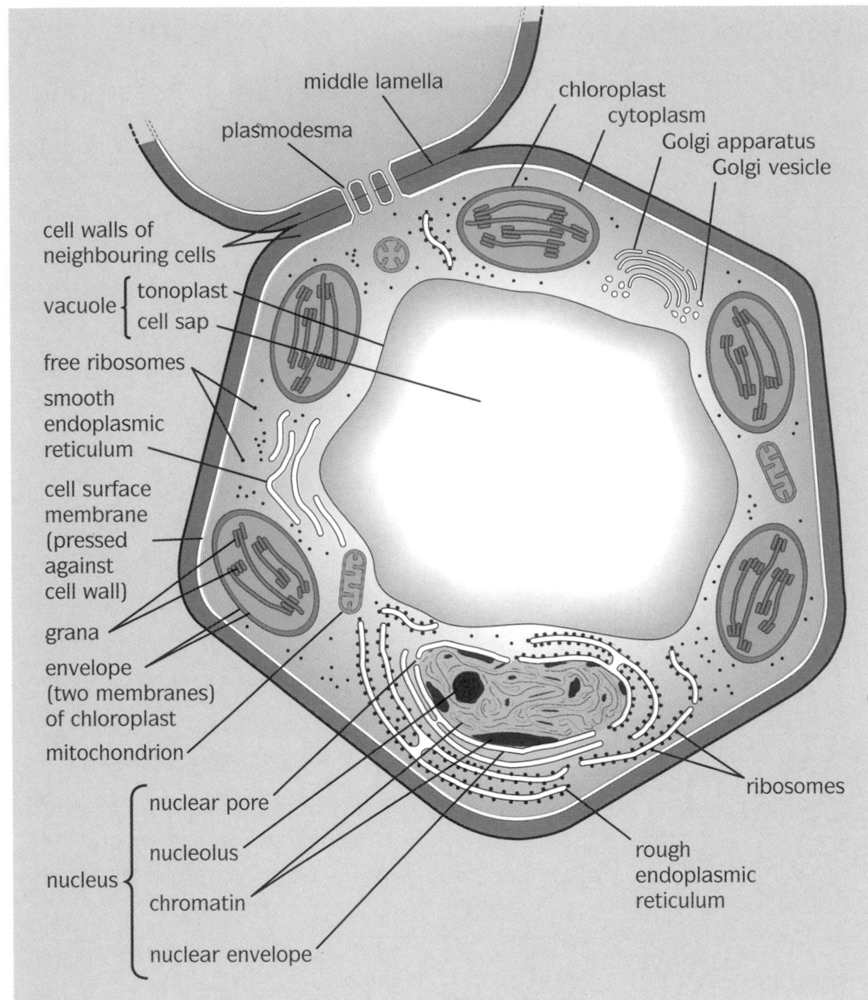

● ***Figure 1.14*** Ultrastructure of a typical plant cell as seen with the electron microscope. NB The ER is more extensive in reality than shown. Free ribosomes may also be more extensive.

● ***Figure 1.15*** False-colour scanning electron micrograph (SEM) of the head of a cat flea (×75).

white' picture. The stains used to improve the contrast of biological specimens for electron microscopy contain heavy metal atoms which stop the passage of electrons. The resulting picture is therefore similar in principle to an X-ray photograph, with the more dense parts of the specimen appearing blacker.

To add to the difficulties of electron microscopy, the electron beam, and therefore the specimen and the fluorescent screen, must be in a vacuum. If electrons collided with air molecules, they would scatter, making it impossible to achieve a sharp picture. Also, water boils in a vacuum, so all specimens must be dehydrated before being placed in the microscope. This means that only dead material can be examined. Great efforts are therefore made to try to preserve material in a life-like state when preparing it for the microscope.

Two fundamentally different types of cell

At one time it was common practice to try to classify *all* living organisms as either animals or plants. With advances in our knowledge of living things, it has become obvious that the living world is not that simple. Fungi and bacteria, for example, are very different from animals and plants, and from each other. Eventually it was realised that there are two fundamentally different types of cell. The most obvious difference between these types is that one *possesses a nucleus* and the other does not. Organisms that lack nuclei are called **prokaryotes** (*pro* means before; *karyon* means nucleus). All prokaryotes are now referred to as **bacteria** *(figure 1.16)*. They are, on average, about 1000 to 10 000 times smaller in *volume* than cells with nuclei and are much simpler in structure, for example their DNA lies free in the cytoplasm. Organisms whose cells possess nuclei are called **eukaryotes** (*eu* means true). Their DNA lies inside a nucleus. Eukaryotes include **animals, plants, fungi** and a group containing most of the unicellular eukaryotes known as **protoctists.** Most biologists believe that eukaryotes evolved from prokaryotes some one and a half thousand million years after prokaryotes first appeared on Earth. Although we mainly study animals and plants in this book, **all** eukaryotic cells have certain features in common. A comparison of prokaryotic and eukaryotic cells is given in *table 1.3*.

Tissues and organs

So far we have studied life at the cell level. Some organisms, such as bacteria, consist of one cell only. However, many organisms are multicellular, consisting of collections of cells from several hundred to billions in total. One great advantage that multicellular organisms gain over unicellular

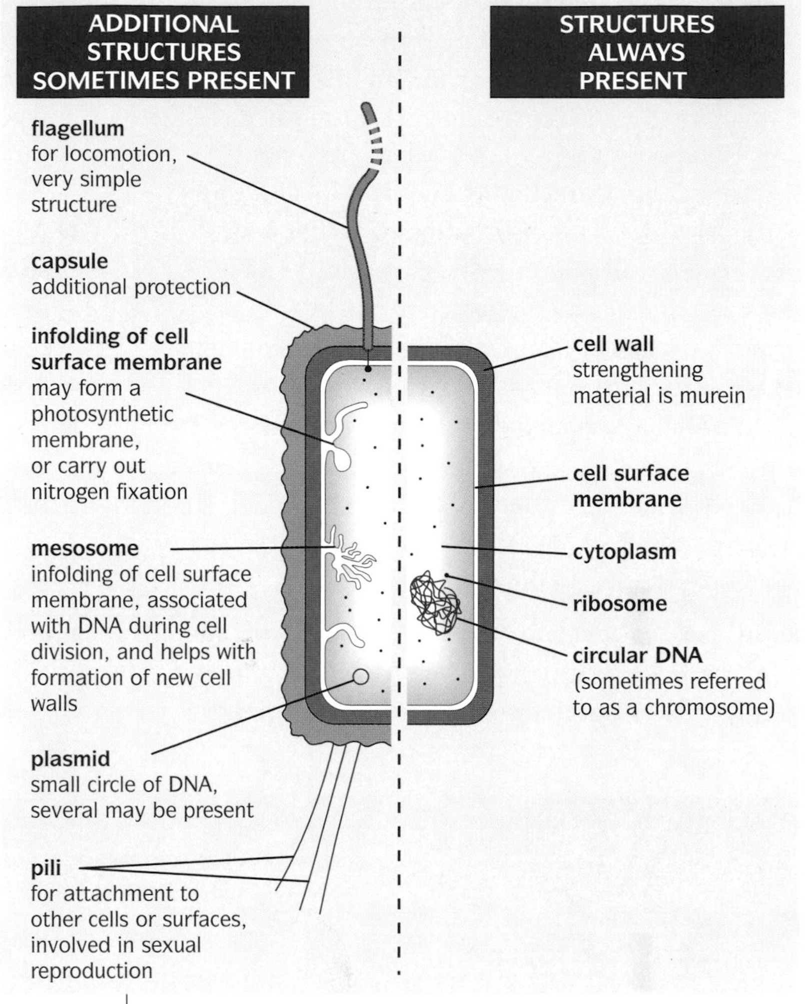

● ***Figure 1.16*** Diagram of a generalised bacterium showing the typical features of a prokaryotic cell.

Prokaryotes	*Eukaryotes*
Average diameter of cell 0.5–5 µm	Cells commonly up to 40 µm diameter and commonly 1000–10 000 times the volume of prokaryotic cells
DNA is circular and lies free in the cytoplasm	DNA is not circular and is contained in a nucleus. The nucleus is surrounded by an envelope of two membranes
DNA is naked	DNA is associated with protein, forming structures called chromosomes
Slightly smaller ribosomes (about 18 nm diameter)	Slightly larger ribosomes (about 22 nm diameter)
No ER present	ER present, to which ribosomes may be attached
Very few cell organelles; none are surrounded by an envelope of two membranes	Many types of cell organelle present (extensive compartmentation and division of labour). Some organelles are bounded by a single membrane, e.g. lysosomes, Golgi apparatus, vacuoles; some are bounded by two membranes (an envelope), e.g. nucleus, mitochondrion; some have no membrane, e.g. ribosomes
Cell wall present	Cell wall sometimes present e.g. in plants

● ***Table 1.3*** A comparison of prokaryotic and eukaryotic cells organisms is greater independence from the environment, but a full discussion of this is outside the scope of this book. In these communities of cells, it is usual for the functions of the organism to be divided among groups of cells which become specialised, both structurally and functionally, for particular roles. This distribution of function we have seen already *within* cells, particularly eukaryotic cells, and has been referred to as 'division of labour'. Usually, specialised cells show division of labour by being grouped into 'tissues'; the tissues may be further grouped into 'organs' and the organs into 'systems'. Each tissue, organ or system has a particular function and a structure appropriate to that function. More precisely, we can define the terms as follows.

- A **tissue** is a collection of cells, together with any intercellular secretion produced by them, that is specialised to perform a particular function or functions. The cells may be of the same type, such as parenchyma in plants and cuboidal epithelium in animals. They may be of mixed type, such as xylem and phloem in plants and cartilage, bone and connective tissue in animals. The study of tissues is called **histology**.
- An **organ** is a part of the body which forms a structural and functional unit and is composed of more than one tissue. Examples of plant organs are leaves and roots; animal organs include the brain, heart, liver, kidney and eye.
- A **system** is a collection of organs with a particular function, such as the excretory, reproductive, cardiovascular and digestive systems.

Figure 1.17 shows some examples of plant tissues within a leaf. *Figure 1.18* shows some examples of tissues in animals.

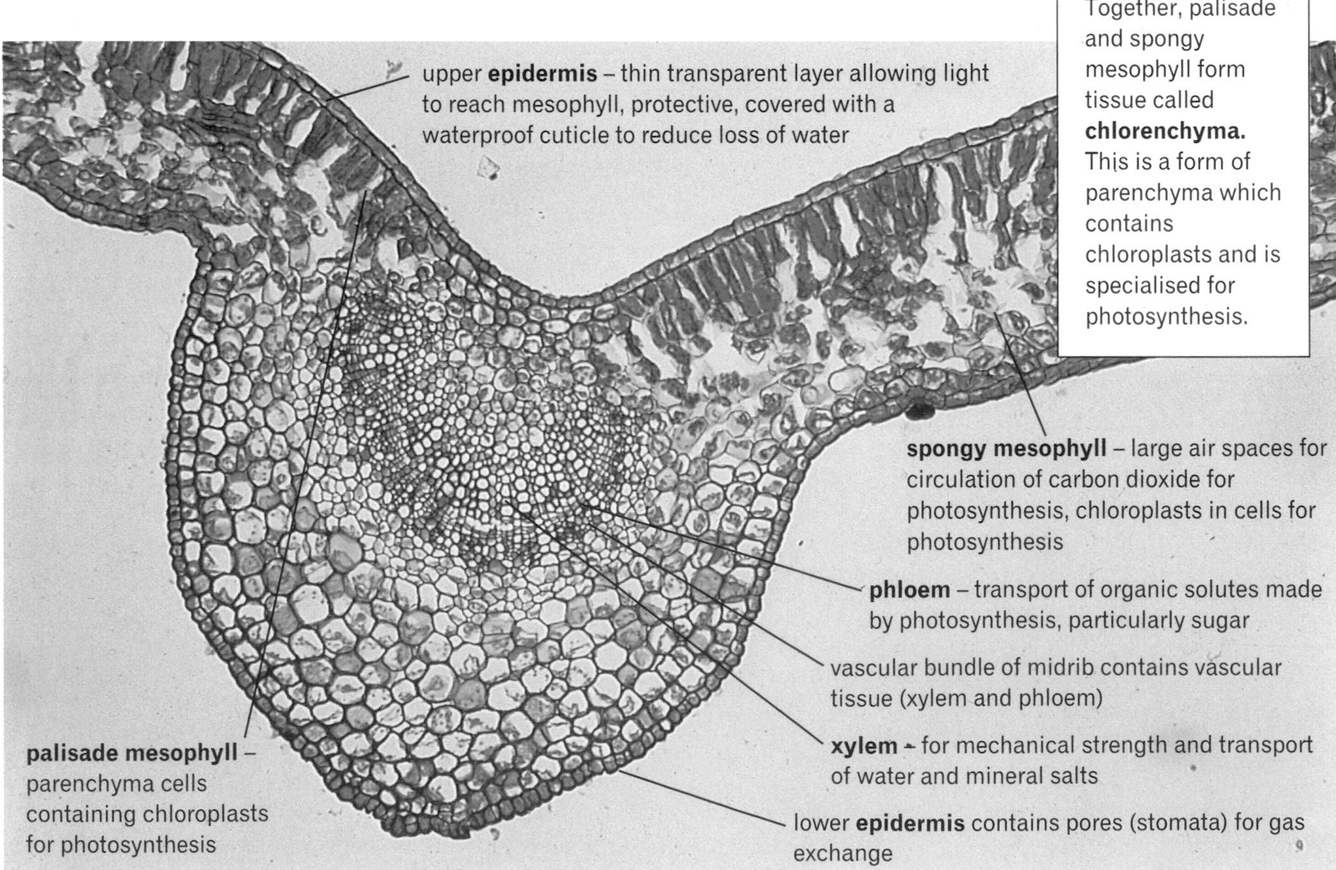

● ***Figure 1.17*** Transverse section through the midrib of a dicotyledonous leaf, *Ligustrum* (privet) (magnification ×50). Tissues are indicated in bold type.

● ***Figure 1.18*** Some examples of animal tissues.

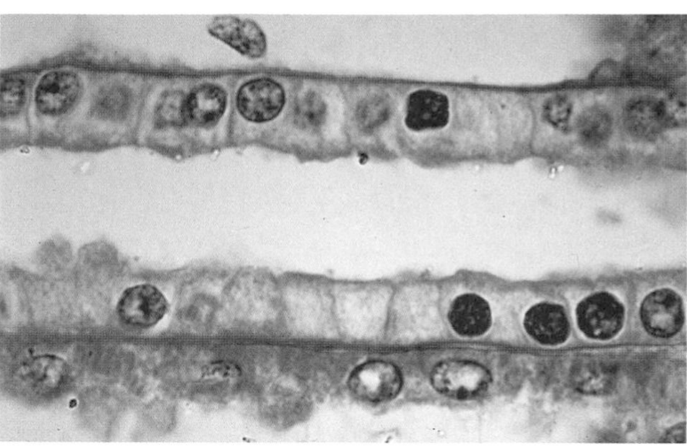

a Cuboidal epithelium from kidney (×800). Epithelial tissues line all the body's surfaces and cavities and are involved in a variety of functions such as absorption, secretion and protection.

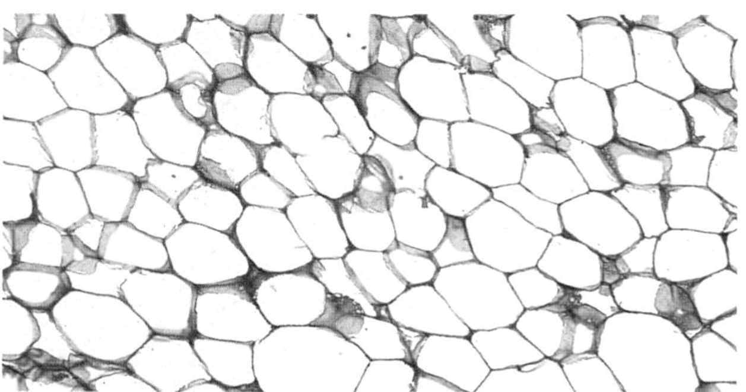

b Adipose (fat) tissue (×200). This tissue comprises up to 20% of total body mass in normal male adult humans and 25% in females. Each cell normally contains a single large globule of fat, but this has been lost during preparation of the material, leaving a large unstained white area in each cell. Cytoplasm (stained purple) is confined to a tiny rim around the edge of the cell.

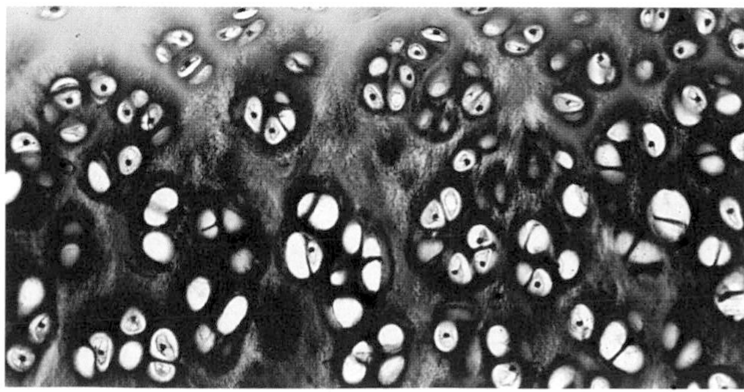

c Hyaline cartilage (×50). The darkly staining nuclei of cells can be seen in clear spaces scattered throughout the uniform background (**matrix**). The cells secrete the matrix, which is hard but not brittle. Cartilage is widely used in vertebrates as a mechanically strong tissue, for example at the ends of bones where it is an effective shock absorber.

SUMMARY

- All organisms are composed of units called cells.
- All cells are surrounded by a partially permeable membrane to control exchange between the cell and its environment.
- The cells of animals and plants contain many similar structures: cell surface membrane; cytoplasm containing mitochondria, endoplasmic reticulum, lysosomes and ribosomes; and a nucleus with a nucleolus and chromatin.
- Animal cells also have centrioles, whereas most plant cells have chloroplasts and a large central vacuole. Plant cells are also surrounded by rigid cell walls.
- Some of these structures are not visible with the light microscope because of the limit of resolution allowed by the use of light waves.
- Greater detail and smaller structures are seen with electron microscopes which use electron beams transmitted through (transmission electron microscope) or bounced off (scanning electron microscope) the specimen. However, only dead material can be viewed in electron microscopes.
- Prokaryote cells differ from eukaryote cells in being smaller, having free DNA in the cytoplasm, no endoplasmic reticulum or nucleus, few organelles and smaller ribosomes.

Questions

1 Briefly explain the differences between the following:

a rough ER and smooth ER*, **b** cell wall and cell surface membrane*, **c** prokaryote and eukaryote, **d** chromatin and chromosome*, **e** nucleus and nucleolus*, **f** resolution and magnification, **g** scanning electron microscope and transmission electron microscope, **h** light microscope and electron microscope, **i** tissue and organ.

(* With reference to both structure and function.)

2 What is meant by division of labour? Show how it is important within eukaryotic cells.

3 Summarise the similarities and differences in structure between **a** prokaryote and eukaryote cells, and **b** animal and plant cells.

Nuclear and cell division

By the end of this chapter you should be able to:

1 describe how nuclear division comes before cell division and know that replication of DNA takes place during interphase;

2 explain that as a result of mitosis, growth, repair and asexual reproduction of living organisms is possible;

3 explain the need for the production of genetically identical cells within an organism, and hence for precise control of nuclear and cell division;

4 explain how cancers are a result of uncontrolled cell division and list factors which can cause cancers;

5 describe, with the aid of diagrams, the behaviour of chromosomes during mitosis and the associated behaviour of the nuclear envelope, cell surface membrane and centrioles;

6 name the main stages of mitosis;

7 distinguish between haploid and diploid;

8 explain what is meant by homologous pairs of chromosomes;

9 explain why gametes must be haploid and how this is achieved by meiosis (reduction division);

10 describe, with the aid of diagrams, the behaviour of chromosomes during meiosis and the associated behaviour of the nuclear envelope, cell surface membrane and centrioles;

11 name the main stages of meiosis;

12 explain how meiosis can lead to variation.

All living organisms grow and reproduce. Since living organisms are made of cells, this means that cells must be able to grow and reproduce. Cells reproduce by dividing and passing on their genes (hereditary information) to 'daughter cells'. The process must be very precisely controlled so that no vital information is lost. In this chapter we shall examine how eukaryotic cells achieve this.

In chapter 1 it was seen that one of the most conspicuous structures in eukaryotic cells is the nucleus. Its importance has been obvious ever since it was realised that the nucleus always divides before a cell divides. So each new cell, or 'daughter cell', contains its own nucleus. This is important because the nucleus controls the cell's activities. It does this through the genetic material DNA. The book *Central Concepts in Biology*, in this series, shows how DNA is able to act as a set of instructions, or code, for life.

So, nuclear division combined with cell division allows cells, and therefore whole organisms, to reproduce themselves. It also allows multicellular organisms to grow. The cells in your body, for example, are all genetically identical (apart from the gametes); they were all derived from one cell, the zygote, which was the cell formed when two gametes from your parents fused.

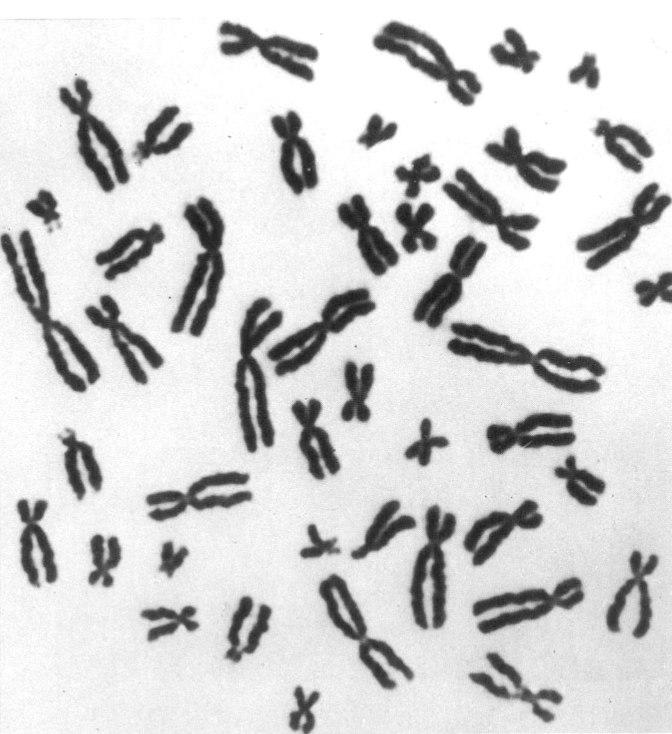

● ***Figure 2.1*** Photograph of a set of chromosomes in a human male, just before cell division. Each chromosome is composed of two chromatids held at the centromere. Note the different sizes of the chromosomes and positions of the centromeres.

The nucleus contains chromosomes

Just before a eukaryotic cell divides, a number of characteristic thread-like structures gradually become visible in the nucleus. They are easily seen because they stain intensely with particular stains. They were originally described as chromosomes (*chromo* means coloured; *somes* means bodies). The number of chromosomes is characteristic of the species. For example, in humans there are 46 chromosomes, and in fruit flies there are only 8. *Figure 2.1* shows the appearance of a set of chromosomes in the nucleus of a human cell. *Figure 2.2* shows the same chromosomes rearranged and *figure 2.3* a diagram of the same chromosomes.

SAQ 2.1

Look at the figures and try to decide why the chromosomes are arranged in that particular order.

A photograph such as *figure 2.2* is called a **karyotype**. It is prepared by cutting out individual chromosomes from a picture like *figure 2.1* and rearranging them. Note the following.

- There are matching pairs of chromosomes. These are called **homologous pairs**. Each pair is given a number.
- Chromosomes of similar size may be grouped together. The pairs can be distinguished because each pair has a distinctive banding pattern when stained.
- Two chromosomes are displayed to one side. These are the **sex chromosomes**, which determine the sex. All the other chromosomes are called **autosomes**. It is conventional to position the two sex chromosomes to one side so that the sex of the organism can be recognised quickly. In humans, females have two X chromosomes, and males have one X and one Y chromosome. The Y chromosome has a portion missing and is therefore smaller than the X chromosome.

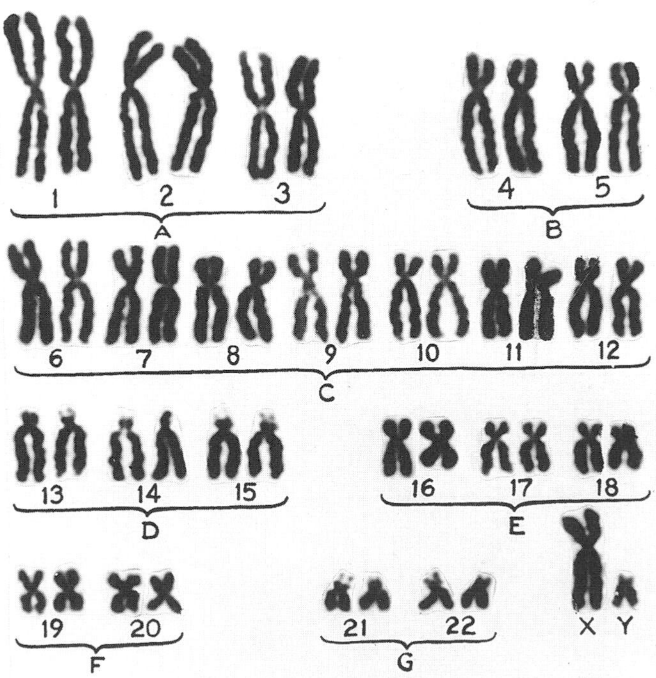

● ***Figure 2.2*** Karyotype of a human male, prepared from figure 2.1. Non-sex chromosomes (autosomes) are placed in the groups A to G. The sex chromosomes (X, female; Y, male) are placed separately.

Figures 2.1, 2.2 and *2.3* show that human cells contain 46 chromosomes, arranged in homologous pairs. There are therefore two **sets** of chromosomes, each set containing 23 chromosomes. In the original zygote, one of these sets came from the mother, and one from the father. Accurate and precise nuclear division during growth results in all cells of the body containing two sets of chromosomes.

Each chromosome has a characteristic set of genes which code for different features. Much research is currently being done to find out which genes are on which chromosomes. In 1989, for example, it was discovered that the gene for the genetic disease cystic fibrosis is located on chromosome 7. This subject is covered in more detail in *Central Concepts in Biology* and *Applications of Genetics* in this series.

Haploid and diploid cells

When animals other than humans are examined, we again find that cells usually contain two sets of chromosomes. Such cells are described as **diploid.** This is represented as **2n**, where n = number of chromosomes in one set of chromosomes.

Not all cells are diploid. As we shall see, gametes have only one set of chromosomes. Plants show an alternation of generations in which a generation with one set of chromosomes in each cell alternates with one containing two sets. A cell which contains only one set of chromosomes is described as **haploid**. This is represented as **n**.

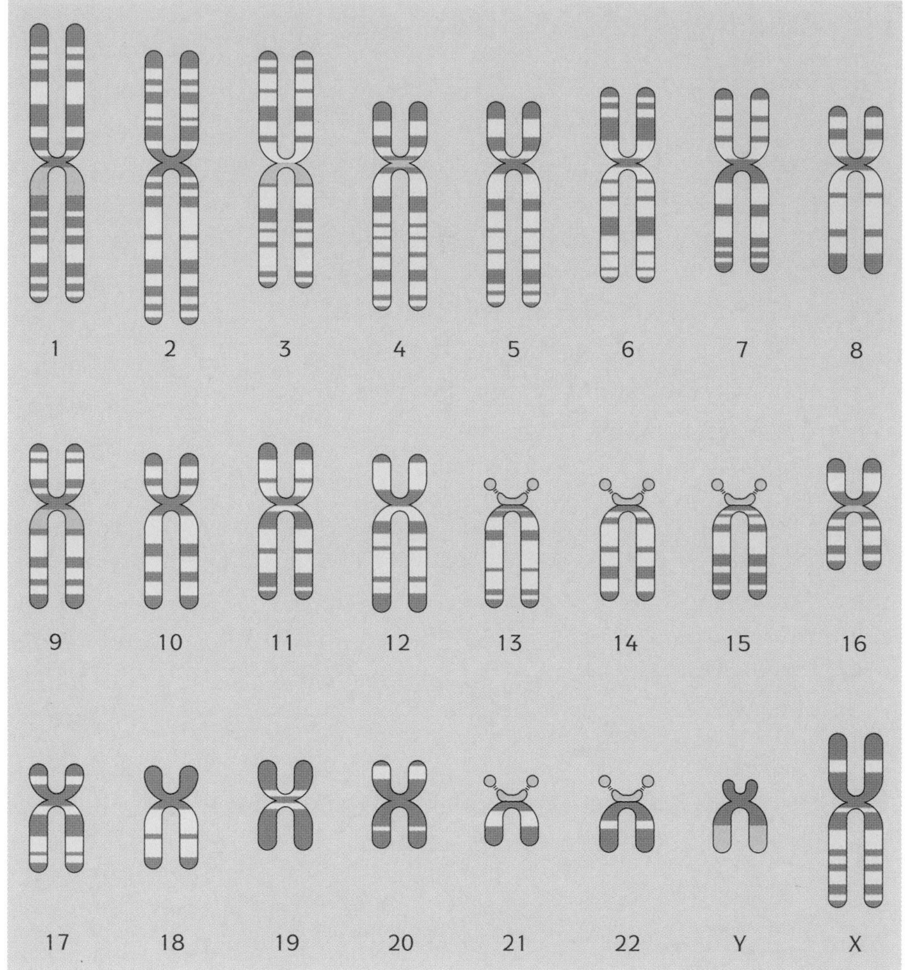

● ***Figure 2.3*** Diagram showing banding patterns of human chromosomes when stained. Green areas represent those regions that stain with ultraviolet fluorescence staining; orange areas are variable bands. NB The number of genes is greater than the number of stained bands. Only one chromosome of each pair is shown except for the sex chromosomes which are both shown.

Structure of chromosomes

Before studying nuclear division, you need to understand a little about the structure of chromosomes. *Figure 2.4* is a simplified diagram of the structure of a chromosome. It can be seen that the chromosome is really a double structure. It is made of two identical structures called **chromatids**. This is because during the period between nuclear divisions, which is known as **interphase**, each DNA molecule in a nucleus makes an identical copy of itself. Each copy is contained in a structure known as a chromatid and the two chromatids are held together by a characteristic narrow region called the **centromere**, forming a chromosome. The centromere can be found anywhere along the length of the chromosome, but the position is characteristic for a particular chromosome, as *figures* 2.2 and 2.3 show. **Each chromatid contains one DNA molecule.** DNA is the molecule of inheritance and is made up of a series of genes. Each gene is one unit of inheritance, controlling one characteristic of the organism. The fact that the two DNA molecules in sister chromatids, and hence their genes, are identical is the key to precise nuclear division.

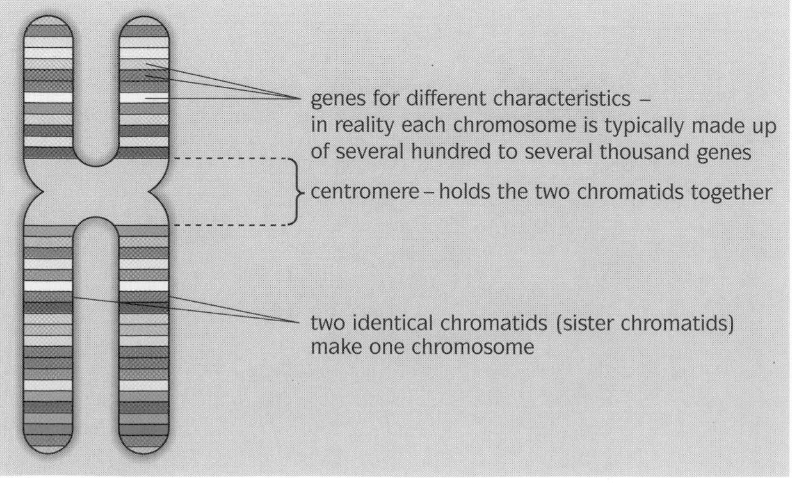

● ***Figure 2.4*** Simplified diagram of the structure of a chromosome.

The gene for a particular characteristic is always found at the same position, or **locus** (plural loci), on a chromosome. *Figure 2.5* shows a map of some of the genes on the human female sex chromosome which are involved in known genetic diseases.

Each chromosome typically has several hundred to several thousand gene loci, many more than shown in *figure 2.4*. The total number of different genes in humans is thought to be somewhere between 30 000 and 120 000.

Homologous pairs of chromosomes

The word homologous means similar in structure and composition. The two members of a homologous pair of chromosomes come from different parents. In humans 23 chromosomes come from the female parent (the **maternal chromosomes**), and 23 from the male parent (the **paternal chromosomes**). There are therefore 23 homologous pairs. Each member of a pair possesses genes for the same characteristics.

Genes controlling a characteristic may exist in different forms which are expressed differently. In the condition known as cystic fibrosis the gene exists in two forms **or alleles**. The normal allele controls production of a protein needed to produce normal mucus. A mutant (changed) allele of the gene controls production of very thick mucus which leads to cystic fibrosis. If both homologous chromosomes have a copy of the faulty allele, the person will suffer the disease; if only one copy of the faulty allele is present the person will not suffer the disease, but is termed a **carrier**. The possibilities are shown in *figure 2.6*.

The need for two types of nuclear division

Figure 2.7a shows a brief summary of the life cycle of an animal, such as a human. Two requirements must be satisfied.

1 **Growth** When a diploid zygote (one cell) grows into a multicellular diploid adult the daughter cells must keep the same number of chromosomes as the parent cell. The type of nuclear division that occurs here is called **mitosis.**

2 **Sexual reproduction** If the life cycle contains sexual reproduction, there must be a point in the life cycle when the number of chromosomes is halved (see *figure 2.7b*). This means that the gametes contain only one set of chromosomes rather than two sets. If there was no point in the

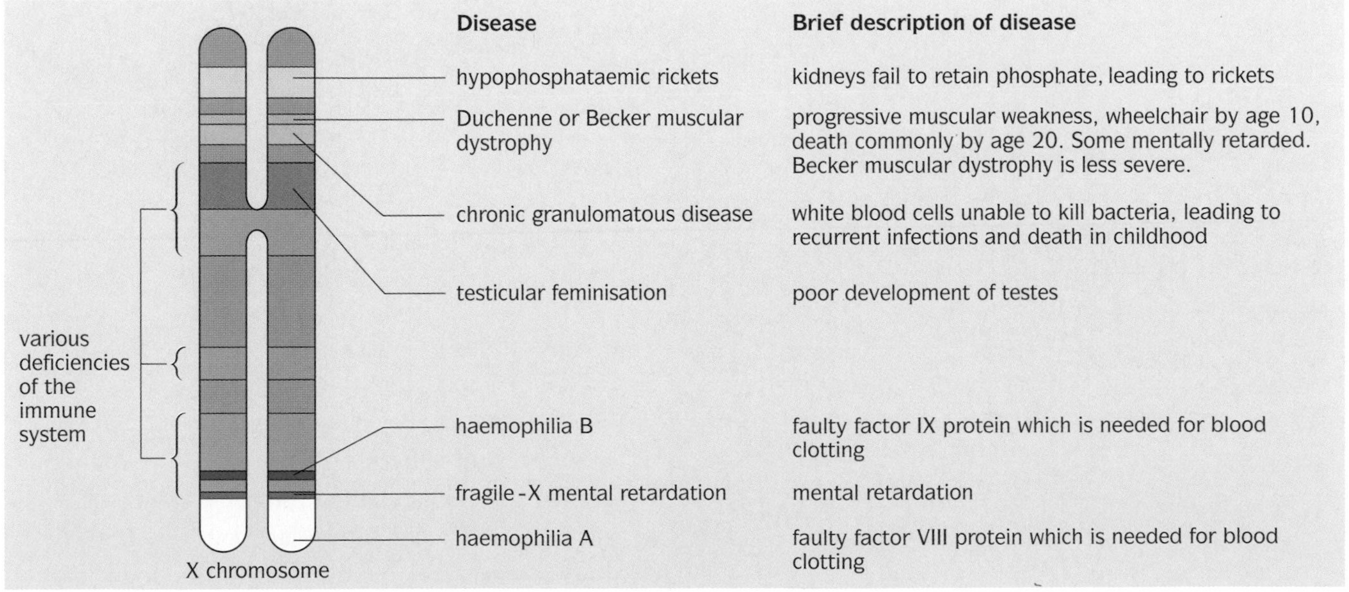

● ***Figure 2.5*** Locations of some of the genes on the human female sex chromosome (the X chromosome) which are involved in known diseases. The complete map would include at least 150 diseases. (Some locations are not yet known precisely.)

life cycle when the number of chromosomes halved then it would double every generation. The type of nuclear division that halves the chromosome number is called **meiosis**. Gametes are always haploid as a result of meiosis.

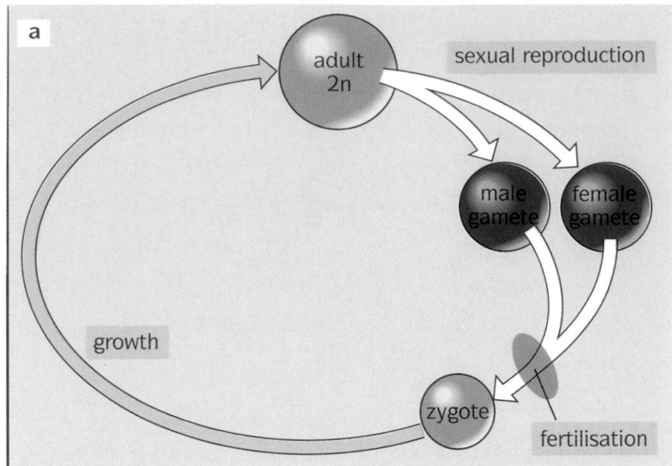

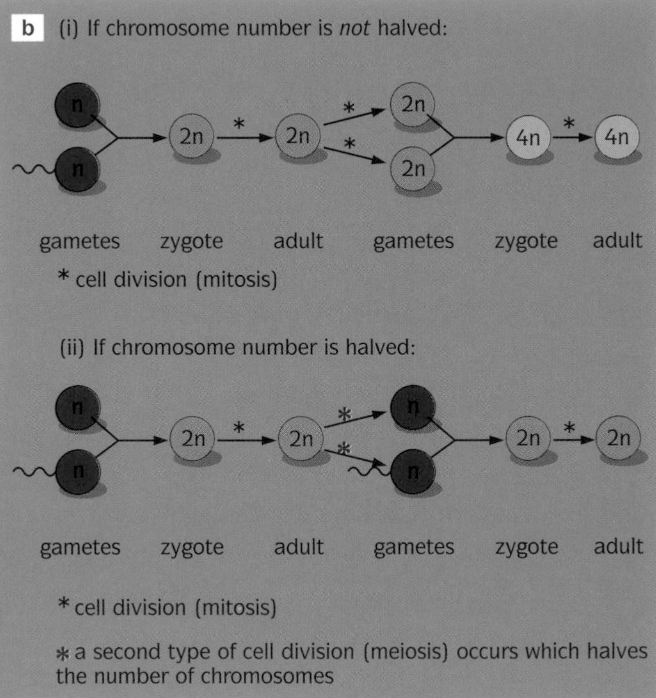

● ***Figure 2.7*** **a** Outline of the life cycle of an animal. **b** A life cycle in which the chromosome number is (i) not halved, (ii) halved.

Mitosis in an animal cell

Mitosis is nuclear division to produce two genetically identical daughter nuclei, each containing the same number of chromosomes as the parent nucleus. A diploid nucleus that divides by mitosis produces two diploid nuclei; a haploid nucleus produces two haploid nuclei. Mitosis, like meiosis, is a form of **nuclear division** which is followed by the separate process of **cell division.** In animal cells, this involves constriction of the cytoplasm between the two new nuclei, a process called **cytokinesis.** In plant cells it involves the formation of a new cell wall between the two new nuclei.

The process of mitosis is best described by annotated diagrams (diagrams with notes) as shown in *figure 2.8*. Although in reality the process is continuous, it is divided into four main stages for convenience, like four snapshots from a film. The four stages are called **prophase, metaphase, anaphase** and **telophase.** The period between nuclear divisions is called **interphase**, but this is not part of mitosis. Interphase is normally the longest stage. As previously mentioned, during interphase the important event of DNA replication takes place, so that at the beginning of nuclear division each chromosome consists of two

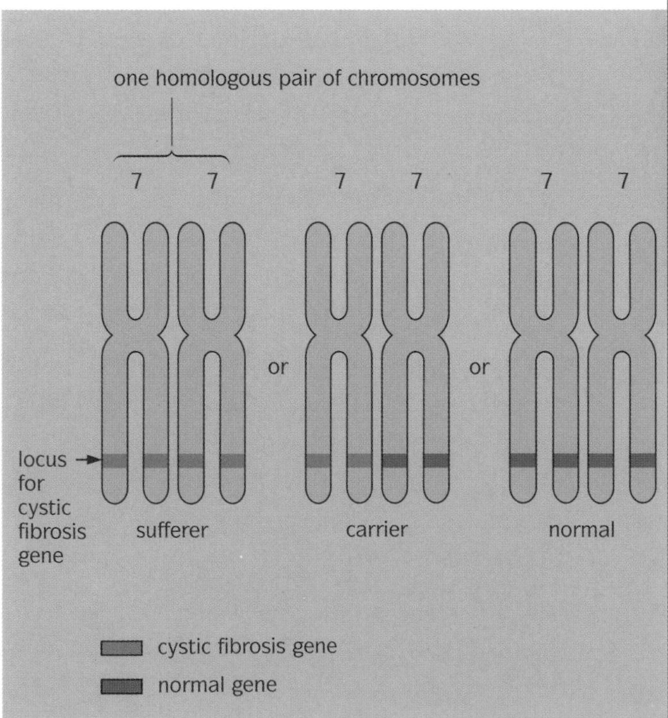

● ***Figure 2.6*** An example of a gene locus on a homologous pair of chromosomes (chromosome number 7). Note that each sister chromatid has an identical copy of the gene.

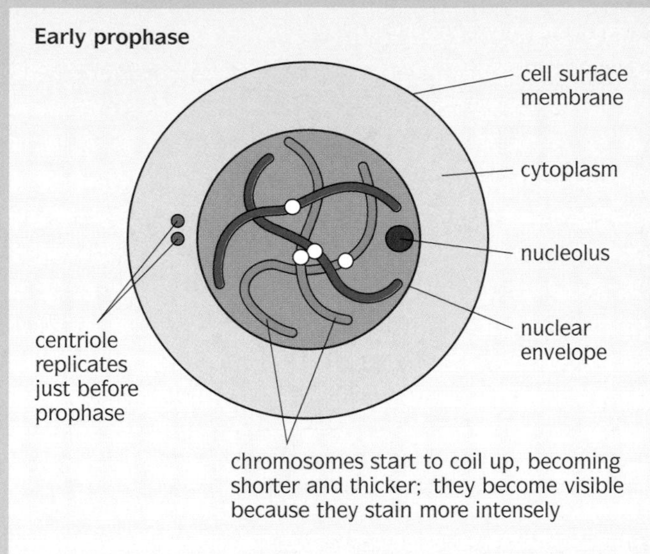

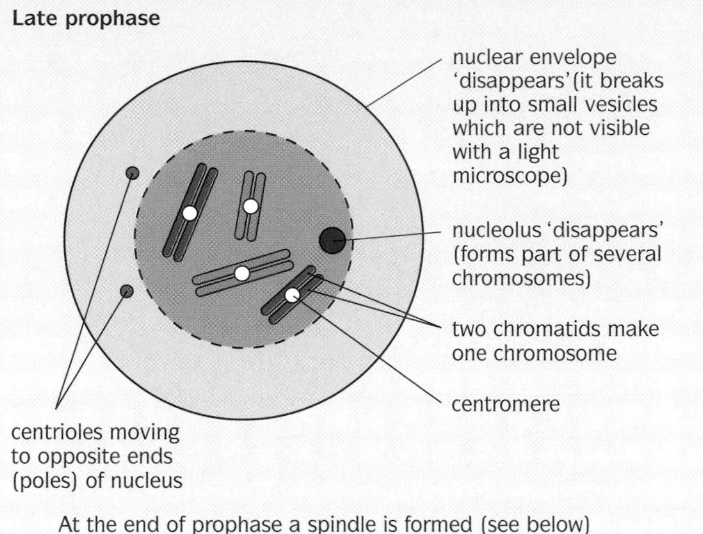

Metaphase

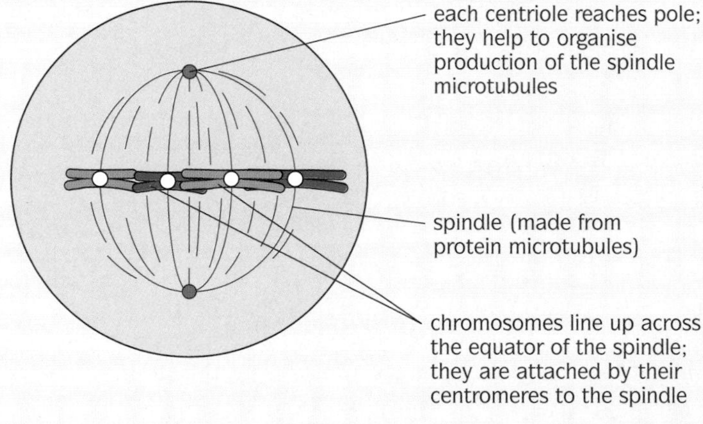

Three–dimensional view of spindle:

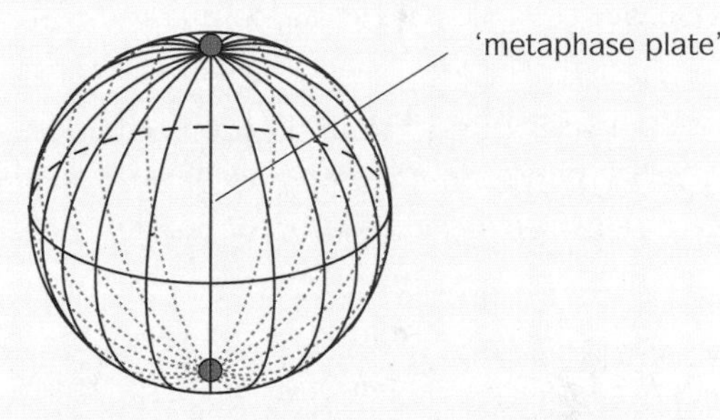

The spindle is circular at the equator, forming the 'metaphase plate'. The chromosomes are arranged around the edge of the plate.

Anaphase

centromeres divide into two

chromatids move to opposite poles, centromeres first, pulled by the microtubules

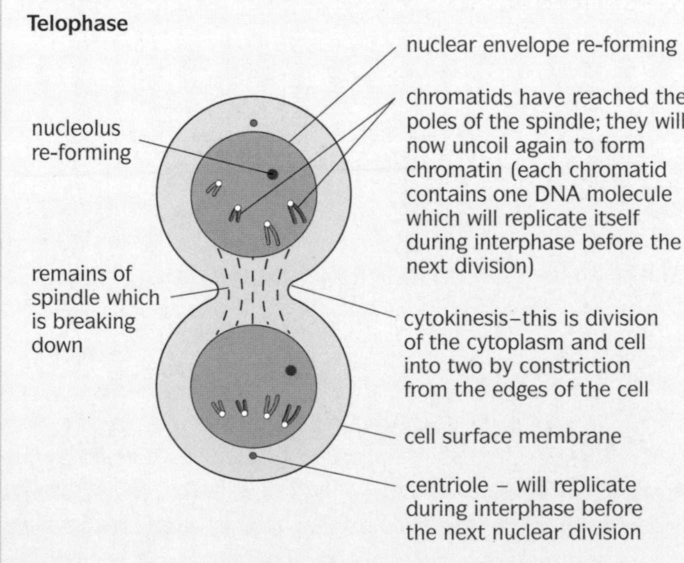

● ***Figure 2.8*** Mitosis and cytokinesis in an animal cell.

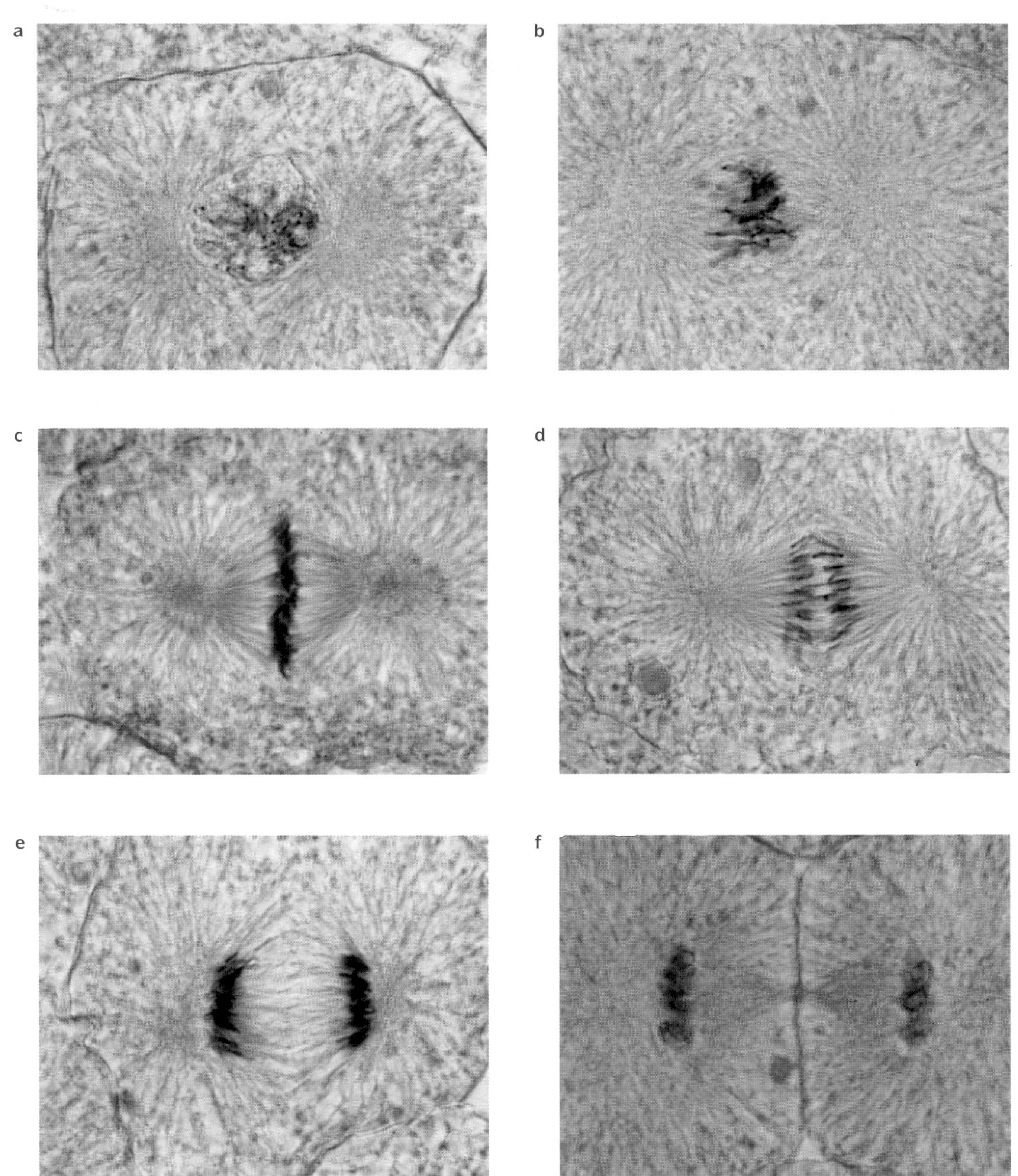

● ***Figure 2.9*** Stages of mitosis and cell division in an animal cell (whitefish) (×1000). Chromosomes are stained dark purple: **a** *prophase*; **b** stage intermediate between prophase and metaphase; **c** *metaphase*, the spindle fibres (microtubules) are now clearly visible and the centrioles are located at opposite ends of the spindle in the centre of a star-shaped arrangement of radiating microtubules; **d** *early anaphase*; **e** *anaphase*; **f** *telophase* and cell division (*cytokinesis*).

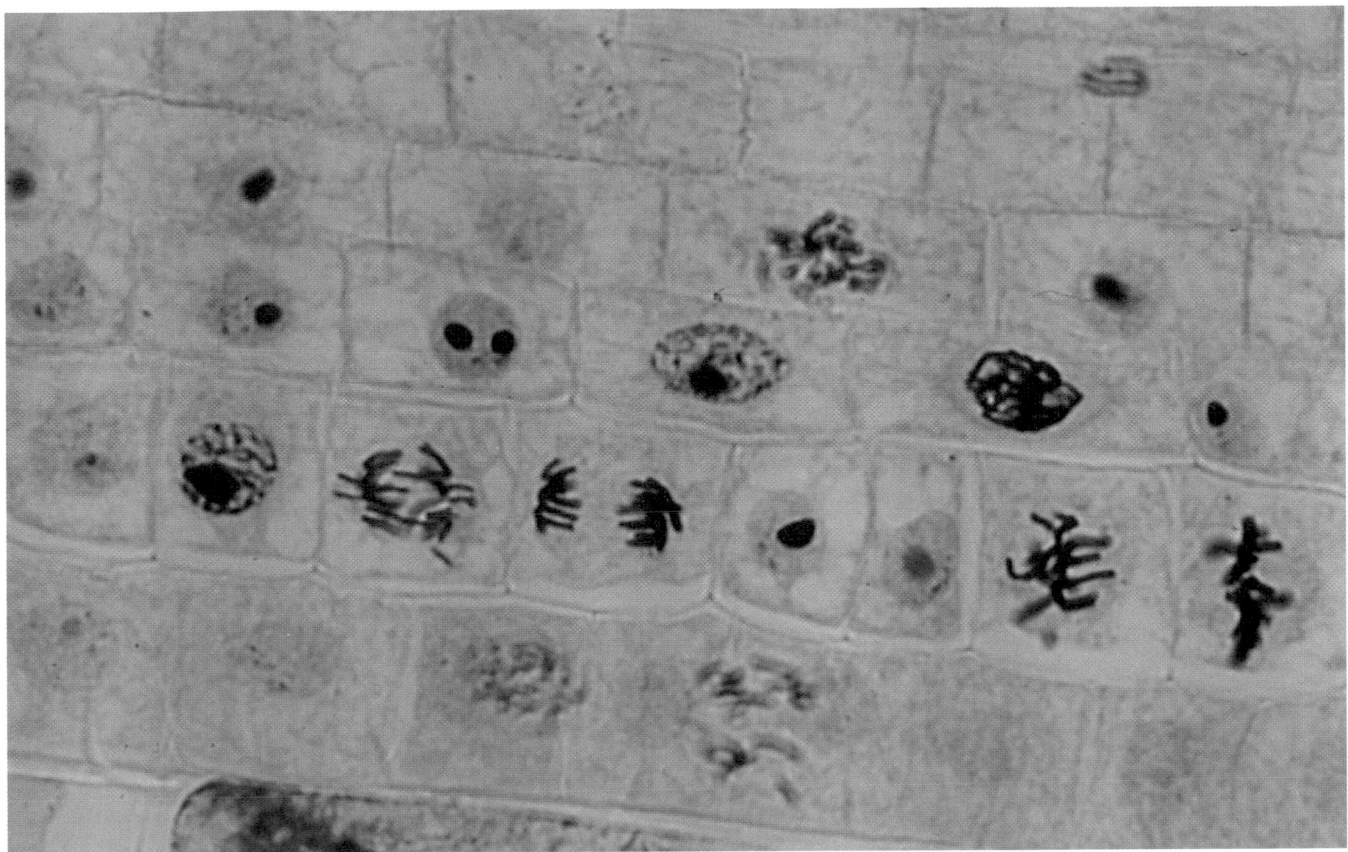

● ***Figure 2.10*** LS root tip showing stages of mitosis and cell division typical of plant cells (×130). Try to identify the stages based on information given in figure 2.9.

identical chromatids. The complete cycle of events from one mitosis to the next is called the **cell cycle.**

Most nuclei contain many chromosomes, but the diagrams in *figure 2.8* show a cell containing only four chromosomes for convenience ($2n = 4$). Colours are used to show whether the chromosomes are from the female or male parent. An animal cell is used as an example. The behaviour of chromosomes in plant cells is identical. However, plant cells do not contain centrioles and, after nuclear division, a new cell wall must form between the daughter nuclei. It is chromosome behaviour, though, that is of particular interest. *Figure 2.8* summarises the process of mitosis diagrammatically, as seen with the light microscope. *Figures 2.9* (animal) and *2.10* (plant) show photographs of the process as seen with a light microscope.

Biological significance of mitosis

- The nuclei of the two daughter cells formed have the same number of chromosomes as the parent nucleus and are genetically identical. This allows growth of multicellular organisms from unicellular zygotes. Growth may occur over the entire body, as in animals, or be confined to certain regions, as in the meristems (growing points) of plants.
- Replacement of cells and repair of tissues is possible using mitosis followed by cell division. Cells are constantly dying and being replaced by identical cells. In the human body, for example, cell replacement is particularly rapid in the skin and in the lining of the gut. Some animals are able to regenerate whole parts of the body, as, for example, the arms of a starfish.
- Mitosis is the basis of asexual reproduction, the production of new individuals of a species by

one parent organism. This can take many forms. For a unicellular organism, such as a bacterium or *Amoeba*, cell division inevitably results in reproduction. For multicellular organisms, new individuals may be produced which bud off from the parent in various ways *(figure 2.11)*. This is particularly common in plants, where it is most commonly a form of vegetative propagation in which a bud on part of the stem simply grows a new plant. This eventually becomes detached from the parent and lives independently. The bud may be part of the stem of an overwintering structure such as a bulb or tuber. The ability to generate whole organisms from single cells, or small groups of cells, is becoming important in biotechnology and genetic engineering.

Meiosis in an animal cell

As with mitosis, the process is best described by means of annotated diagrams *(figure 2.12)*. Again, an animal cell is shown where $2n = 4$, and different colours represent maternal and paternal chromosomes.

Unlike mitosis, meiosis involves two divisions, called meiosis I and meiosis II. **Meiosis I** is a reduction division, resulting in two daughter nuclei with **half** the number of chromosomes of the parent nucleus. In **meiosis II**, the chromosomes behave as in mitosis, so that each of the two haploid daughter nuclei divides again. Meiosis therefore results in a total of four haploid nuclei. Note that it is the behaviour of chromosomes in *meiosis I* that is particularly important and contrasts with mitosis.

Figure 2.12 summarises the process of meiosis diagrammatically. *Figure 2.13* shows photographs of the process as seen with a light microscope.

Meiosis and genetic variation

Meiosis leads to genetic variation in two ways, through independent assortment of homologous chromosomes and through crossing over of chromatids.

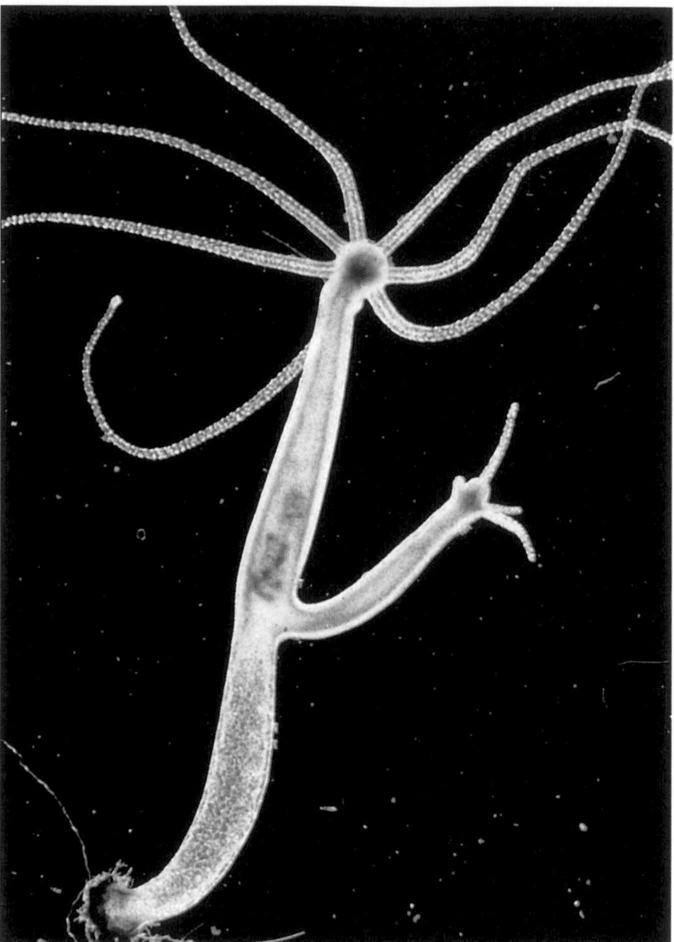

● ***Figure 2.11*** Asexual reproduction by budding in *Hydra*. *Hydra* lives in fresh water, catching its prey with the aid of its tentacles. The bud growing from its side is genetically identical to the parent and will eventually break free and live independently.

Independent assortment of homologous chromosomes

Figure 2.14 shows two possible ways in which the bivalents of a cell with a diploid number of 4 can line up on the equator of the spindle during metaphase I. Either way is equally likely because the orientation of each homologous pair is independent of all the other homologous pairs. This results in 'independent assortment' of chromosomes. In other words, which chromosome of a given pair goes to which pole is independent of (unaffected by) the behaviour of the chromosomes in other pairs. This in turn leads to the maximum possible variation in the chromosome composition of the gametes.

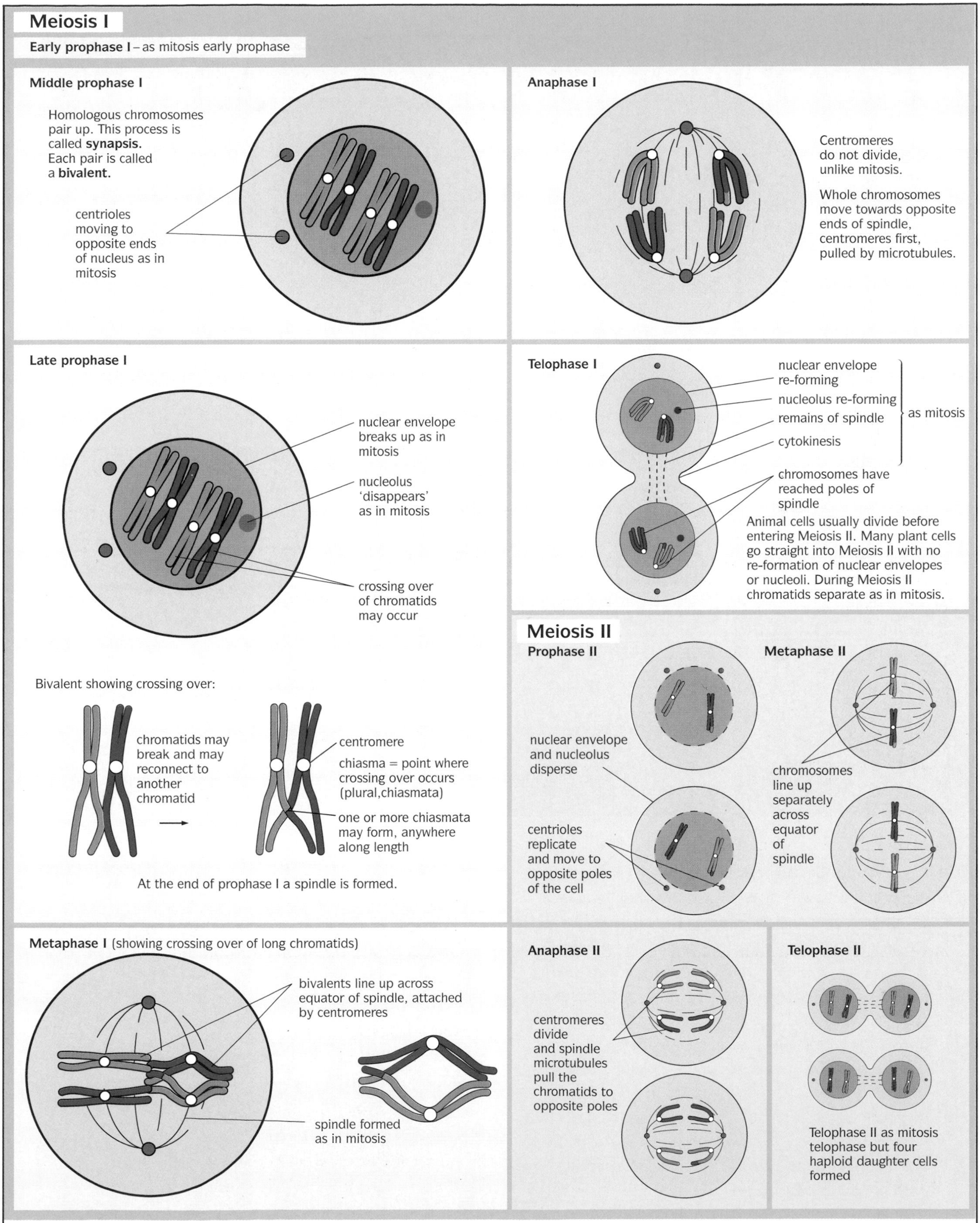

Meiosis I

Early prophase I – as mitosis early prophase

Middle prophase I

Homologous chromosomes pair up. This process is called **synapsis.** Each pair is called a **bivalent.**

centrioles moving to opposite ends of nucleus as in mitosis

Anaphase I

Centromeres do not divide, unlike mitosis.

Whole chromosomes move towards opposite ends of spindle, centromeres first, pulled by microtubules.

Late prophase I

nuclear envelope breaks up as in mitosis

nucleolus 'disappears' as in mitosis

crossing over of chromatids may occur

Bivalent showing crossing over:

chromatids may break and may reconnect to another chromatid

centromere

chiasma = point where crossing over occurs (plural,chiasmata)

one or more chiasmata may form, anywhere along length

At the end of prophase I a spindle is formed.

Telophase I

nuclear envelope re-forming

nucleolus re-forming

remains of spindle

cytokinesis

} as mitosis

chromosomes have reached poles of spindle

Animal cells usually divide before entering Meiosis II. Many plant cells go straight into Meiosis II with no re-formation of nuclear envelopes or nucleoli. During Meiosis II chromatids separate as in mitosis.

Metaphase I (showing crossing over of long chromatids)

bivalents line up across equator of spindle, attached by centromeres

spindle formed as in mitosis

Meiosis II

Prophase II

nuclear envelope and nucleolus disperse

centrioles replicate and move to opposite poles of the cell

Metaphase II

chromosomes line up separately across equator of spindle

Anaphase II

centromeres divide and spindle microtubules pull the chromatids to opposite poles

Telophase II

Telophase II as mitosis telophase but four haploid daughter cells formed

● ***Figure 2.12*** Meiosis and cytokinesis in an animal cell.

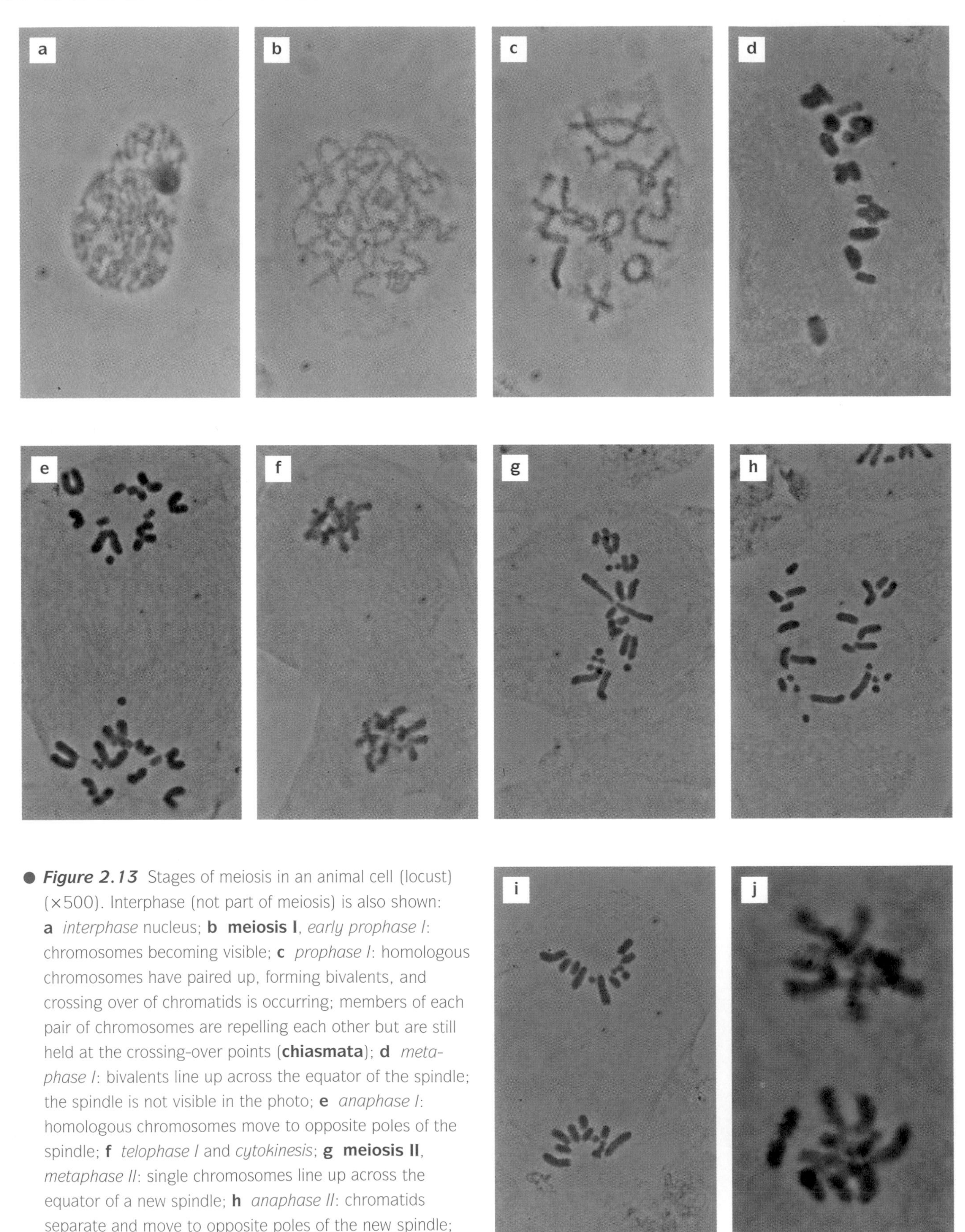

● ***Figure 2.13*** Stages of meiosis in an animal cell (locust) (×500). Interphase (not part of meiosis) is also shown: **a** *interphase* nucleus; **b** **meiosis I**, *early prophase I*: chromosomes becoming visible; **c** *prophase I*: homologous chromosomes have paired up, forming bivalents, and crossing over of chromatids is occurring; members of each pair of chromosomes are repelling each other but are still held at the crossing-over points (**chiasmata**); **d** *metaphase I*: bivalents line up across the equator of the spindle; the spindle is not visible in the photo; **e** *anaphase I*: homologous chromosomes move to opposite poles of the spindle; **f** *telophase I* and *cytokinesis*; **g** **meiosis II**, *metaphase II*: single chromosomes line up across the equator of a new spindle; **h** *anaphase II*: chromatids separate and move to opposite poles of the new spindle; **i** *late anaphase II*; **j** *telophase II*.

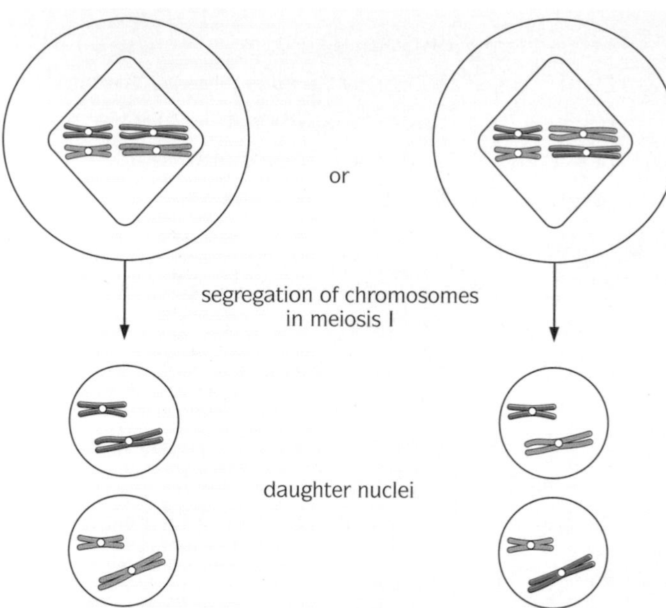

Nuclei of the four possible types of gamete. Each is equally likely.

● ***Figure 2.14*** Possible arrangements of bivalents at metaphase I in a cell with 4 chromosomes. Daughter nuclei that are formed as a result are also shown.

SAQ 2.2

Draw diagrams, as in *figure 2.14*, to show the chromosome content of the nuclei of all possible types of gamete produced as a result of independent assortment of chromosomes in a parent cell containing a nucleus with a diploid number of 6.

SAQ 2.3

From your answer to SAQ 2.2, what is the formula for predicting how many possible types of gamete can be formed by independent assortment from one parent cell?

SAQ 2.4

Using your formula, calculate how many different types of gamete a human can produce as a result of independent assortment of chromosomes.

SAQ 2.5

From your answer to SAQ 2.4 how many genetically different offspring can a human couple theoretically produce as a result of independent assortment?

Crossing over

When chromatids cross over in prophase I of meiosis, it is possible for genes from a maternal chromatid to exchange places with genes from a paternal chromatid. This increases variation among the daughter cells, as seen at the end of *figure 2.12*, where all the daughter cells are different. As a result of this the amount of variation possible is enormous.

Cancer

Cancer is one of the most common diseases of developed countries, accounting for roughly one in five deaths. Lung cancer alone caused about one in 18 deaths in Britain in the 1980s *(figure 2.15)*. It is the most common form of cancer in men, while breast cancer is the leading form of cancer in women. There are, in fact, more than a hundred different forms of cancer and the medical profession does not think of it as a single disease. Cancers show us the importance of controlling cell division precisely, because cancers are a result of uncontrolled mitosis. Cancerous cells divide repeatedly, out of control, and a **tumour** develops which is an irregular mass of cells. The cells usually show abnormal changes in shape *(figure 2.16)*. Sometimes cells break away from the developing tumour and are carried in blood or lymph to other parts of the body, starting **secondary tumours.**

Cancers are thought to start when changes occur in genes which control cell division. A change in a gene is called a **mutation.** A factor which brings about mutation is called a **mutagen** and is described as **mutagenic.** Mutagens can therefore cause cancer. Mutations are not unusual events, and *most* mutated cells, unlike those that cause cancer, are either crippled in some way that results in their early death, or are destroyed by the body's immune system. Since most cells can be replaced, this usually has no detrimental effect on the body.

Any agent which causes cancer is described as **carcinogenic.** The mutation may only occur in one cell, but since it is a genetic change, it is passed on to all that cell's descendants. By the time it is usually detected, a typical tumour contains about a thousand million cells. The genes that cause cancer are called **oncogenes** (*onco* from the Greek word *onkos* meaning a bulk or mass). They are the mutated forms of genes which normally regulate cell division. It is thought that a single mutation cannot be responsible for cancer, but that several independent rare 'accidents' must occur in one cell.

Some of the factors which can increase mutation rates, and hence cancer, are as follows.

- *Ionising radiation*
  This includes X-rays, gamma rays and particles from the decay of radioactive elements. They cause the formation of damaging ions inside cells which can break DNA strands. Ultraviolet light, although it does not cause the formation of damaging ions, can also damage genes. Depletion of the ozone layer is causing concern because, as a result, more ultraviolet light will penetrate to the Earth's surface and could result in an increase in skin cancer.
- *Chemicals*
  Many different chemicals have been shown to be carcinogenic. About 25% of all cancer deaths in developed countries are due to carcinogens in the tar of tobacco smoke. Certain dyes, such as a group known as the aniline dyes, are also well-known carcinogens. All these chemicals damage DNA molecules.
- *Virus infection*
  Some cancers in animals, including humans, are known to be caused by viruses. Burkitt's lymphoma, the most common cancer in children in certain parts of Africa, is caused by a

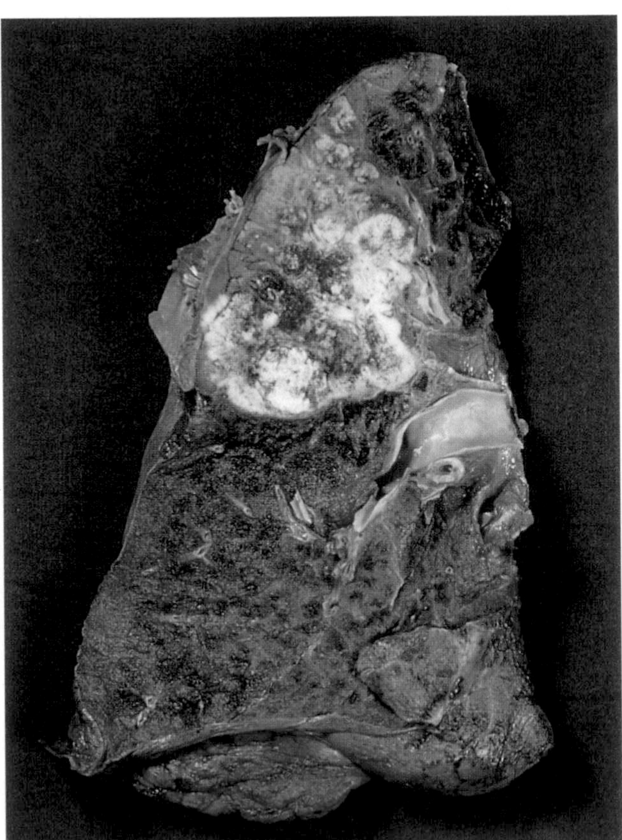

● ***Figure 2.15*** **a** Lung of a patient who died of lung cancer. The tumour appears as a black and white mouldy area towards the top of the lung and black tarry deposits throughout the lung show the patient was a heavy smoker.

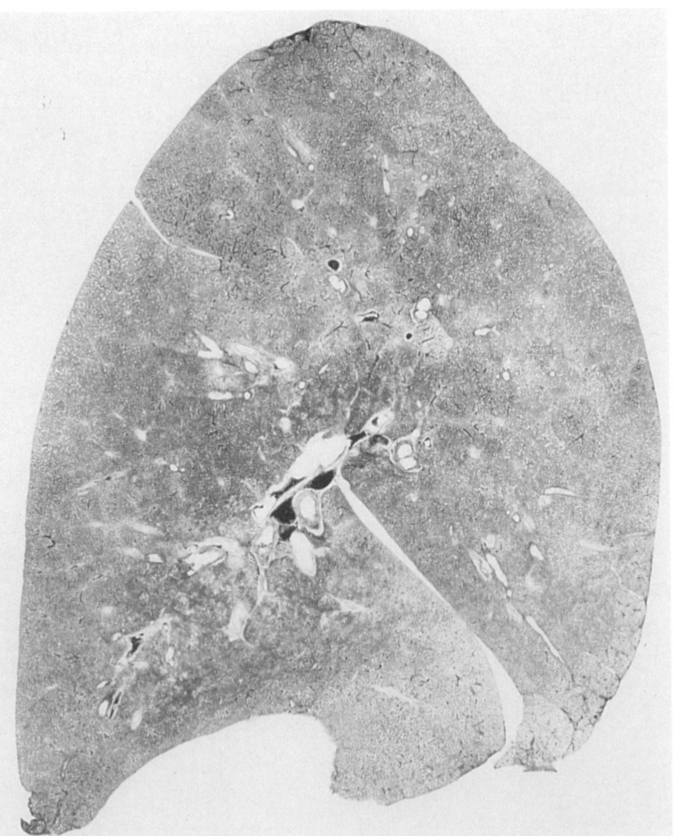

b Section of a healthy human lung. No black tar deposits are visible.

virus. Another causes a form of leukaemia (cancer of the white blood cells). Papilloma viruses are responsible for some cancers, and include two types that have been linked with cervical cancer, a disease that can be transmitted sexually. Viruses that cause cancer usually carry oncogenes, or regulatory genes that can become oncogenes.

- *Hereditary predisposition* Cancer tends to be more common in some families than others, indicating a genetic link. In most cases it is believed that the disease *itself* is not inherited, but susceptibility to the factors that cause the disease is inherited. However, some forms of cancer do appear to be caused by inheritance of a single faulty gene. For example, retinoblastoma, which starts in one or both eyes during childhood and spreads to the brain, causing death if untreated, is caused by a dominant gene.

a

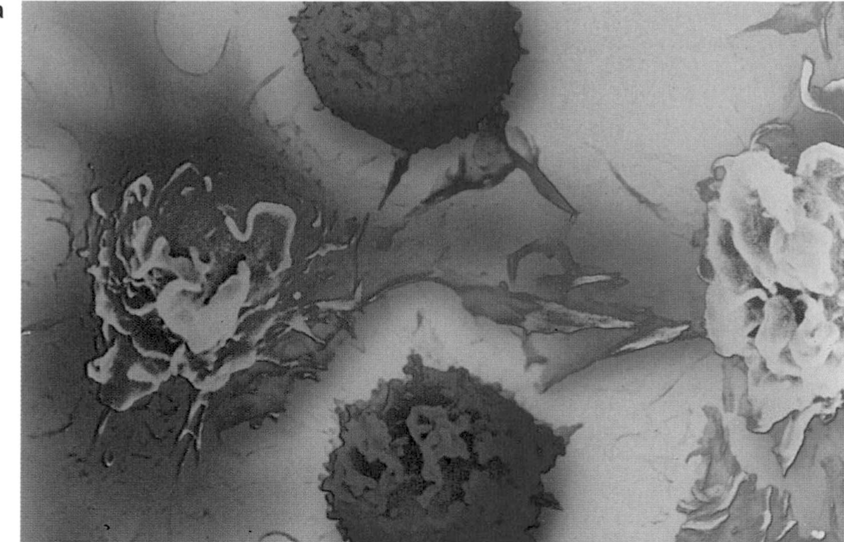

b

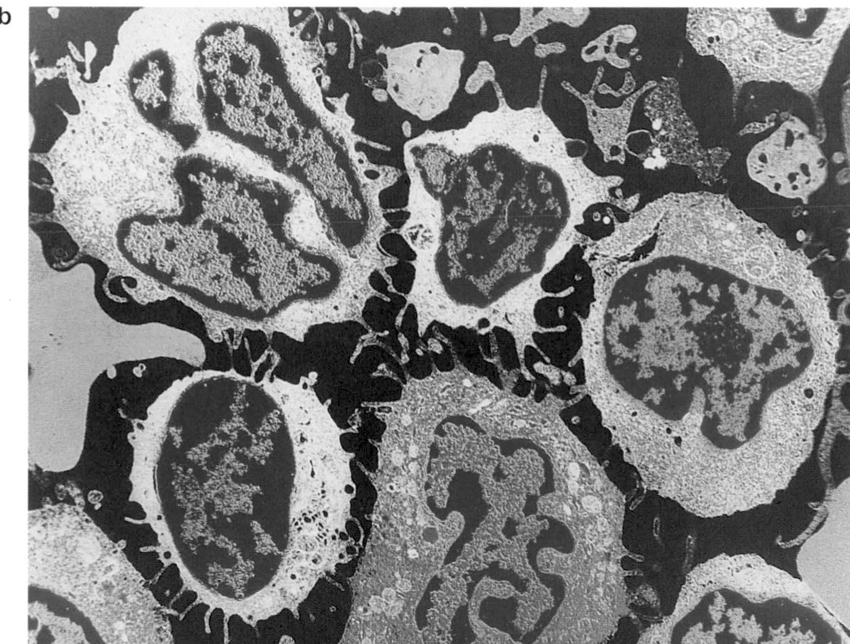

● ***Figure 2.16*** **a** False-colour SEM of cancer cells (yellow) and white blood cells (red). The two cancer cells have an uneven surface, with cytoplasmic projections which may be used for movement. These cells form tumours which invade and destroy surrounding tissues and travel to distant parts of the body to start secondary tumours. White blood cells gather at these sites as an immune response. They may serve as natural killer cells, attacking both foreign invaders and cancers. The white blood cells have just undergone cell division.

b False-colour TEM of abnormal white blood cells isolated from the blood of a person suffering from hairy-cell leukaemia. The white blood cells are covered with characteristic hair-like, cytoplasmic projections. Leukaemia is a disease in which the bone marrow and other blood-forming organs produce too many of certain types of white blood cells. These immature or abnormal cells suppress the normal production of white and red blood cells, and increase the sufferer's susceptibility to infection (×3100).

SUMMARY

- Cell division is needed so that organisms can grow and reproduce. It involves division of the nucleus followed by division of the cytoplasm.
- During nuclear division the chromosomes become visible. Each is seen to be formed of two chromatids. The chromosomes of a body cell can be photographed and arranged in order of size as a karyotype. This shows that each cell has either one set of chromosomes, known as haploid, or two sets of chromosomes known as diploid. In the diploid condition, one set comes from the female parent and one from the male parent. Gametes are haploid cells.
- Body cells divide in the process of mitosis to produce two identical daughter cells whose nuclei contain the same number of chromosomes as the parent cell. This allows growth and repair of a multicellular organism and is the basis of asexual reproduction.
- Meiosis halves the number of chromosomes in the nucleus. This prevents chromosome number doubling in each generation of organisms which reproduce sexually. Meiosis contributes to genetic variation because during meiosis there is exchange of genetic material between chromosomes (crossing over), and independent assortment of chromosomes before division. This makes it possible for all four daughter cells to have a genetically different set of chromosomes.
- Cancers are caused by uncontrolled mitosis, possibly as the result of a mutation in a gene or genes which control cell division. Agents which cause cancer are known as carcinogens and include ionising radiation, many chemicals and viruses. Some cancers may have a hereditary link.

Questions

1 With reference to chromosome behaviour only, compare the processes of mitosis and meiosis I in an animal cell. (If you wish, you may answer the question by the use of annotated diagrams of the different stages placed side by side for comparison.)

2 Explain how meiosis leads to genetic variation among the gametes of a parent organism.

3 Summarise the biological significance of **a** mitosis, and **b** meiosis.

4 Explain the link between cancer and mitosis. Describe how the chances of cancer developing in the human body may be increased.

5 Draw a diagram to show the arrangement of chromosomes **a** at metaphase I, meiosis, in an animal cell with a diploid number of 2 and **b** at anaphase of mitosis in a plant cell with a diploid number of 6.

6 Using photographs, such as shown in *figure 2.10*, how could you estimate the relative length of each stage of mitosis?

7 Explain clearly the meaning of the following terms: haploid, diploid, zygote, homologous pair of chromosomes, bivalent, synapsis, centromere, autosome, chromatid, chiasma.

Biological molecules

By the end of this chapter you should be able to:

1 understand the importance in biology of carbohydrates, lipids and proteins;

2 understand that although some important biological molecules are very large, they are made by the relatively simple process of joining together many small repeating subunits;

3 describe the basic structure of the main types of carbohydrates, namely monosaccharides, disaccharides and polysaccharides;

4 describe the structure of the ring form of α- and β-glucose;

5 describe the formation and breakage of a glycosidic bond, and its significance;

6 describe the structure of the polysaccharides starch, glycogen and cellulose and show how these structures are related to their functions in living organisms;

7 describe the basic structure and properties of triglycerides and phospholipids and relate these structures to their functions in living organisms;

8 distinguish between saturated and unsaturated fatty acids and lipids;

9 describe the structure of amino acids and the way in which peptide bonds are formed;

10 describe the primary structure of polypeptides and proteins and how it affects their secondary and tertiary structure;

11 explain that the quaternary structure of a protein is formed by the combination of two or more polypeptide chains;

12 describe the importance of hydrogen bonds, disulphide bonds, ionic bonds and van der Waals forces in maintaining the three-dimensional structure of a protein;

13 discuss the ways in which the structures of haemoglobin and collagen are related to their functions;

14 describe the crucial role that water plays in maintaining life on Earth, both as a constituent of living organisms and as an environment.

The study of the structure and functioning of biological molecules now forms an important branch of biology known as **molecular biology**. This is a relatively young science, but the importance of the subject is clear from the relatively large number of Nobel prizes that have been awarded in this field. It has attracted some of the best scientists, even from other disciplines like physics and mathematics.

Molecular biology is closely linked with biochemistry, which looks at the chemical reactions of biological molecules. The sum total of all the biochemical reactions in the body is known as **metabolism**. Metabolism is complex, but it has an underlying simplicity. For example, there are only 20 common amino acids used to make proteins, whereas theoretically there could be millions. Why is there this economy? One possibility is that all the manufacture and interactions of biological molecules must be controlled and regulated and, the more there are, the more complex the control becomes. Control and regulation by enzymes will be examined in chapter 4.

Another striking principle of molecular biology is how closely the structures of molecules are related to their functions. This will become clear in this chapter and in chapter 4. Our understanding of how structure is related to function may, in the next century, lead to the creation of designer molecules which will be able to carry out a vast range of functions, from large-scale industrial reactions to precise targetting of cells in medical treatment.

The building blocks of life

The four most common elements in living organisms are, in order of abundance, hydrogen, carbon, oxygen and nitrogen. They account for more than 99% of the atoms found in all living things. Carbon is particularly important because carbon atoms tend to join together, forming long chains or ring structures. They can be thought of as the basic skeletons of organic molecules to which other groups of atoms are attached. Organic molecules always contain carbon.

It is believed that, before life evolved, there was a period of chemical evolution in which a whole variety of simple carbon-based molecules evolved from the more simple molecules that existed on the young planet Earth. Such mixtures can be created relatively easily today given similar raw ingredients, such as methane (CH_4), carbon dioxide (CO_2), hydrogen (H_2), water (H_2O), nitrogen (N_2), ammonia (NH_3), hydrogen sulphide (H_2S) and an energy source. Key biological molecules such as amino acids and the bases found in nucleic acids form in such mixtures if provided with large amounts of energy, for example an electrical discharge. These simple molecules, which are relatively few in number, then act as the building blocks for larger molecules. The main ones are shown in *figure 3.1*.

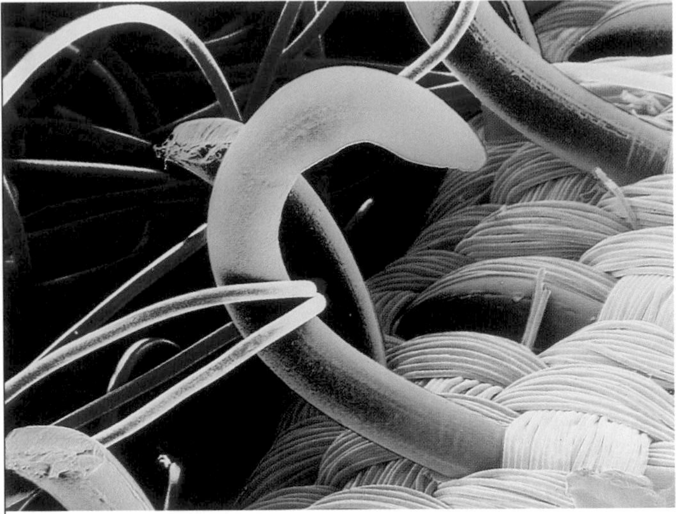

● ***Figure 3.2*** False-colour SEM of Velcro, which is a nylon material manufactured in two separate pieces and used as a fastener. One piece has a hooked surface (right) made by weaving loops into the fabric (yellow) and then cutting them. The other piece has a surface covered with loops (left).

Polymers and macromolecules

The term **macromolecule** means giant molecule. There are three types of macromolecule in living organisms, namely polysaccharides, proteins (polypeptides) and nucleic acids (polynucleotides). The prefix *poly* means that these molecules are **polymers**, that is macromolecules made up of repeating subunits that are similar or identical which are joined end to end like beads on a string. Making such molecules is relatively easy because the same reaction is repeated many times. There are many examples of industrially produced polymers, such as polyester, polythene, PVC (polyvinyl chloride), nylon and plastics *(figure 3.2)*.

All these are made up of carbon-based subunits and contain thousands of carbon atoms joined end to end. Natural examples of polymers are cellulose (cotton is about 99% cellulose) and rubber. The subunits from which polysaccharides, proteins and nucleic acids are made are monosaccharides, amino acids and nucleotides respectively. *Figure 3.1* shows two further types of molecule which, although not polymers, are made up of simpler biochemicals. These are lipids and nucleotides.

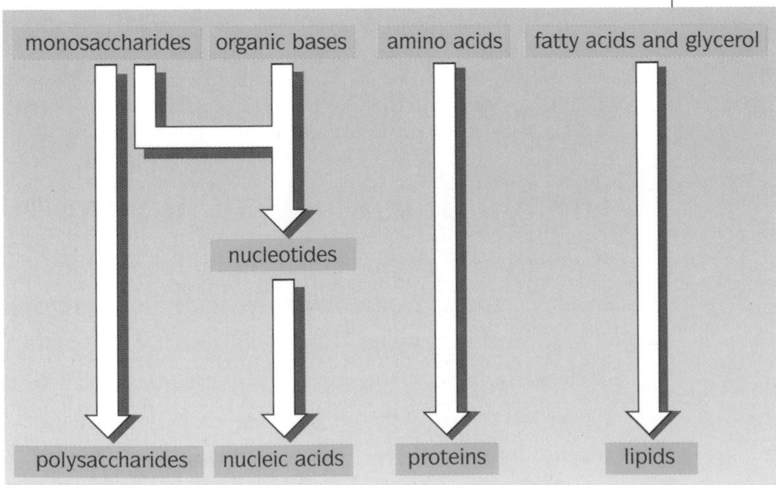

● ***Figure 3.1*** The building blocks of life.

We shall now take a closer look at the small biological molecules and the larger molecules made from them, starting with a group of molecules called carbohydrates.

Carbohydrates

Carbohydrates contain the elements carbon, hydrogen and oxygen. The name comes from the fact that hydrogen and oxygen atoms are present in the ratio of 2:1, as in water (*hydrate* refers to water). The **general formula** for a carbohydrate can therefore be written as $C_x(H_2O)_y$.

Carbohydrates are divided into three main groups, namely monosaccharides, disaccharides and polysaccharides.

Monosaccharides

Monosaccharides and disaccharides are **sugars**. They dissolve easily in water to form sweet solutions (*saccharide* refers to sweet or sugar). Monosaccharides have the general formula $(CH_2O)_n$ and consist of a **single** sugar molecule (*mono* means one). A disaccharide molecule is made by joining **two** monosaccharide molecules together. The main types of monosaccharides, if they are classified according to the number of carbon atoms, are **trioses** (3C), **pentoses** (5C) and **hexoses** (6C). The names of all sugars end with **-ose**.

SAQ 3.1

The formula for a hexose is $C_6H_{12}O_6$ or $(CH_2O)_6$. What would be the formula of **a** a triose and **b** a pentose?

Molecular and structural formulae

The formula for a hexose has been written as $C_6H_{12}O_6$. This is known as the **molecular formula**. It is also useful to show the arrangements of the atoms which can be done by a diagram known as the **structural formula**. *Figure 3.3* shows the structural formula of glucose, a hexose which is the most common monosaccharide.

Ring structures

One important aspect of the structure of pentoses and hexoses is that the chain of carbon atoms is long enough to close up on itself and form a more stable ring structure. This can be illustrated using glucose as an example. When glucose forms a ring, carbon atom number 1 joins to the oxygen on carbon atom number 5 *(figure 3.4)*. The ring therefore contains oxygen, and carbon atom number 6 is not part of the ring.

You will see from *figure 3.4* that the hydroxyl group, –OH, on carbon atom 1 may be **above** or **below** the plane of the ring. The form of glucose where it is below the ring is known as **α-glucose (alpha-glucose)** and the form where it is above as **β-glucose (beta-glucose)**. Two forms of the same chemical are known as **isomers**, and the extra variety provided by the existence of α- and β-isomers has important biological consequences, as we shall see in the structure of starch, glycogen and cellulose.

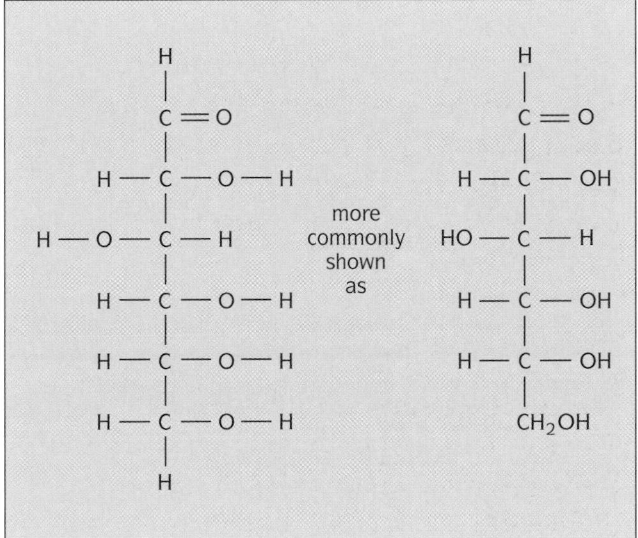

● **Figure 3.3** Structural formula of glucose. –OH is known as a hydroxyl group. There are five in glucose.

Roles of monosaccharides in living organisms

Monosaccharides have two major functions. Firstly, they are commonly used as a source of energy in respiration. This is due to the large number of carbon–hydrogen bonds. These bonds can be broken to release a lot of energy which is transferred to help make ATP (adenosine triphosphate) from ADP (adenosine diphosphate) and phosphate. The most important monosaccharide in energy metabolism is glucose.

Secondly, they are important as building blocks for larger molecules. For example, glucose is used to make the polysaccharides starch, glycogen and cellulose. Ribose (a pentose) is used to make RNA (ribonucleic acid) and ATP. Deoxyribose (a pentose) is used to make DNA.

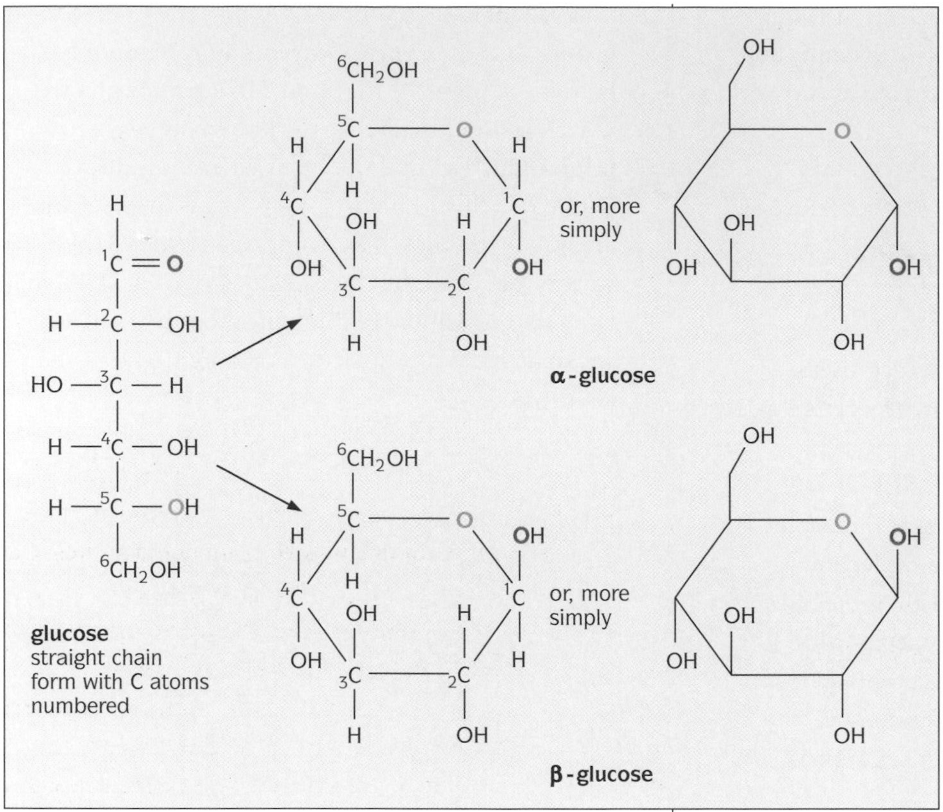

● **Figure 3.4** Structural formulae for the straight-chain and ring forms of glucose. Chemists often leave out the C and H atoms from the structural formula for simplicity.

Glycosidic bonds

Figure 3.5 shows how two monosaccharides may be joined together by a process known as **condensation**. Two hydroxyl (–OH) groups line up alongside each other. One combines with a hydrogen atom from the other to form a water molecule. This allows an oxygen 'bridge' to form between the two molecules, holding them together and forming a **disaccharide**. The bridge is called a **glycosidic bond**. In theory any two –OH groups can line up and, since monosaccharides have many –OH groups, there are a large number of possible disaccharides. However, only a few of these are common.

The reverse of this kind of condensation is the **addition** of water which is known as **hydrolysis** (*figure 3.5*). This takes place during the digestion of disaccharides and polysaccharides when they are broken back down to monosaccharides. Like most chemical reactions in cells, hydrolysis and condensation reactions are controlled by enzymes.

Polysaccharides

Polysaccharides are polymers whose subunits are monosaccharides. They are made by joining many monosaccharide molecules by condensation. Each successive monosaccharide is added by means of a glycosidic bond, as in disaccharides. The final molecule may be several thousand monosaccharide units long, forming a macromolecule. The most important polysaccharides are starch, glycogen and cellulose, all of which are polymers of glucose.

Since glucose is the main source of energy for cells, it is important for living organisms to store it in an appropriate form. If glucose itself accumulated in cells, it would dissolve and make the contents of the cell too concentrated, which would seriously affect its osmotic properties (see page 63). It is also a very reactive molecule and would interfere with normal cell chemistry. These problems are avoided by converting it, by condensation reactions, to a storage polysaccharide, which is a convenient, compact, inert and insoluble molecule. Starch is made in plants and glycogen in animals. Glucose can be made available again quickly by an enzyme-controlled reaction.

SAQ 3.2

What type of chemical reaction would be involved in the formation of glucose from starch or glycogen?

Starch (amylose)

Starch is made by many condensations between α-glucose molecules, as shown in *figure 3.5*. In this way a long, unbranching chain of several thousand 1,4 linked glucose molecules is built up. (1,4 linked means they are linked between carbon atoms 1 and

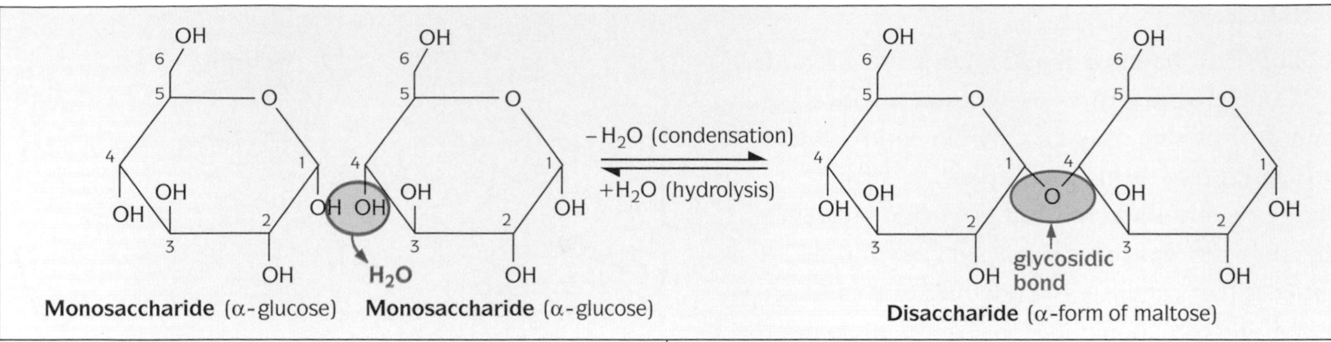

● ***Figure 3.5*** Formation of a disaccharide from two monosaccharides. In this example, the glycosidic bond is formed between carbon atoms 1 and 4 of neighbouring monosaccharides. The process may be repeated many times to form a polysaccharide.

4 of successive glucose units.) The chains are curved and coil up into helical structures like springs, making the final molecule more compact *(figure 3.6a)*. This unbranching form of starch is called **amylose**; there is a branching form also. A suspension of amylose in water stains a blue-black colour with iodine–potassium iodide solution. The molecules build up into relatively large starch grains which are commonly found in chloroplasts and in storage organs such as the potato tuber and the seeds of cereals and legumes *(figure 3.6b)*. Starch grains are easily seen with a light microscope, especially if stained; rubbing a freshly cut potato tuber on a glass slide and staining with iodine–potassium iodide solution is a quick method of preparing a specimen for viewing.

Glycogen

Glycogen resembles amylose in containing chains of 1,4 linked α-glucose units, but it also has many branches formed by 1,6 linkages as shown in *figure 3.7*. So it can form even more compact granules than amylose. These granules are clearly visible in liver cells *(figures 1.10 and 6.5)* and can form up to 10% of the mass of the liver. The balance between blood glucose and liver glycogen is controlled by hormones, particularly insulin (see page 71). The other main storage site of glycogen in humans is muscle tissue, where an energy reserve is an obvious advantage.

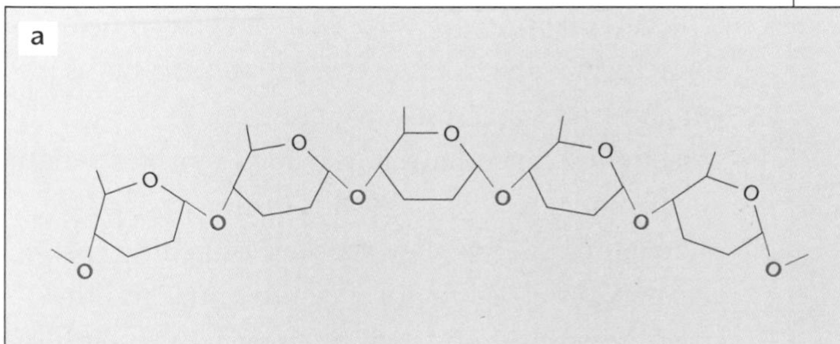

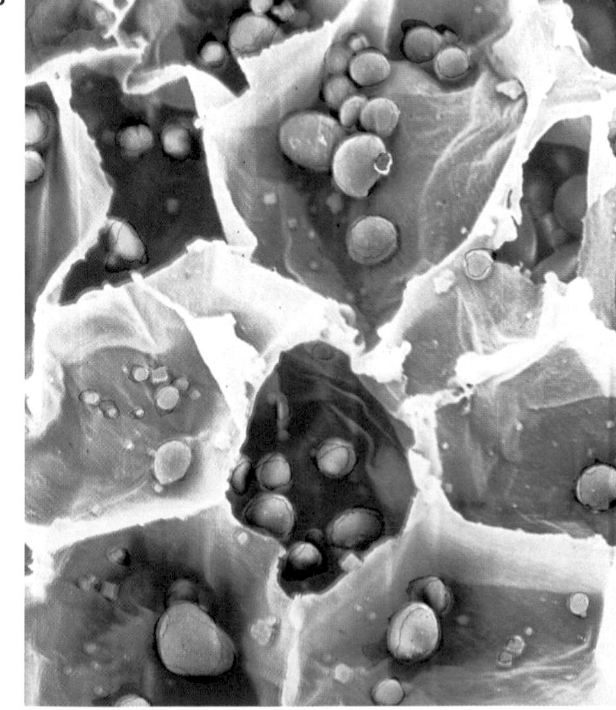

● ***Figure 3.6*** Arrangement of α-glucose units in starch (amylose). **a** The 1,4 linkages cause the chain to turn and coil.The glycosidic bonds are shown in red and the hydroxyl groups are omitted. **b** False-colour SEM of a slice through a raw potato showing starch grains or starch-containing organelles (coloured green) within their cellular compartments (×400).

Cellulose

Cellulose is the most abundant organic molecule on the planet due to its presence in plant cell walls and its slow rate of breakdown in nature. It has a structural role, being a mechanically strong molecule, unlike starch and glycogen. However the only difference between cellulose and the latter is that cellulose is a polymer of β-glucose, not α-glucose. Remember that in the β-isomer the –OH group on carbon atom 1 projects **above** the ring. In order to form a glycosidic bond with carbon atom 4, where the –OH group is **below** the ring, one glucose molecule must be upside down relative to the other, that is rotated 180°. Thus successive glucose units are linked at 180° to each other, as shown in *figure 3.8*.

This results in a strong molecule because of hydrogen bonding: the hydrogen atoms of –OH groups are weakly attracted to oxygen atoms in the same cellulose molecule (the oxygen of the glucose ring) and also to oxygen atoms of –OH groups in neighbouring molecules. Individually these bonds are weak, but so many can form, due to the large number of –OH groups, that collectively they develop enormous strength. Between 60 and 70 cellulose molecules become tightly cross-linked to form bundles called **microfibrils**. Microfibrils are in turn held together in bundles called **fibres** by hydrogen bonding. A cell wall typically has several layers of fibres, running in different directions to increase strength *(figure 3.9)*. Cellulose comprises about 20–40% of the average cell wall; other molecules help to cross-link the cellulose fibres and some form a glue-like matrix around the fibres which further increases strength.

Cellulose fibres have a very high tensile strength, almost equal to that of steel. This means that if pulled at both ends they are very difficult to break, and makes it possible for a cell to withstand the large pressures that develop within it as a result of osmosis (page 64). Without the wall it would burst when in a dilute solution. These pressures help provide support for the plant by making tissues rigid, and are responsible for cell expansion during

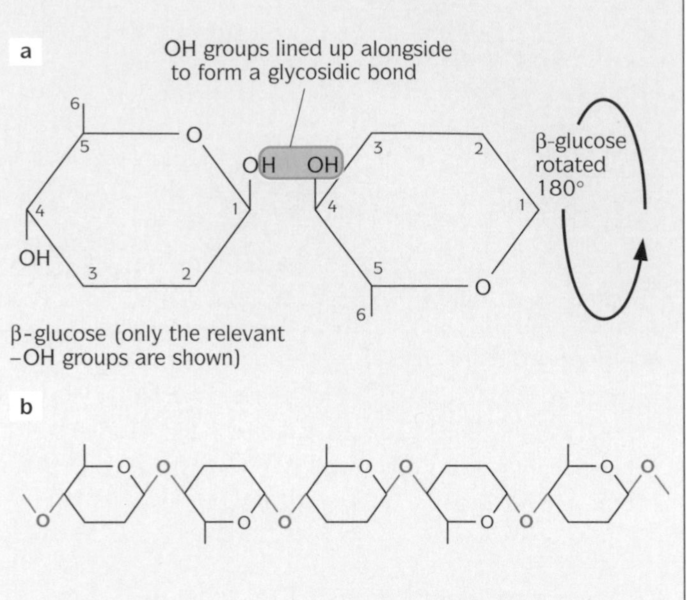

● ***Figure 3.8*** **a** Two β-glucose molecules lined up to form a 1,4 link; **b** arrangement of β-glucose units in cellulose: glycosidic bonds are shown in red and hydroxyl groups are omitted.

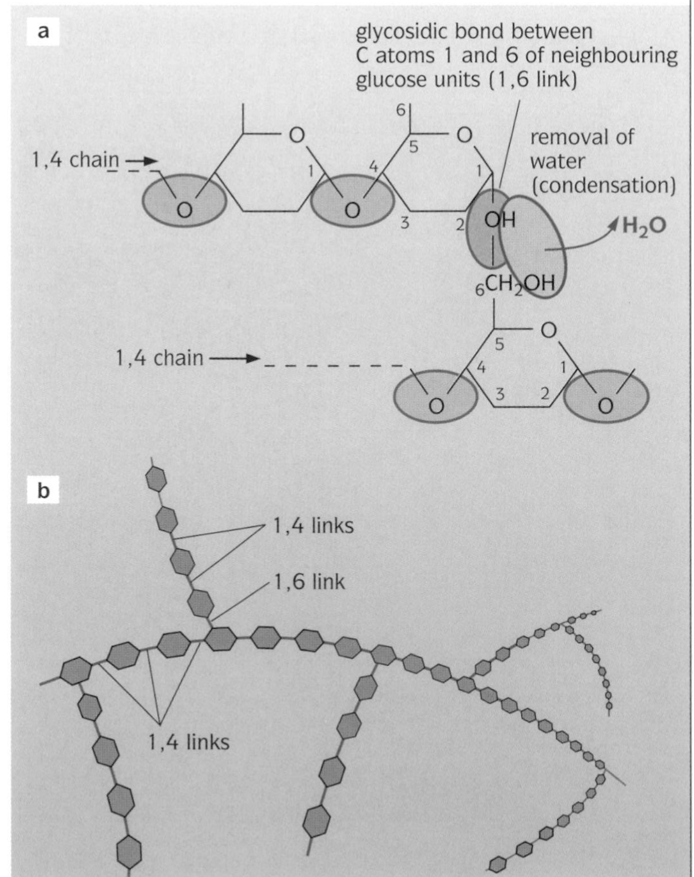

● ***Figure 3.7*** Branching structure of glycogen: **a** formation of a 1,6 link, a branchpoint; **b** overall structure of a glycogen molecule.

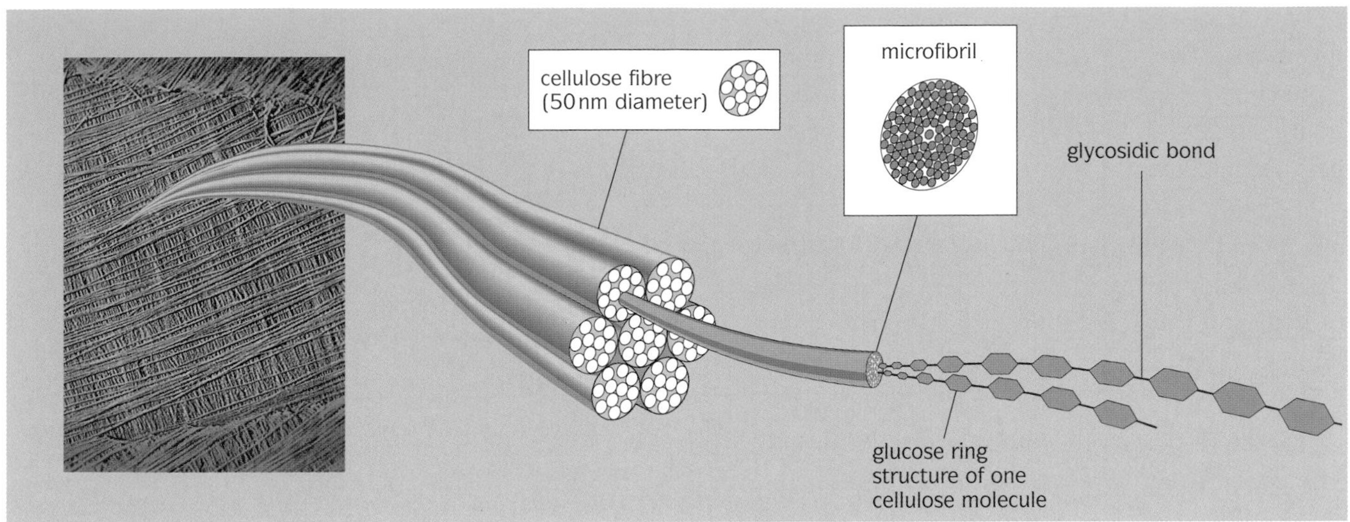

● ***Figure 3.9*** Structure of cellulose.

growth. The arrangement of fibres around the cell helps to determine the shape of the cell as it grows. Despite their strength, cellulose fibres are freely permeable, allowing water and solutes to reach the cell surface membrane.

Lipids

Lipids are a diverse group of chemicals. The most common type are the **triglycerides** which are usually known as fats and oils. The main difference between them is that, at room temperature, fats are solid whereas oils are liquid.

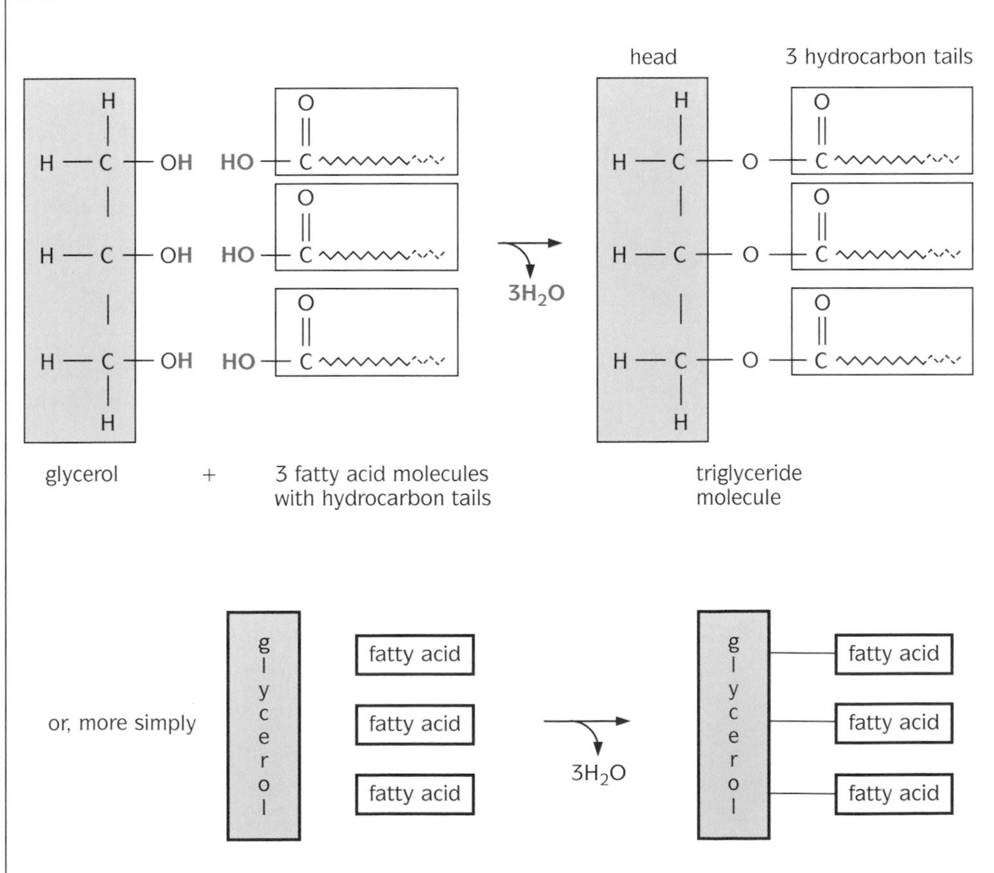

● ***Figure 3.10*** Formation of a triglyceride from glycerol and three fatty acid molecules.

Triglycerides

Triglycerides are made by the combination of three fatty acid molecules with one glycerol molecule. Glycerol is a type of alcohol.

Triglycerides are insoluble in water but are soluble in certain organic solvents, such as ether and chloroform. Each of the three fatty acid molecules joins to glycerol by a condensation reaction as shown in *figure 3.10*. You can see that glycerol contains three carbon atoms and three –OH groups. When a fatty acid combines with glycerol, it forms a glyceride. Therefore, the final molecule is called a **triglyceride** because it is made from three fatty acids.

Each fatty acid has a long hydrocarbon tail. This means that it consists of a chain of carbon atoms (often 15 or 17 carbon atoms long) combined with hydrogen *(figure 3.11)*. These tails are important because they remain free in triglycerides and explain why triglycerides are insoluble in water. They are described as water-hating, or **hydrophobic** because they do not dissolve in water. They are **non-polar** as there is no uneven distribution of electrical charge within the molecule, and so the molecules do not form hydrogen bonds with water. Consequently, they will not mix freely with water molecules. Triglycerides are therefore non-polar and hydrophobic. The triglyceride molecule can be represented diagrammatically as shown in *figure 3.12*. The tails vary in length, depending on the fatty acids used.

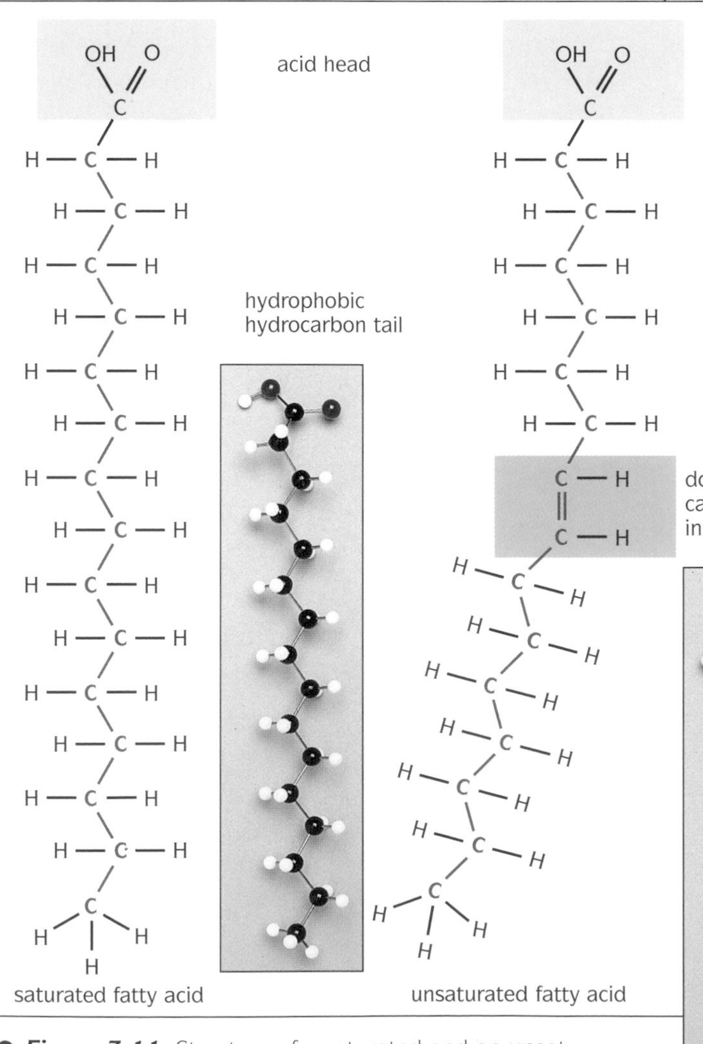

● ***Figure 3.11*** Structure of a saturated and an unsaturated fatty acid. Photographs of models are shown to the right of each structure. In the models hydrogen is white, carbon is black and oxygen is red.

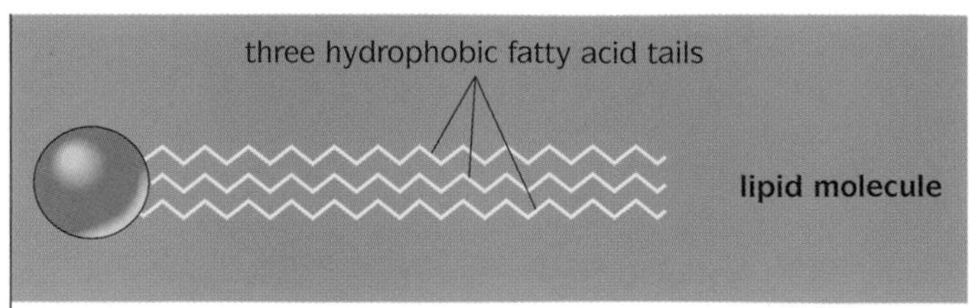

● ***Figure 3.12*** Diagrammatic representation of a lipid molecule.

Saturated and unsaturated fatty acids and lipids

Some fatty acids have double bonds between neighbouring carbon atoms, like this:
–C–C=C–C– (see also *figure 3.11*). Such fatty acids are described as **unsaturated** (meaning unsaturated with hydrogen) and form unsaturated lipids. Double bonds make fatty acids and lipids melt more easily, for example most oils are unsaturated. If there is more than one double bond, the fatty acid or lipid is described as **polyunsaturated**; if there is only one it is **monounsaturated.** Animal lipids are often saturated and occur as fats, whereas plant lipids are often unsaturated and occur as oils, such as olive oil and sunflower oil.

Roles of triglycerides

Lipids make excellent **energy reserves** because they are even richer in carbon–hydrogen bonds than carbohydrates. A given mass of lipid will therefore yield more energy on oxidation than the same mass of carbohydrate (it has a higher calorific value), an important advantage for a storage product.

Fat is stored in a number of places in the human body, particularly just below the dermis of the skin and around the kidneys. Below the skin it also acts as an **insulator** against loss of heat. Blubber, a lipid

● ***Figure 3.13*** The desert kangaroo rat uses metabolism of food to provide the water it needs.

found in sea mammals like whales, has a similar function, as well as providing buoyancy. An unusual role for lipids is as a **metabolic source of water**. When oxidised in respiration they are converted to carbon dioxide and water. The water may be of importance in very dry habitats. For example, the desert kangaroo rat *(figure 3.13)* never drinks water and survives on metabolic water from its fat intake.

Phospholipids

Phospholipids are a special type of lipid. Each molecule has the unusual property of having one end which is soluble in water. This is because one of the three fatty acid molecules is replaced by a phosphate group which carries an electrical charge and can therefore dissolve in water. The phosphate group is described as water-loving or **hydrophilic** and makes the head of a phospholipid molecule hydrophilic, though the two remaining tails are hydrophobic *(figure 3.14)*. The biological significance of this will become apparent when we study membrane structure (page 59).

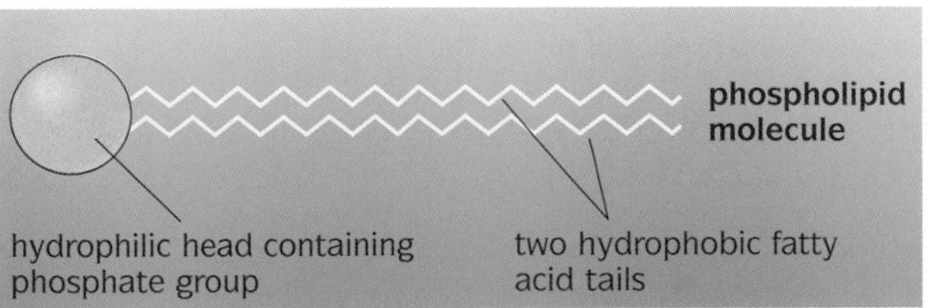

● ***Figure 3.14*** Diagrammatic representation of a phospholipid molecule.

Proteins and amino acids

Proteins are an extremely important class of molecules in living organisms. More than 50% of the dry mass of most cells is protein. They have many important functions. For example:

- they are essential components of cell membranes;
- the oxygen-carrying pigment haemoglobin is a protein;
- antibodies which attack and destroy invading microorganisms are proteins;
- all enzymes are proteins;
- hair and the surface layers of your skin contain the protein keratin;
- collagen, another protein, adds strength to many tissues, such as bone and the walls of arteries.

Despite their tremendous range of functions, all proteins are made from the same basic components. These are **amino acids**.

Amino acids

Figure 3.15 shows the structure of glycine, the most simple amino acid. Like all amino acids, it

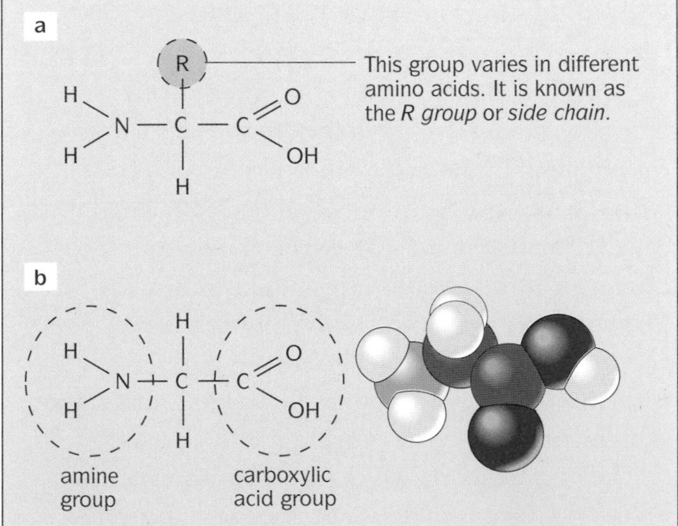

● ***Figure 3.15*** **a** The general structure of an amino acid. **b** Structure of the simplest amino acid, glycine, in which the R group is hydrogen, H. R groups for the 20 naturally occurring amino acids are shown in the appendix.

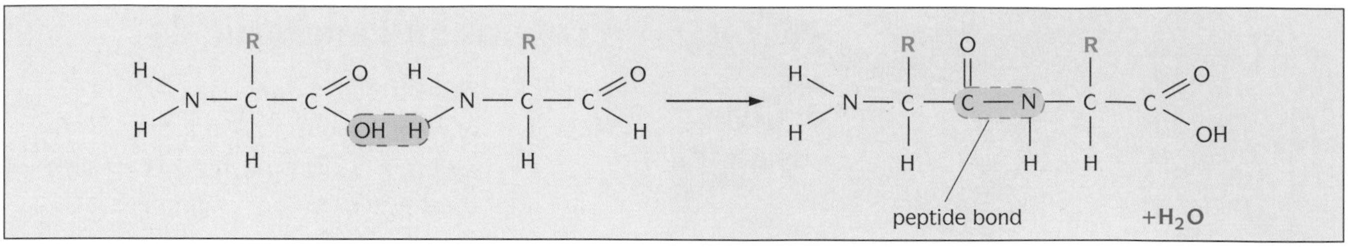

● ***Figure 3.16*** Amino acids link together by the loss of a molecule of water to form a peptide bond.

has an **amine** group, $-NH_2$, and a **carboxylic acid** group, –COOH. It is these two groups which give amino acids their name. There are 20 different amino acids which occur naturally in the proteins of living organisms. (Many others have been synthesised in laboratories.) You can see their molecular formulae in the appendix.

All amino acids have a 'central' carbon atom, to which is bonded a hydrogen atom, an amine group and a carboxylic acid group. The only way in which they differ from each other is in the remaining group of atoms bonded to the central carbon. This is called the **R group** of which there are many different kinds. (You do not need to remember all of the different R groups!) However, it is often these R groups that are responsible for the three-dimensional shapes of protein molecules and hence their functions (page 43).

The peptide bond

Figure 3.16 shows how two amino acids can join together. One loses a hydroxyl (OH) group from its carboxylic acid group, while the other loses a hydrogen atom from its amine group. This leaves a carbon atom of the first amino acid free to bond with the nitrogen atom of the second. The bond is called a **peptide bond**. The oxygen and two hydrogen atoms removed from the amino acids form a water molecule. This type of reaction, a condensation reaction, is also involved in the formation of glycosidic bonds *(figure 3.5)* and in the synthesis of triglycerides *(figure 3.10)*.

The new molecule which has been formed, made up of two linked amino acids, is called a **dipeptide**. Any number of extra amino acids could be added to the chain, in a series of condensation reactions. A molecule made up of many amino acids linked together by peptide bonds is called a **polypeptide**. A polypeptide is another example of a polymer and a macromolecule, like polysaccharides and nucleic acids. A complete **protein** molecule may contain just one polypeptide chain, or it may have two or more chains which interact with each other.

In living cells, **ribosomes** are the sites where amino acids are linked together to form polypeptides. The reaction is controlled by enzymes. You can read more about this in *Central Concepts in Biology* in this series.

Primary structure

A polypeptide or protein molecule may contain several hundred amino acids linked into a long chain. The types of amino acids contained in the chain, and the sequence in which they are joined, is called the **primary structure** of the protein. *Figure 3.17* shows the primary structure of ribonuclease.

There is an enormous number of different *possible* primary structures. Even a change in one amino acid in a chain made up of thousands may completely alter the properties of the polypeptide or protein.

Secondary structure

The amino acids in a polypeptide chain interact with each other. A polypeptide chain often coils into an **α-helix** *(figure 3.18)*. The helix is held in shape by attraction between the oxygen of the CO group of one amino acid and the hydrogen of the NH group of the amino acid four places ahead of it. This attraction is called a **hydrogen bond**. It is the result of electron sharing in the NH group, which leaves the hydrogen slightly positive, and in the CO group, which leaves the oxygen slightly negative. So the oxygen and hydrogen are attracted to each other. A similar situation happens with the OH group in water (page 48).

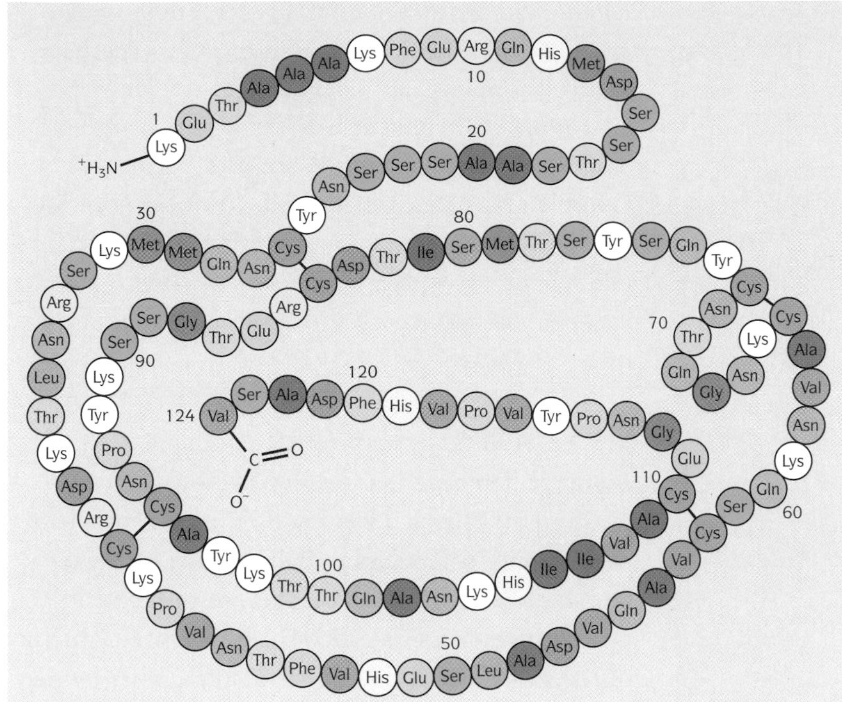

● ***Figure 3.17*** The primary structure of ribonuclease. Ribonuclease is an enzyme found in pancreatic juice which hydrolyses (digests) RNA. Notice that at one end of the amino acid chain there is an NH_3^+ group, while at the other end there is a COO^- group. These are known as the amino and carboxyl ends respectively.

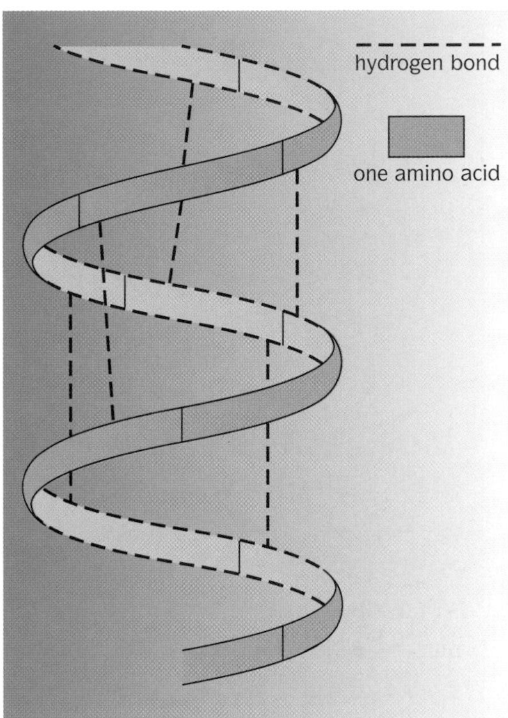

● ***Figure 3.18*** Polypeptide chains often coil into a tightly wound α-helix. The helix is held in shape by hydrogen bonds between the amino acids.

Hydrogen bonds, although strong enough to hold the α-helix in shape, are easily broken by high temperatures. As you will see on page 56, the effect of high temperatures on hydrogen bonds in proteins has important consequences for living organisms.

Not all proteins coil into an α-helix. Sometimes a much looser, straighter shape is formed, called a **β-pleated sheet.** Other proteins show no regular arrangement at all. It all depends on which R groups are present.

Tertiary structure

In many proteins, the α-helix itself is coiled or folded. *Figure 3.19* shows the complex way in which a molecule of the protein myoglobin folds.

At first sight, the myoglobin molecule looks like a disorganised tangle, but this is not so. The shape of the molecule is very precise, and held in this exact shape by bonds between amino acids in different parts of the chain. The way in which a protein coils up to form a precise three-dimensional shape is known as its **tertiary structure.**

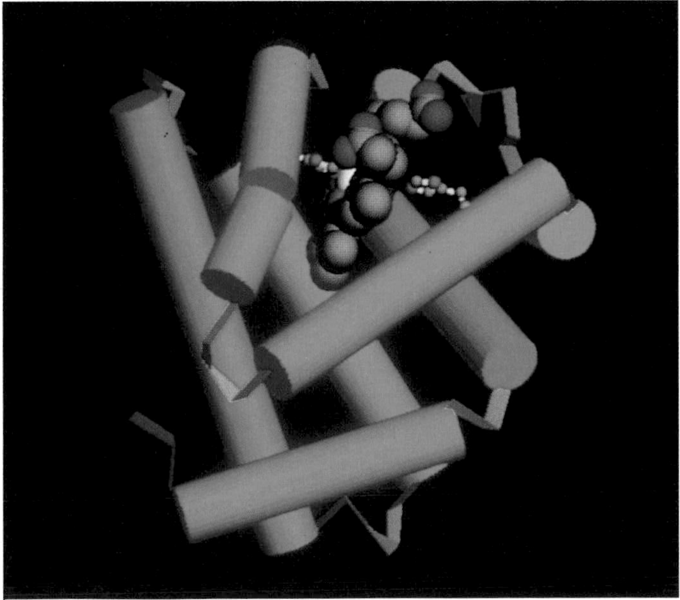

● ***Figure 3.19*** A computer graphic showing the shape of a myoglobin molecule. Myoglobin is the substance which makes meat look red. It is found in muscle, where it acts as an oxygen-storing molecule. The blue sections are alpha helixes, which are linked by sections of polypeptide chain which are more stretched out – these are shown in red. At the top right is an iron-containing haem group.

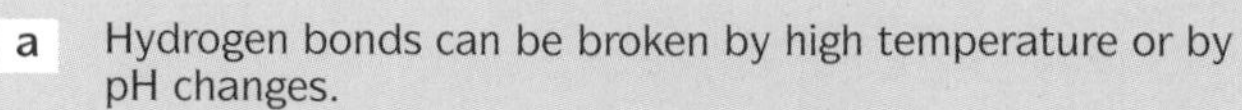

a Hydrogen bonds can be broken by high temperature or by pH changes.

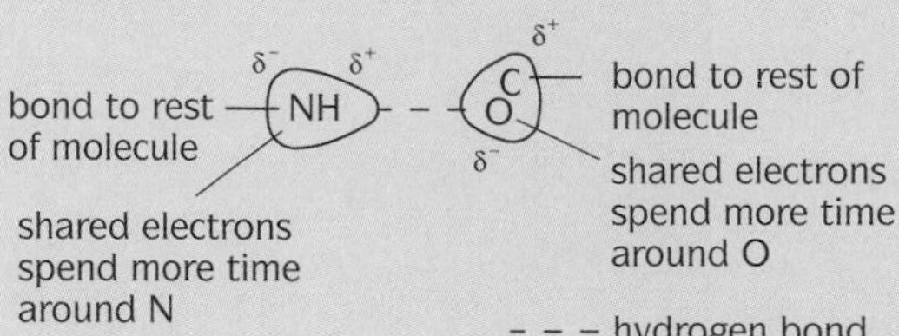

The NH group and CO group are said to be dipoles in this condition. Another important group which forms a dipole is OH (see figure 3.25)

b Disulphide bonds form between cysteine molecules. The bonds can be broken by reducing agents.

cysteine
CH_2
SH
SH
CH_2
cysteine
CH_2
S
S
CH_2
disulphide bond

c Ionic bonds form between ionised amine and carboxylic acid groups.

asparagine
CH_2
C
O
NH_3^+
ionic bond
O
O^-
C
CH_2
CH_2
glutamic acid
ionic bonds can be broken by pH changes

d Intermolecular or van der Waals forces attract non-polar side chains to each other.

tyrosine
CH_2
OH
CH
CH_3
CH_3
valine

● ***Figure 3.20*** The four bonds which are important in protein secondary and tertiary structure: **a** hydrogen bonds, **b** disulphide bonds, **c** ionic bonds, **d** van der Waals forces.

Figure 3.20 shows the four types of bonds which help to hold folded proteins in their precise shape. **Hydrogen bonds** can form between a wide variety of R groups, including those of tryptophan, arginine and asparagine. **Disulphide bonds** form between two cysteine molecules. **Ionic bonds** form between R groups containing amine and carboxyl groups. (Which amino acids have these?). Van der Waals forces occur between R groups which are non-polar, or hydrophobic.

Quaternary structure

Many proteins are made up of two or more polypeptide chains. Haemoglobin is an example of this, having four polypeptide chains in each haemoglobin molecule. The association of different polypeptide chains is called the **quaternary structure** of the protein. The chains are held together by the same four types of bond as in the tertiary structure.

Globular and fibrous proteins

A protein whose molecules coil up into a 'ball' shape, such as myoglobin and haemoglobin, is known as a **globular protein**. In a living organism, proteins may be found in cells, in tissue fluid, or in fluids being transported, such as blood or in the phloem. All these environments contain water. Globular proteins usually curl up so that their non-polar, hydrophobic side-chains point into the centre of the molecule, away from their watery surroundings. Water molecules are excluded from the centre of the folded protein molecule. The polar, hydrophilic, side-chains remain on the outside of the molecule. Globular proteins, therefore, are usually soluble, because water molecules cluster around their outward-pointing hydrophilic side-chains (*figure 3.21*).

Many globular proteins have roles in metabolic reactions. Enzymes, for example, are globular proteins.

Many protein molecules do not curl up into a ball, but form long chains. These are known as **fibrous proteins**. Fibrous proteins are usually insoluble. Many fibrous proteins have structural roles. Examples include **keratin** in hair and the outer layers of skin, and **collagen** (see page 46).

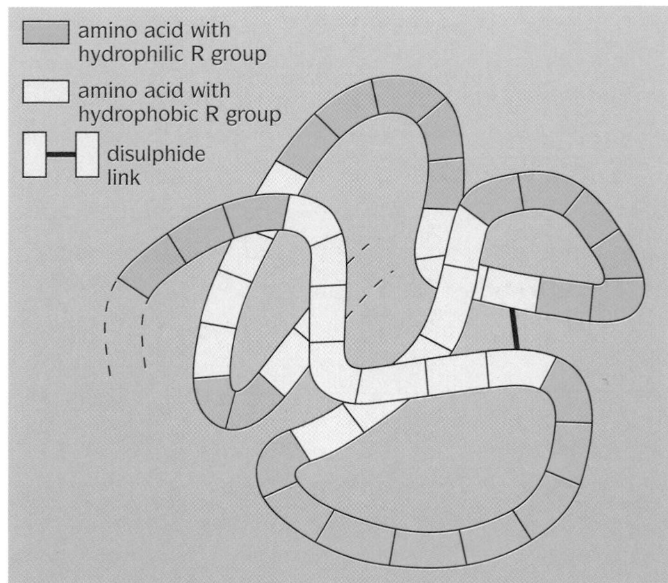

● ***Figure 3.21*** A schematic section through part of a globular protein molecule. The polypeptide chain coils up with hydrophilic R groups outside and hydrophobic ones inside, which makes the molecule soluble.

Haemoglobin

Haemoglobin, the red, oxygen-carrying pigment found in red blood cells, is a globular protein. It is made up of four polypeptide chains. Two of these are identical to each other, and are called α-chains. The other two, also identical to each other, are called β-chains.

The haemoglobin molecule is nearly spherical. The four polypeptide chains coil closely together, their hydrophobic side-chains pointing in towards the centre of the molecule and their hydrophilic ones pointing outwards. Each chain has a tertiary structure very similar to that of myoglobin *(figures 3.19* and *3.22)*.

The interactions between the hydrophobic side-chains inside the molecule are important in holding it in its correct three-dimensional shape. The outward-pointing hydrophilic side-chains on the surface of the molecule are important in maintaining its solubility. In the disease sickle cell anaemia one amino acid, which occurs in a part of the amino acid chain of the β polypeptides on the surface of the curled-up molecule, is replaced with a different amino acid. The correct amino acid is glutamic acid which is polar. The substitute is valine which is non-polar. Having a non-polar side-chain on the outside of the molecule makes the haemoglobin much less soluble, and causes unpleasant and dangerous symptoms in anyone whose haemoglobin is all of this 'faulty' type.

Each polypeptide chain contains a **haem group**. *Figure 3.22b* shows the structure of a haem

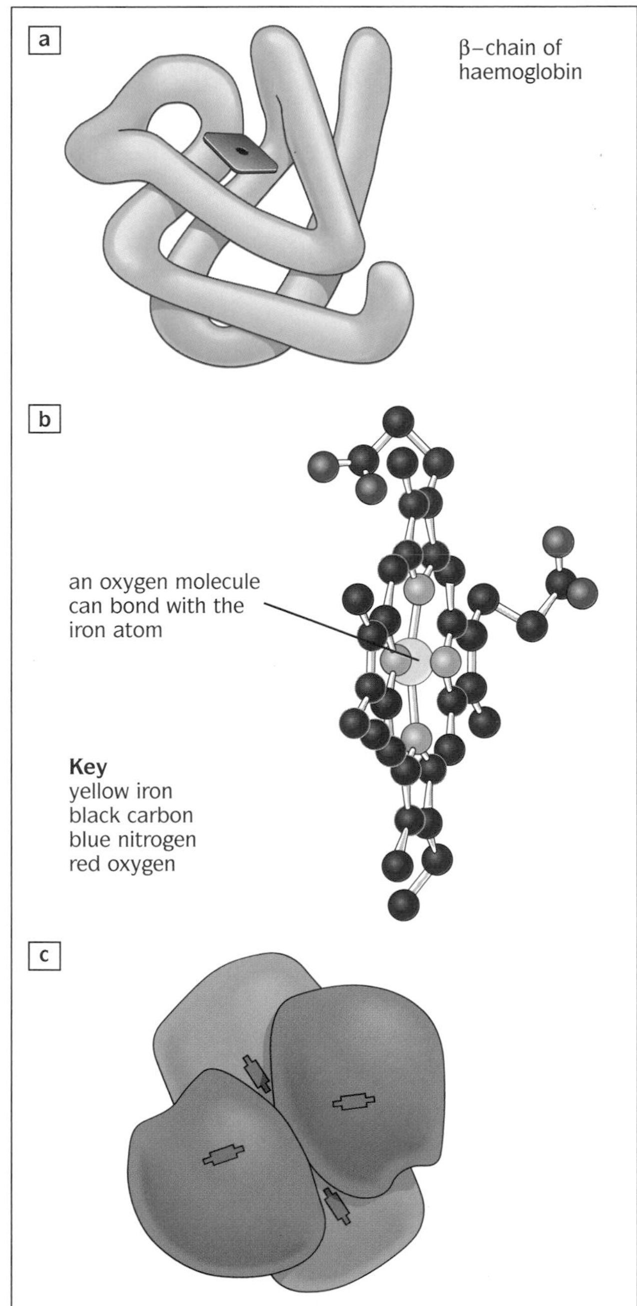

● ***Figure 3.22*** Haemoglobin. **a** Each haemoglobin molecule contains four polypeptide chains, one of which is shown here. Each polypeptide chain contains a haem group, shown in red. **b** the haem group contains an iron ion which can bond reversibly with an oxygen molecule. **c** the complete haemoglobin molecule is nearly spherical.

● *Figure 3.23* Human red blood cells. Each cell contains about 250 million haemoglobin molecules (× 6000).

group. A group like this, which is an important, permanent, part of a protein molecule but is not made of amino acids, is called a **prosthetic group**.

Each haem group contains an iron ion, Fe^{2+}. An oxygen molecule, O_2, can bind with each iron ion. So a complete haemoglobin molecule, with four haem groups, can carry four oxygen molecules (eight oxygen atoms) at a time.

It is the haem group which is responsible for the colour of haemoglobin. This colour changes depending on whether or not the iron ions are combined with oxygen. If they are, the molecule is known as **oxyhaemoglobin**, and is bright red. If not, the colour is purplish.

Collagen

Collagen is a fibrous protein that is found in skin, tendons, cartilage, bones, teeth and the walls of blood vessels. It is an important **structural protein**, not only in humans but in almost all animals, and is found in structures ranging from the body wall of sea anemones to the egg cases of dogfish.

A collagen molecule consists of three polypeptide chains wound around each other in a triple helix *(figure 3.24)*. Each chain contains about one thousand amino acids and almost every third amino acid in the chain is glycine, the smallest amino acid.

Each of the polypeptide chains is in the shape of a helix. (This is not an α-helix as it is not tightly wound.) The three helical polypeptides then wind around each other to form a three-stranded 'rope'. The three strands are held together by hydrogen bonds. The small size of glycine allows the three strands to lie close together and so form a tight coil. Any other amino acid would be too large.

Each complete, three-stranded molecule of collagen interacts with other collagen molecules running parallel to it. Bonds form between the side-chains of lysines in chains lying next to each other. These cross-links hold many collagen molecules side by side, forming **fibres**. The ends of molecules in parallel chains are staggered; if they were not, there would be a weak spot running right across the collagen fibre. As it is, collagen has tremendous tensile strength; that is it can withstand large pulling forces. The human Achilles tendon, which is almost all collagen fibres, can withstand a pulling force of 300 N per mm^2 of cross-sectional area, about one-quarter the tensile strength of mild steel.

Water

Water is arguably the most important biochemical of all. Without water, life would not exist on this planet. It is important for two reasons. Firstly, it is a major component of cells, typically forming between 70 and 95% of the mass of the cell. You yourself are about 60% water. Secondly, it provides an environment for those organisms that live in water. Three-quarters of the planet is covered in water.

Although it is a simple molecule, water has some surprising properties. For example, such a small molecule would exist as a gas at normal Earth temperatures were it not for its special property of hydrogen bonding to other water molecules (see page 48). Also, because it is a liquid, it provides a medium for molecules and ions to move around and interact in and hence a medium in which life could evolve.

The most important property of water molecules is their ability to form hydrogen bonds

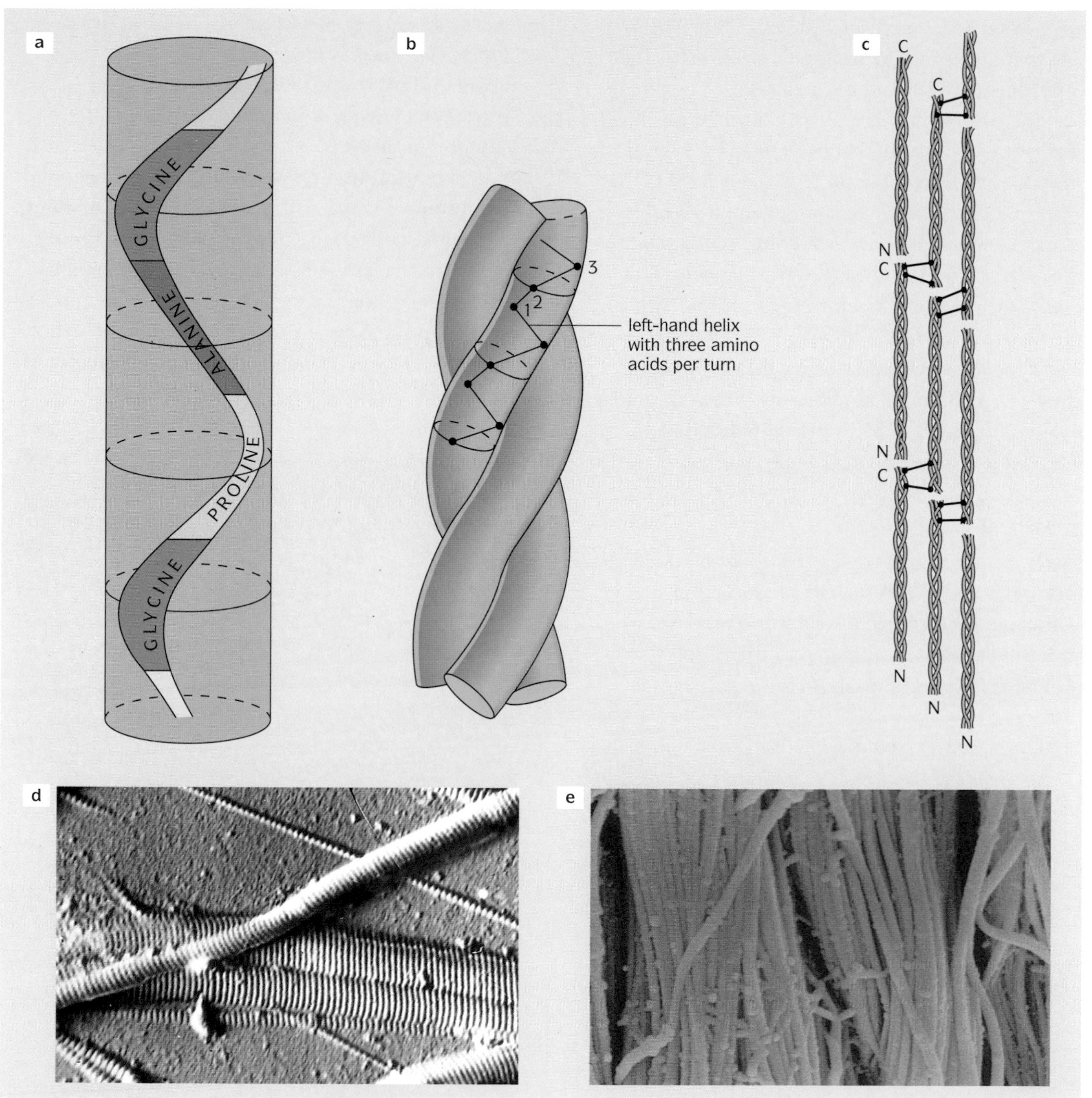

● ***Figure 3.24*** Collagen. The diagrams and photographs begin with the very small and work up to the not-so-small. Thus three of the polypeptide chains shown in **a** make up a collagen molecule shown in **b**; many of these molecules make up a fibril, shown in **c** and **d**; and many fibrils make up a fibre, shown in **e**.
a The polypeptides which make up a collagen molecule are in the shape of a stretched-out helix. Every third amino acid is glycine. **b** Three helices wind together to form a collagen molecule. These strands are held together by hydrogen bonds. **c** Many of these triple helices lie side by side, linked to each other by covalent cross-links between the carboxyl end of one molecule and the amino end of another. Notice that these cross-links are out-of-step with each other; this gives collagen greater strength. **d** An SEM of collagen fibrils (×15 000). Each fibril is made up of many triple helixes lying parallel with one another. The banded appearance is caused by the regular way in which these helices are arranged, with the staggered gaps between the molecules (shown in **c**) appearing darker. **e** An SEM of human collagen fibres (×10 000). Each fibre is made up of many fibrils lying side by side. These fibres are large enough to be seen with an ordinary light microscope.

with other water molecules *(figure 3.25)*. This is due to an uneven distribution of electrons as they orbit the hydrogen and oxygen atoms. They tend to be drawn towards the oxygen atom, creating a slight negative charge there ($2\delta^-$), and leaving a slight positive charge at the hydrogen atom (δ^+). Opposite charges on different molecules weakly attract each other, and so water molecules tend to stick to each other like very weak magnets. This makes them more difficult to separate and affects the physical properties of water. For example, more energy is needed to break these bonds and convert water from a liquid to a gas than in similar compounds, such as hydrogen sulphide (H_2S) which is a gas at normal air temperatures.

Water as a solvent

Water is an excellent solvent for ions and polar molecules (molecules such as sugars and glycerol with an uneven charge distribution) because the water molecules are attracted to them, collect around and separate them *(figure 3.26)*. This is

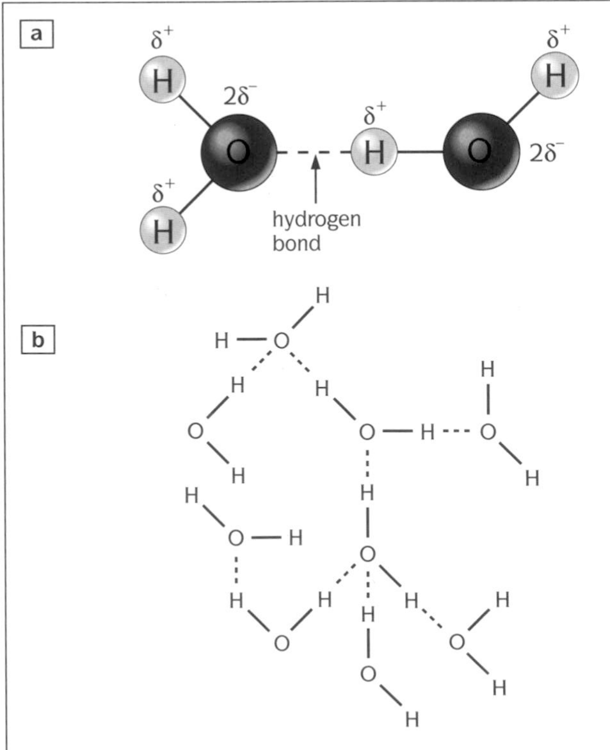

● ***Figure 3.25*** Hydrogen bond formation between water molecules. **a** Two water molecules. **b** Cluster of hydrogen-bonded water molecules. Such clusters are constantly forming and breaking in liquid water.

what happens when a chemical dissolves in water. Once a chemical is in solution, it is free to move about and react with other chemicals. Most processes in living organisms take place in solution in this way.

By contrast, non-polar molecules such as lipids are insoluble in water and, if surrounded by water, tend to be pushed together by the water since the water molecules are attracted to *each other*. This is important, for example, in hydrophobic interactions in protein structure and in membrane structure (see chapter 5) and it increases the stability of these structures.

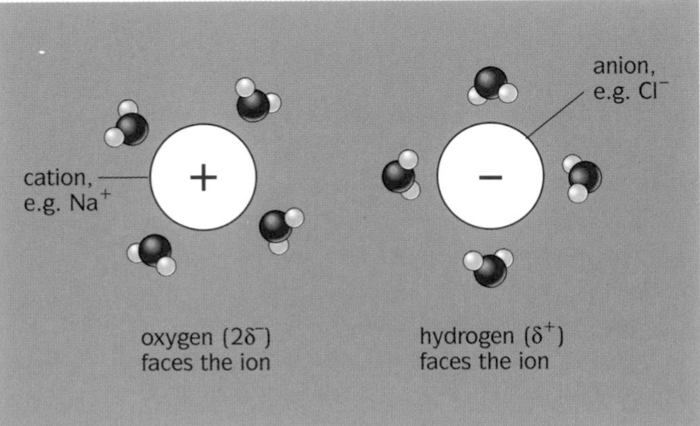

● ***Figure 3.26*** Distribution of water molecules around ions in a solution.

Water as a transport medium

Water is the transport medium in the blood, lymphatic, excretory and digestive systems of animals, and in the vascular tissues of plants. Here again its solvent properties are essential.

Thermal properties

As hydrogen bonding restricts the movement of water molecules, a relatively large amount of energy is needed to raise the temperature of water. This means that large bodies of water are slow to change temperature as environmental temperature changes. As a result they are more stable habitats. Internal changes in body temperature are also minimised, making it easier to achieve a stable body temperature.

Since a relatively large amount of energy is needed to convert water to a gas, the process of evaporation transfers a correspondingly large amount of energy and can be an effective means of cooling the body, as in sweating and panting. Conversely, a relatively large amount of energy must be transferred from water before it is converted from a liquid to a solid (ice). This makes it less likely that water will freeze, an advantage both for the bodies of living organisms and for organisms which live in water.

Density and freezing properties

Water is the only chemical where the solid form, ice, is less dense than its liquid form. Below 4 °C the density of water starts to decrease. Ice therefore floats on liquid water and insulates the water under it. This reduces the tendency for large bodies of water such as oceans and lakes to freeze completely, and increases the chances of life surviving in cold conditions.

Changes in density of water with temperature cause currents which help to maintain the circulation of nutrients in the oceans.

High surface tension and cohesion

Water molecules have very high cohesion, in other words they tend to stick to each other. This is exploited in the way water moves in long, unbroken columns through the vascular tissue in plants and is an important property in cells. High cohesion also results in high surface tension at the surface of water. This allows certain small organisms, such as the pond skater, to exploit the surface of water as a habitat, allowing them to settle on or skate over its surface *(figure 3.27)*.

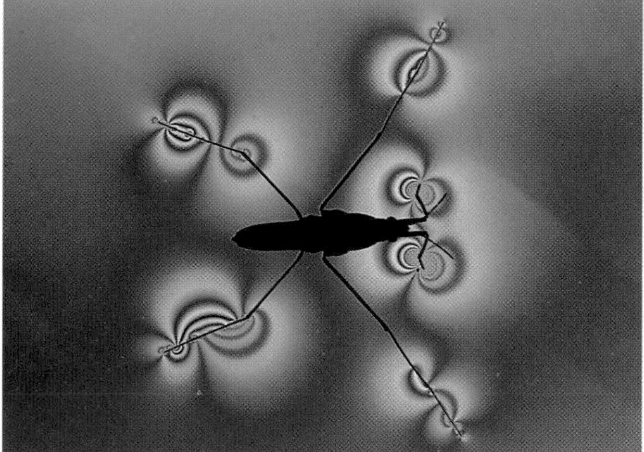

● ***Figure 3.27*** A pond skater standing on the surface of pond water. This was photographed through an interferometer which shows interference patterns made by the pond skater as it walks on the water's surface. The surface tension of the water means the pond skater never breaks through the surface.

Questions

1 Discuss the biological importance of hydrogen bonding in **a** water, and **b** proteins.

2 Show how the structure of **a** glycogen, and **b** cellulose, is related to its function in each case.

3 What is a monosaccharide? In what ways can the structure of monosaccharides vary?

4 With reference to one named protein, describe the meanings of the terms primary structure, secondary structure, tertiary structure and quaternary structure.

5 Discuss the ways in which the molecular structures of haemoglobin and collagen are related to their functions.

6 Copy and complete this table to summarise the molecular structure and functions of the main groups of chemicals found in living organisms. Your table will need to be large, so that you have plenty of space to include several examples in the last column, and several kinds of bonds in the penultimate column for proteins. (There is no example for water, of course!)

Chemical	*Elements which it contains*	*Subunits from which it is made*	*Types of bonds which hold units together*	*Types of bonds which hold molecules in shape, or to other molecules*	*Examples and their functions*
water		–	–		
carbohydrates					
proteins					
lipids					

SUMMARY

- Molecular biology is the study of the structure and function of biological molecules.
- Many biological molecules are formed from smaller units that bond together. These include carbohydrates, lipids, proteins and nucleic acids. Molecules which are formed from repeating identical or similar subunits are called polymers.
- Carbohydrates have the general formula $C_x(H_2O)_y$. Monosaccharides are the smallest carbohydrate units, of which glucose is the most common form. They are important energy sources in cells and also important building blocks for larger molecules. They may form straight-chain or ring structures and may exist in different isomeric forms. These are important because they bond together in different ways and so affect the structure of polysaccharides, such as starch, glycogen and cellulose. The glycosidic bond forms between monosaccharides by condensation.
- Starch is formed from some straight and some branched chains of α-glucose molecules and is an energy storage compound in plants. Glycogen is a branched α-glucose chain and is an energy storage compound in animals. Cellulose is a polymer of β-glucose molecules in which the chains are grouped together by hydrogen bonding to form strong fibres that are found in plant cell walls.
- Lipids are made from fatty acids and glycerol. They are hydrophobic and do not mix with water. They are energy storage compounds in animals, as well as having other functions such as insulation and buoyancy in marine mammals. Phospholipids have a hydrophilic phosphate head and hydrophobic fatty acid tails. This is important in the formation of membranes.
- Proteins are long chains of amino acids which fold into precise shapes. The sequence of amino acids in a protein, known as its primary structure, determines the way that it folds and hence determines its three-dimensional shape and function.
- Many proteins contain areas where the amino acid chain is twisted into an α-helix; this is an example of secondary structure. Further folding produces the tertiary structure. Often, more than one polypeptide associates to form a protein molecule. The association between different polypeptide chains is the quaternary structure of the protein.
- Proteins may be globular or fibrous. A molecule of a globular protein is roughly spherical. Most globular proteins are soluble and metabolically active. A molecule of a fibrous protein is less folded and forms long chains. Fibrous proteins are insoluble. They often have a structural role.
- Water is important within bodies where it forms a large part of the mass of the cell. It is also an environment in which organisms can live. As a result of extensive hydrogen bonding, it has properties that are important for life: it is liquid at most temperatures on the Earth's surface; its highest density occurs above its freezing point so that ice floats and insulates water below from freezing air temperatures; it acts as a solvent for ions and polar molecules and causes non-polar molecules to group together; it has a high surface tension which affects the way it moves through narrow tubes and forms a surface on which some organisms can live.

Chapter four

Enzymes

By the end of this chapter you should be able to:

1 explain that enzymes are globular proteins which act as catalysts;

2 explain the way in which enzymes act as catalysts by lowering activation energy;

3 describe examples of enzyme-catalysed reactions;

4 describe methods of following the time-course of an enzyme-controlled reaction;

5 discuss the ways in which temperature, pH, concentration of enzyme, concentration of substrate, and competitive and non-competitive inhibition affect the rate of enzyme-controlled reactions;

6 describe methods of investigating the effects of these factors experimentally.

Enzymes are protein molecules which can be defined as **biological catalysts.** A catalyst is a molecule which speeds up a chemical reaction, but remains unchanged at the end of the reaction. Virtually every metabolic reaction which takes place within a living organism is catalysed by an enzyme.

Enzymes are globular proteins. Like all globular proteins, enzyme molecules are coiled into a precise three-dimensional shape, with hydrophilic side-chains on the outside of the molecule ensuring that they are soluble. Enzyme molecules also have a special feature in that they possess an **active site** *(figure 4.1)*. The active site of an enzyme is a region of the molecule, usually a cleft or depression, to which another molecule or molecules can bind. This molecule is the **substrate** of the enzyme. The shape of the active site allows the substrate to fit perfectly, and to be held in place by temporary bonds which form between the substrate and some of the side- chains of the enzyme's amino acids.

Each type of enzyme will usually act on only one type of substrate molecule. This is because the shape of the active site will only allow one

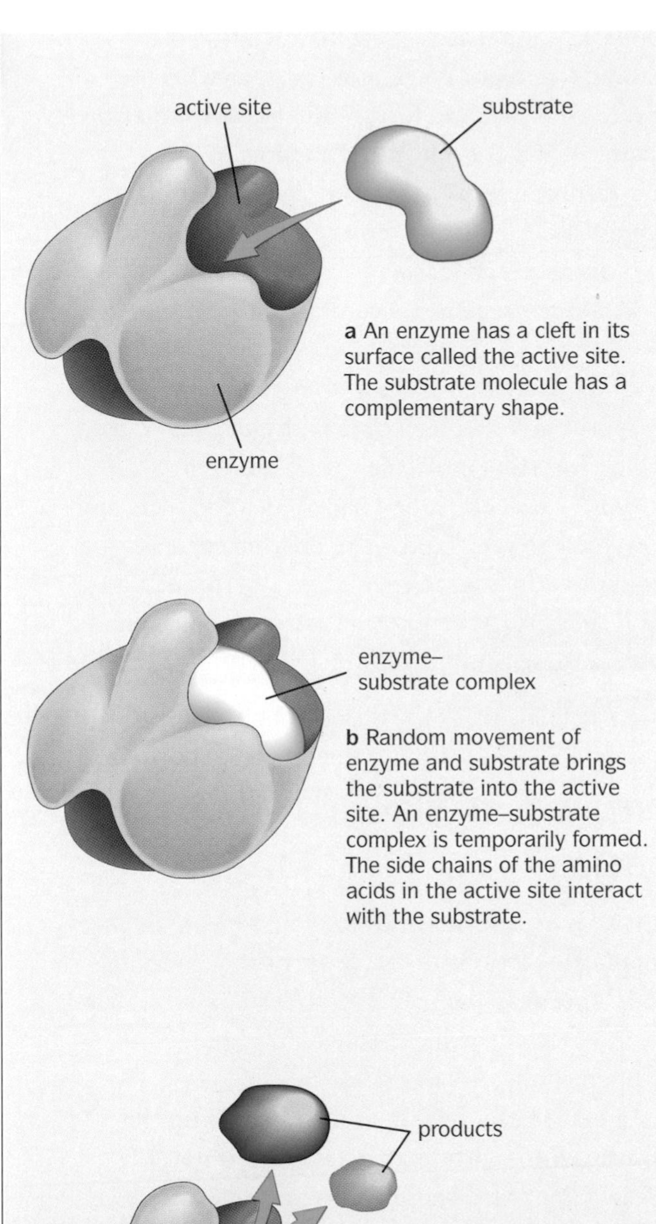

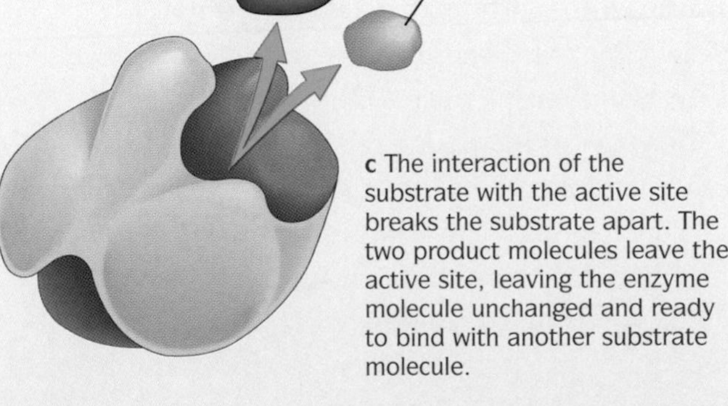

● ***Figure 4.1*** How an enzyme catalyses the breakdown of a substrate molecule to two product molecules.

shape of molecule to fit. The enzyme is said to be **specific** for this substrate.

The enzyme may catalyse a reaction in which the substrate molecule is split into two or more molecules. Alternatively, it may catalyse the joining together of two molecules, as when making a dipeptide. Interaction between the side-chains of the enzyme and the atoms of the substrate can break, or encourage formation of, bonds in the substrate molecule, forming one, two or more **products**.

When the reaction is complete, the product or products leave the active site. The enzyme is unchanged by this process, so it is now available to receive another substrate molecule. The rate at which substrate molecules can bind to the enzyme's active site, be formed into products and leave can be very rapid. The enzyme catalase, for example, can bind with hydrogen peroxide molecules, split them into water and oxygen and release these products at a rate of 10^7 molecules per second.

Enzymes reduce activation energy

As catalysts, enzymes increase the rate at which chemical reactions occur. Most of the reactions which occur in living cells would occur so slowly without enzymes that they would virtually not happen at all.

In many reactions, the substrate will not be converted to a product unless it is temporarily given some extra energy. This energy is called **activation energy** *(figure 4.2)*.

One way of increasing the rate of many chemical reactions is to increase the energy of the reactants by heating them. You have probably done this on many occasions by heating substances which you want to react together. In the Benedict's test for reducing sugar, for example, you need to heat the Benedict's reagent and sugar solution together before they will react.

Mammals, such as humans, also use this method of speeding up their metabolic reactions.

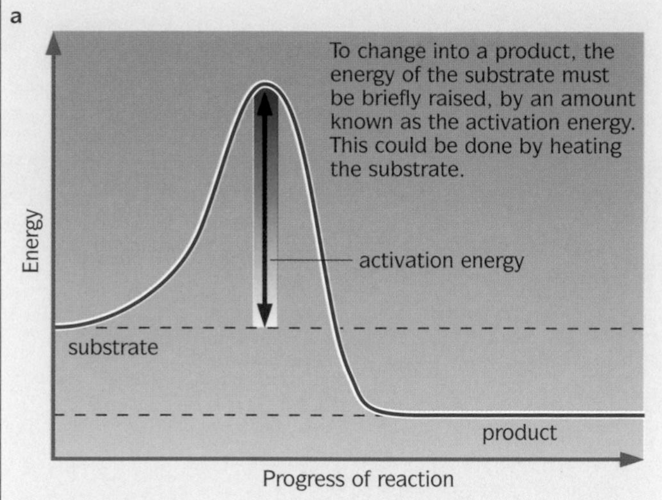

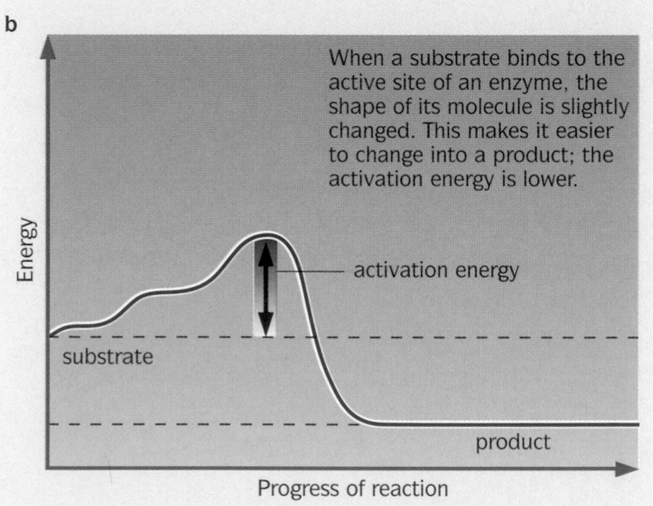

● ***Figure 4.2*** Activation energy **a** without enzyme, **b** with enzyme.

Our body temperature is maintained at 37 °C, which is usually much warmer than the temperature of the air around us. But even raising the temperature of cells to 37 °C is not enough to give most substrates the activation energy which they need to change into products. We cannot raise body temperature much more than this, as temperatures above about 40 °C begin to cause irreversible damage to many of the molecules from which we are made, especially protein molecules. Enzymes are a solution to this problem because they *decrease the activation energy* of the reaction which they catalyse. They do this by holding the substrate or substrates in such a way that their molecules can react more easily. Reactions catalysed by enzymes will take place rapidly at a much lower temperature than they would without them.

The course of a reaction

You may be able to carry out an investigation into the rate at which substrate is converted into product during an enzyme-controlled reaction. *Figure 4.3* shows the results of such an investigation, using the enzyme catalase. This enzyme is found in the tissues of most living things and catalyses the breakdown of hydrogen peroxide into water and oxygen. (Hydrogen peroxide is a toxic product of several different metabolic reactions.) It is an easy reaction to follow as the oxygen that is released can be collected and measured.

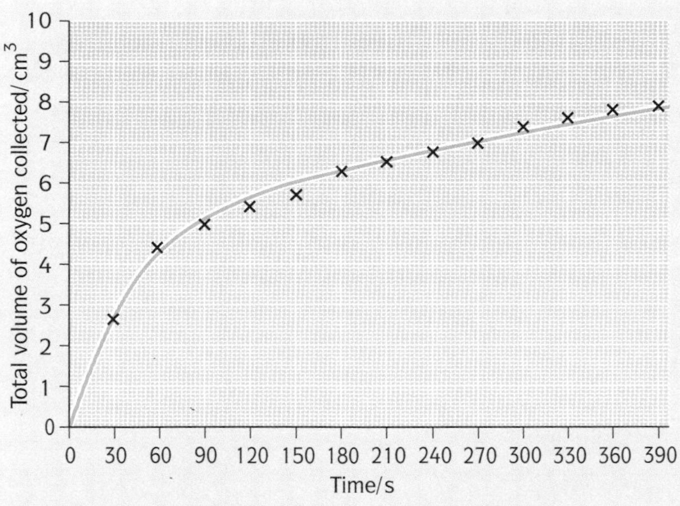

● ***Figure 4.3*** The course of an enzyme-catalysed reaction. Catalase was added to hydrogen peroxide at time 0. The gas released was collected in a gas syringe, the volume being read at 30 s intervals.

The reaction begins very swiftly. As soon as the enzyme and substrate are mixed, bubbles of oxygen are released quickly. A large volume of oxygen is collected in the first minute of the reaction. As the reaction continues, however, the rate at which oxygen is released gradually slows down. The reaction gets slower and slower, until it eventually stops completely.

The explanation for this is quite straightforward. When the enzyme and substrate are first mixed, there is a large number of substrate molecules. At any moment, virtually every enzyme molecule will have a substrate molecule in its active site. The rate at which the reaction occurs will depend only on how many enzyme molecules there are, and the speed at which the enzyme can convert the substrate into product, release it, and then bind with another substrate molecule. However, as more and more substrate is converted into product, there are fewer and fewer substrate molecules to bind with enzymes. Enzyme molecules may be 'waiting' for a substrate molecule to hit their active site. As fewer substrate molecules are left, the reaction gets slower and slower, until it eventually stops.

The curve is therefore steepest at the beginning of the reaction: the rate of an enzyme-controlled reaction is always fastest at the beginning. This rate is called the **initial rate of reaction.** You can measure the initial rate of the reaction by calculating the slope of a tangent to the curve, as close to time 0 as possible. An easier way of doing this is simply to read off the graph the amount of oxygen given off in the first 30 seconds. In this case, the rate of oxygen production in the first 30 seconds is 2.7 cm^3 of oxygen per 30 seconds, or 5.4 cm^3 per minute.

SAQ 4.1

Why is it better to calculate the initial rate of reaction from a curve such as the one in *figure 4.3*, rather than simply measuring how much oxygen is given off in 30 seconds?

The effect of enzyme concentration

Figure 4.4a shows the results of an investigation in which different amounts of catalase were added to the same amount of hydrogen peroxide. You can see that the shape of all five curves is similar. In each case, the reaction begins very quickly (steep curve) and then gradually slows down (curve levels off). Because the amounts of hydrogen peroxide were the same in all five reactions, the total amount of oxygen eventually produced will be the same.

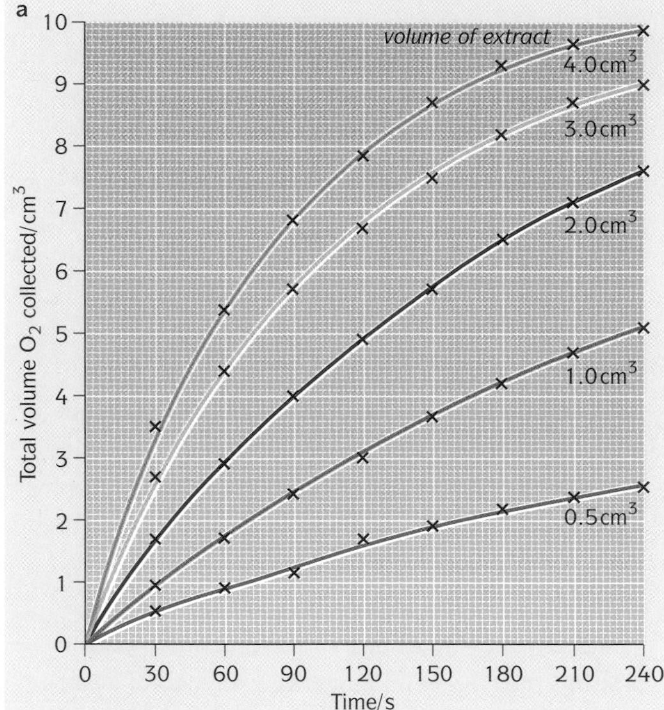

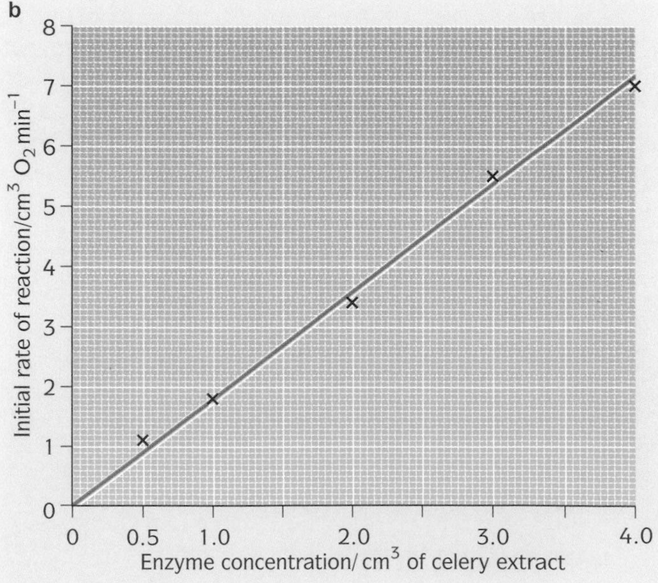

● ***Figure 4.4*** The effect of enzyme concentration on the rate of an enzyme-catalysed reaction. **a** Different volumes of celery extract, which contains catalase, were added to the same volume of hydrogen peroxide. Water was added to make the total volume of the mixture the same in each case. **b** The rate of reaction in the first 30 s was calculated for each enzyme concentration.

To compare the rates of these five reactions, in order to look at the effect of enzyme concentration on reaction rate, it is fairest to look at the rate *right at the beginning* of the reaction. This is because, once the reaction is under way, the amount of substrate in each reaction begins to vary, as substrate is converted to product at different rates in each of the five reactions. It is only at the very beginning of the reaction that we can be sure that differences in reaction rate are caused only by differences in enzyme concentration.

To work out this initial rate for each enzyme concentration, we can calculate the slope of the curve 30 seconds after the beginning of the reaction, as explained earlier. Ideally, we should do this for an even earlier stage of the reaction, but in practice this is impossible. We can then plot a second graph, *figure 4.4b*, showing this initial rate of reaction against enzyme concentration.

This graph shows that the initial rate of reaction increases linearly. In these conditions, reaction rate is directly proportional to the enzyme concentration. This is just what common sense says should happen. The more enzyme present, the more active sites will be available for the substrate to slot into. As long as there is plenty of substrate available, the initial rate of a reaction increases linearly with enzyme concentration.

SAQ 4.2

Sketch the shape of this curve if excess hydrogen peroxide was not available.

Measuring reaction rate

It is easy to measure the rate of the catalase–hydrogen peroxide reaction, because one of the products is a gas, which is released and can be collected. Unfortunately, it is not always so easy to measure the rate of a reaction. If, for example, you wanted to investigate the rate at which amylase breaks down starch, it is very difficult to observe the course of the reaction because the substrate (starch) and the product (maltose) remain as colourless substances in the reaction mixture.

The easiest way to measure the rate of this reaction is to measure the rate at which starch disappears from the reaction mixture. This can be done by taking samples from the mixture at known times, and adding each sample to some iodine in potassium iodide solution. Starch forms a blue-black colour with this solution. Using a colorimeter, you can measure the intensity of the blue-black colour obtained, and use this as a measure of the amount of starch still remaining. If you do this over a period of time, you can plot a curve of amount of starch remaining against time. You can then calculate the initial reaction rate in the same way as for the catalase–hydrogen peroxide reaction.

SAQ 4.3

a Sketch the curve you would expect to obtain if the amount of starch remaining was plotted against time.

b How could you use this curve to calculate the initial reaction rate?

It is even easier to observe the course of this reaction if you mix starch, iodine in potassium iodide solution and amylase in a tube, and take regular readings of the colour of the mixture in a colorimeter. However, this is not ideal, because the iodine interferes with the rate of the reaction and slows it down.

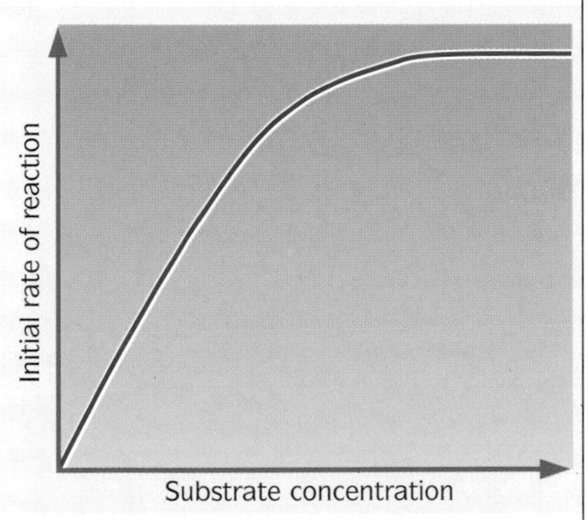

● ***Figure 4.5*** The effect of substrate concentration on the rate of an enzyme-catalysed reaction.

The effect of substrate concentration

Figure 4.5 shows the results of an investigation in which the amount of catalase was kept constant, and the amount of hydrogen peroxide was varied. Once again, curves of oxygen released against time were plotted for each reaction, and the initial rate of reaction calculated for the first 30 seconds. These initial rates of reaction were then plotted against substrate concentration.

As substrate concentration increases, the initial rate of reaction also increases. Again, this is only what we would expect: the more substrate molecules there are around, the more often an enzyme's active site can bind with one. However, if we go on increasing substrate concentration, keeping the enzyme concentration constant, there comes a point where every enzyme active site is working continuously. If more substrate is added, the enzyme simply cannot work faster; substrate molecules are effectively 'queuing up' for an active site to become vacant. The enzyme is working at its maximum possible rate, known as V_{max}.

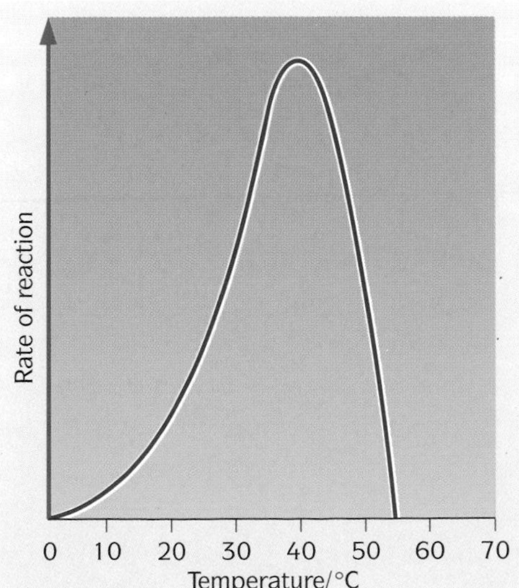

● ***Figure 4.6*** The effect of temperature on the rate of an enzyme-controlled reaction.

Temperature and enzyme activity

Figure 4.6 shows how the rate of a typical enzyme-catalysed reaction varies with temperature. At low temperatures, the reaction takes place only very slowly. This is because molecules are moving relatively slowly. Substrate molecules will not often collide with the active site, and so binding between substrate and enzyme is a rare event. As temperature rises, the enzyme and substrate molecules move faster. Collisions happen more frequently, so that substrate molecules enter the active site more often. Moreover, when they do collide, they do so with more energy. This makes it easier for bonds to be broken so that the reaction can occur.

SAQ 4.4

How could you carry out an experiment to determine the effect of temperature on the rate of breakdown of hydrogen peroxide by catalase?

As temperature continues to increase, the speed of movement of the substrate and enzyme molecules also continues to increase. However, above a certain temperature the structure of the enzyme molecule vibrates so energetically that some of the bonds holding the enzyme molecule in its precise shape begin to break. This is especially true of hydrogen bonds. The enzyme molecule begins to lose its shape and activity and is said to be **denatured**.

At first, the substrate molecule fits less well into the active site of the enzyme, so the rate of the reaction begins to slow down. Eventually the substrate no longer fits at all, or can no longer be held in the correct position for the reaction to occur.

The temperature at which an enzyme catalyses a reaction at the maximum rate is called the **optimum temperature**. Most human enzymes have an optimum temperature of around 40 °C. By keeping our body temperatures at about 37 °C, we ensure that enzyme-catalysed reactions occur at close to their maximum rate. It would be dangerous to maintain a body temperature of 40 °C, as even a slight rise above this would begin to denature enzymes.

Enzymes from other organisms may have different optimum temperatures. Some enzymes, such as those found in bacteria which live in hot springs, have much higher optimum temperatures (*figure 4.7*).

● ***Figure 4.7*** Not all enzymes have optimum temperatures of 40 °C. Bacteria and algae living in hot springs such as this one in Yellowstone National Park, USA, must be able to tolerate very high temperatures. Enzymes from such organisms are proving useful in various industrial applications.

SAQ 4.5

Protein-digesting enzymes are used in biological washing powders.

a How would a protein-digesting enzyme remove a blood stain on clothes?

b Most biological washing powders are recommended for use at low washing temperatures. Why is this?

c Washing powder manufacturers have produced protein-digesting enzymes which can work at higher temperatures than 40°C. Why is this useful?

pH and enzyme activity

Figure 4.8 shows how the activity of an enzyme is affected by pH. Most enzymes work fastest at a pH of somewhere around 7, that is in fairly neutral conditions. Some, however, such as the protease pepsin which is found in the stomach, have a different optimum pH.

pH is a measure of the concentration of hydrogen ions in a solution. The lower the pH, the higher the hydrogen ion concentration. Hydrogen ions can interact with the side-chains of amino acids, affecting the way in which they bond with each other. A pH which is very different from the optimum pH can cause denaturation of an enzyme.

SAQ 4.6

Trypsin is a protein-digesting enzyme secreted in pancreatic juice, which acts in the duodenum. If you make up a suspension of milk powder in water, and add trypsin, the enzyme digests the protein in the milk, so that the suspension becomes clear.

How could you carry out an investigation into the effect of pH on the rate of activity of trypsin? (A suspension of 4 g of milk powder in 100 cm^3 of water will become clear in a few minutes if an equal volume of a 0.5% trypsin solution is added to it.)

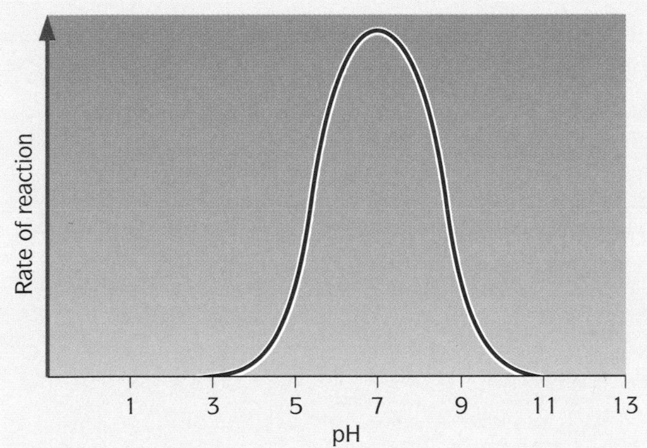

● ***Figure 4.8*** The effect of pH on the rate of an enzyme-controlled reaction.

Enzyme inhibitors

Enzymes are not always required to work at their optimum rate. If an enzyme is converting a substrate into a product, it may be useful for the reaction to stop when sufficient product has been formed. One way of doing this is for the end-product to bind onto the enzyme molecule, usually at a place other than the active site, distorting the enzyme and altering the shape of its active site so that it can no longer bind with its substrate. This is called **end-product inhibition**, and is an important way of regulating enzyme-controlled reactions in living organisms.

Other substances, such as lead and other heavy metal ions, may behave in a similar way, binding to an enzyme at a place other than its active site, and altering its shape. The enzyme can no longer convert substrate to product (*figure 4.9*). This type of inhibitor is known as a **non-competitive inhibitor.**

Competitive inhibitors have a shape similar to that of the enzyme's normal substrate, so that they can fit temporarily into the active site. If a competitive inhibitor molecule is in the active site, then the substrate cannot enter. The inhibitor and substrate *compete* for the active site: whichever gets there first gets in. The likelihood of the inhibitor getting there first depends on the relative concentration of inhibitor and substrate; if the concentration of the substrate is increased, the degree of inhibition is lessened. This is not so with non-competitive inhibition.

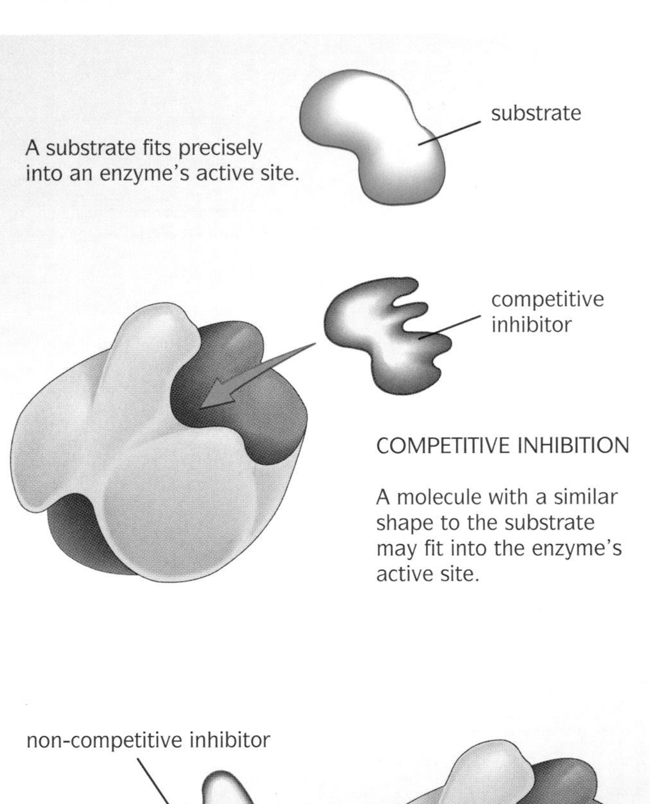

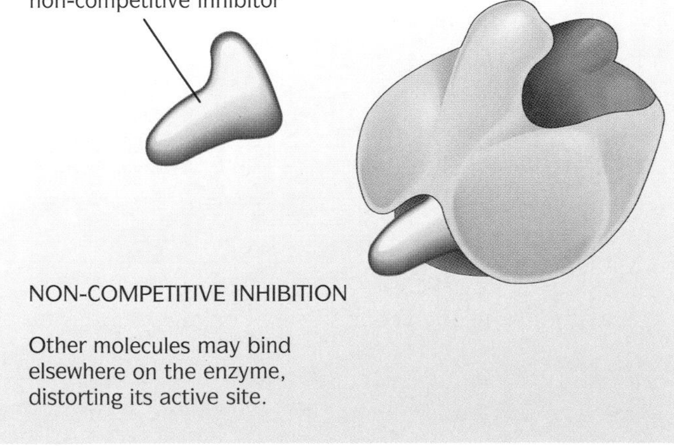

● ***Figure 4.9*** Enzyme inhibition.

An example of competitive inhibition occurs in the treatment of a person who has drunk ethylene glycol. Ethylene glycol is used as antifreeze, and is sometimes drunk accidentally. It has also occasionally been added, illegally, to wine. Ethylene glycol is rapidly converted in the body to oxalic acid, which can cause irreversible kidney damage. However, the active site of the enzyme which converts ethylene glycol to oxalic acid will also accept ethanol. If the poisoned person is given a large dose of ethanol, the ethanol acts as a competitive inhibitor, slowing down the action of the enzyme on ethylene glycol for long enough to allow the ethylene glycol to be excreted.

Reversible inhibition

Competitive inhibition is **reversible**. The enzyme is not permanently bound to the inhibitor. The effect of competitive inhibition can easily be reversed by increasing the relative concentration of the substrate, as this increases the chance of the substrate entering the active site first. Non-competitive inhibition can also be reversible, if the inhibitor only binds temporarily to the enzyme. However, non-competitive inhibition cannot be overcome by increasing substrate concentration, as the likelihood of the inhibitor binding with the enzyme is not affected by the concentration of the substrate, because substrate and inhibitor bind at different sites.

Irreversible inhibition

Inhibition may also be **irreversible**, as some inhibitors bind almost permanently to the enzyme. Some nerve gases use this principle. Where two nerve cells meet, the nerve impulse is carried between them by a chemical known as a transmitter substance (page 83). One transmitter substance is acetylcholine, which is released from the first nerve cell when an impulse arrives, diffuses to the second nerve cell across the gap between them, and starts off an impulse in the second one. The acetylcholine is then rapidly broken down by an enzyme **acetylcholinesterase**; if this did not happen, the second nerve cell would keep sending off impulses, even if no impulse was arriving along the first nerve cell. The nerve gas DIPF binds permanently with acetylcholinesterase, altering its shape so that it can no longer bind with and break down acetylcholine. Impulse after impulse is triggered in the second nerve cell, leading to convulsions and eventually death. Many insecticides, including organophosphorous insecticides, contain enzyme inhibitors which act in a similar way. Prolonged exposure to organophosphorous insecticides can produce nerve and muscle problems in people.

SUMMARY

- Enzymes are globular proteins, which act as catalysts by lowering activation energy.
- Each enzyme acts on only one specific substrate, because there has to be a perfect match between the shape of the substrate and the shape of the enzyme's active site.
- Anything which affects the shape of the active site, such as high temperature, a change of pH or the binding of a non-competitive inhibitor with the enzyme, will slow down the rate of the reaction.
- Competitive inhibitors also slow down the rate of reaction, by competing with the substrate for the active site of the enzyme.

Questions

1 What is an enzyme?

2 In mammals, such as humans, the temperature and pH of body fluids are kept constant. Discuss the reasons for this, in terms of the functioning of enzymes.

Cell membranes

By the end of this chapter you should be able to:

1 describe the fluid mosaic model of membrane structure and explain the underlying reasons for this structure;

2 outline the roles of phospholipids, cholesterol, glycolipids, proteins and glycoproteins in membranes;

3 outline the roles of the cell surface membrane, and the roles of membranes within cells;

4 describe and explain how molecules can get in and out of cells (cross cell membranes) by the processes of diffusion, osmosis, active transport, endocytosis and exocytosis;

5 describe the effects on animal and plant cells of immersion in solutions of different water potential.

In chapter 1 you saw that **all** living cells are surrounded by a membrane which controls the exchange of materials, such as nutrients and waste products, between the cell and its environment. Although extremely thin, the membrane must be capable of regulating this exchange very precisely. Within cells, particularly eukaryotic cells, regulation of transport across the membranes of organelles is vital. Membranes also have other important functions. For example, they enable cells to receive hormone messages. Therefore it is important to study the structure of membranes if we are to understand how these functions are achieved.

Phospholipids

An understanding of the structure of membranes depends on an understanding of the structure of phospholipids (see page 41 and *figure 3.14*). From phospholipids, little bags can be formed in which chemicals can be isolated from the external environment. These bags are the membrane-bound compartments that we know as cells and organelles. *Figure 5.1a* shows what happens if phospholipid molecules are spread over the surface of water.

They form a single layer with their heads in the water, because they are polar (hydrophilic), and their tails projecting out of the water, because they are non-polar (hydrophobic). (The term 'polar' refers to the uneven distribution of charge which occurs in some molecules. The significance of this is also discussed on pages 48 and 50.)

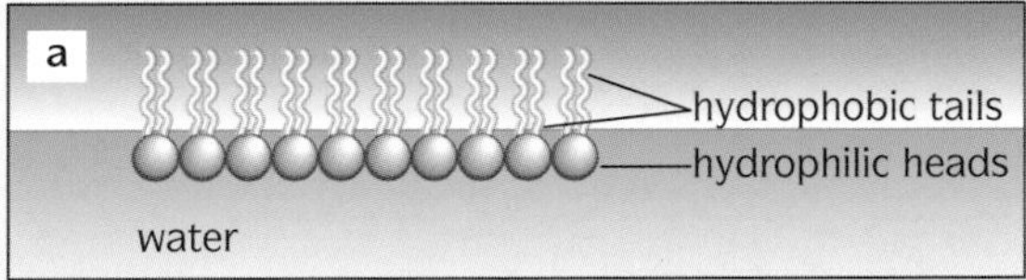

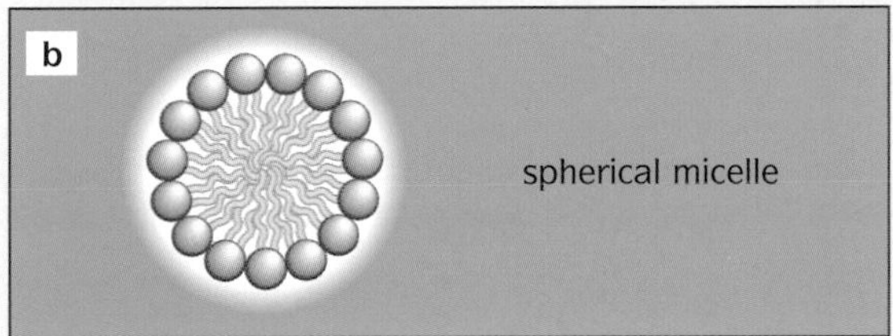

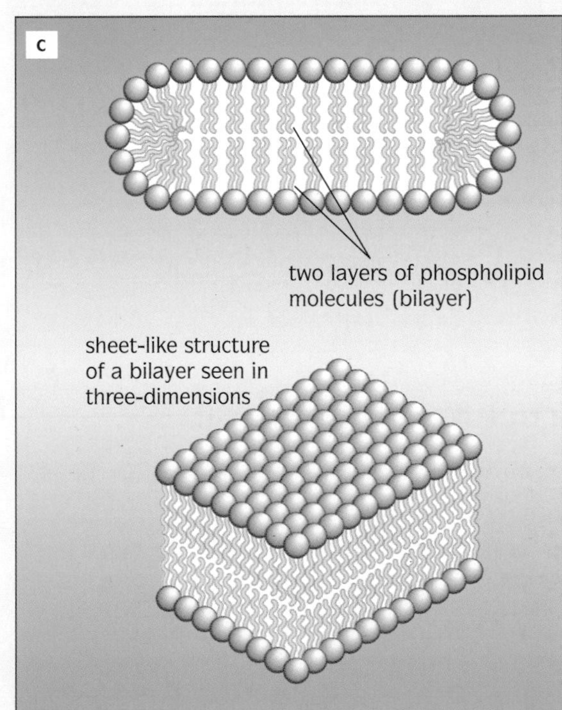

● ***Figure 5.1*** Phospholipids in water **a** spread as a single layer of molecules (a monolayer) on the surface of water, **b** forming micelles surrounded by water, **c** forming bilayers.

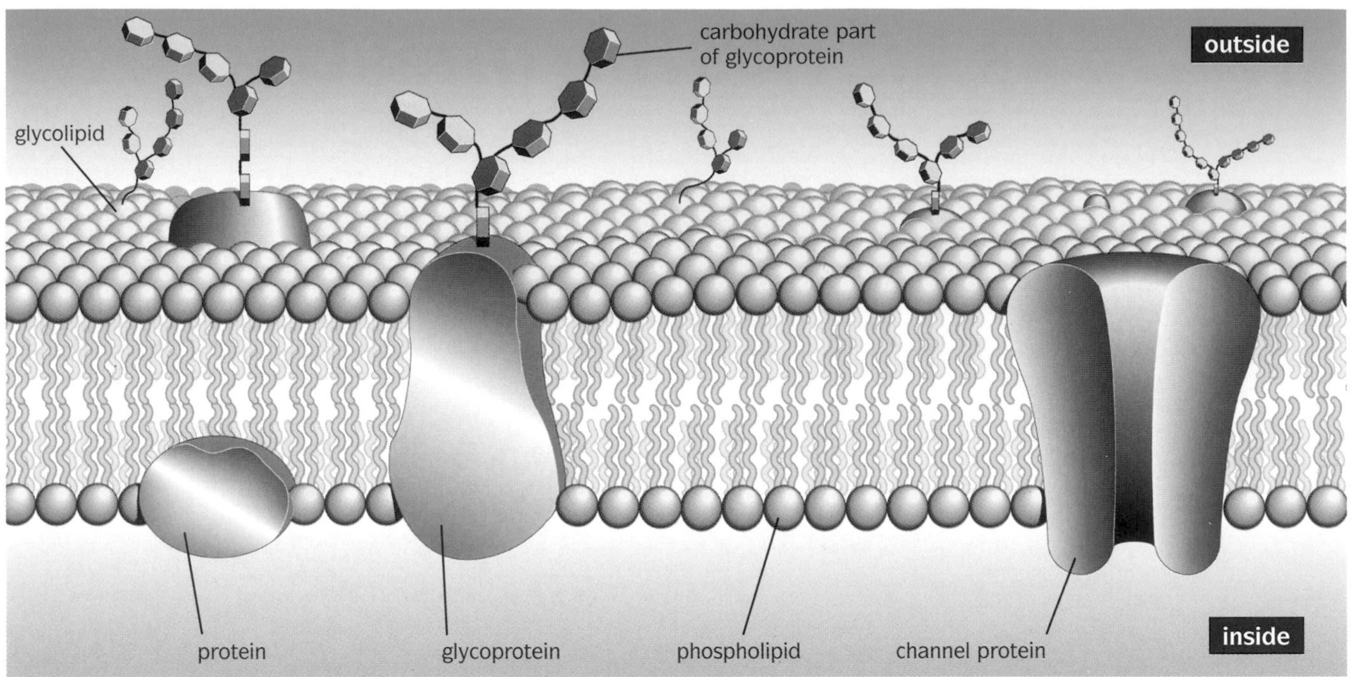

● ***Figure 5.2*** An artist's impression of the fluid mosaic model of membrane structure.

If the phospholipids are shaken up with water they can form stable structures in the water called **micelles** *(figure 5.1b)*. Here all the hydrophilic heads face outwards into the water, shielding the hydrophobic tails, which point towards each other. Alternatively, two-layered structures, called **bilayers**, can form in sheets *(figure 5.1c)*. It is now known that this phospholipid bilayer is the basic structure of membranes.

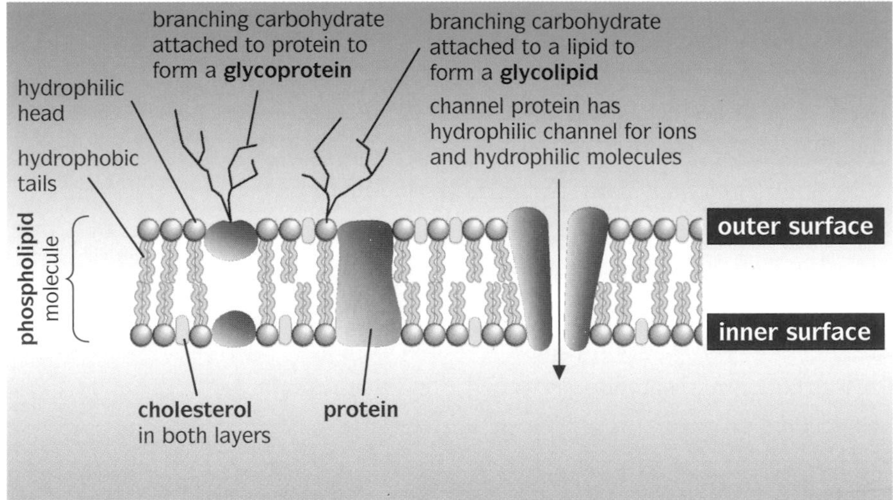

● ***Figure 5.3*** Diagram of the fluid mosaic model of membrane structure.

Structure of membranes

The phospholipid bilayer is visible using the electron microscope at very high magnifications (at least × 100 000 – *figure 1.12g*, page 11). The double black line visible in the electron microscope is thought to show the two phospholipid layers. The bilayer (membrane) is about 7 nm wide.

Chemical analysis of membranes reveals that they also contain proteins. In 1972, Singer and Nicolson suggested a model for the structure which they described as a **fluid mosaic model**. This proposed that the protein molecules float about in the fluid phospholipid bilayer. The protein molecules would therefore form a fluid mosaic pattern, that is isolated 'pieces' floating about and changing in pattern. Probably the best way to try to imagine the fluid phospholipid bilayer is to compare it with the surface of a bubble; it is liquid, like the bubble, and very thin. It has the consistency of olive oil. An artist's impression of a modern interpretation of this model is shown in *figure 5.2* and a diagram of it in *figure 5.3*.

Features of the fluid mosaic model

- The membrane is a double layer (**bilayer**) of phospholipid molecules. The individual phospholipid molecules move about by diffusion within their own monolayer.
- The phospholipid tails point inwards, facing each other and forming a non-polar hydrophobic interior. The phospholipid heads face the aqueous (water-containing) medium that surrounds the membrane.
- Some of the phospholipid tails are saturated and some are unsaturated. The more unsaturated they are, the more fluid the membrane. This is because the unsaturated fatty acid tails are bent *(figure 3.11)* and therefore fit together more loosely. As temperature decreases membranes become less fluid, but some organisms which cannot regulate their own temperature, such as bacteria and yeasts, respond by increasing the proportion of unsaturated fatty acids in their membranes.
- Most of the protein molecules float like mobile icebergs in the phospholipid layers, although some are fixed like islands to structures inside the cell and do not move about.
- Some proteins are embedded in the outer layer, some in the inner layer and some span the whole membrane. They stay in the membrane because they have hydrophobic portions (made from hydrophobic amino acids) which 'sit' among the hydrophobic phospholipid tails. Hydrophilic portions (made from hydrophilic amino acids) face outwards.
- The total thickness is about 7 nm on average.
- Some proteins and lipids have short, branching carbohydrate chains attached to the external surface of the membrane, thus forming **glycoproteins** and **glycolipids** respectively.

Functions of membranes

The phospholipid bilayer provides the basic structure of the membrane and is a barrier to the movement of most water-soluble molecules. The fluidity of the membrane depends partly on the proportions of saturated to unsaturated fatty acids. Another molecule which helps control fluidity is **cholesterol**. Like phospholipids, it has a hydrophilic head and a hydrophobic tail and fits neatly between the phospholipid molecules. It helps to regulate the fluidity of the membrane, preventing it from becoming too fluid or too rigid. It is also important for mechanical stability, as without it membranes quickly break and cells burst open. Cholesterol also reduces uncontrolled leakage, by diffusion, of polar molecules, ions and water through the membrane, ensuring that they must pass through special channels where they can be controlled. This is particularly important in the myelin sheath around nerve cells where leakage of ions would slow down nerve impulses.

The functions of glycolipids are mainly unknown, but they probably act as receptors for chemicals that are used as signals between cells.

Thousands of different types of protein may be found in membranes, which have many different functions, for example:

- **enzymes**, e.g. for digestion of food on the surfaces of microvilli in the gut;
- **receptor molecules**, e.g. for hormones (page 73). Typically the receptor in the membrane recognises the hormone and stimulates another membrane protein to trigger off a particular series of chemical reactions resulting in the desired response. They also act as receptors for neurotransmitters (the chemicals that enable nerve impulses to pass from one nerve cell to another);
- **carrier and channel proteins** (see page 62). These proteins form **hydrophilic tunnels** running from one side of the membrane to the other. These allow water-soluble ions, and molecules such as sugars, amino acids and proteins, into or out of the cell in a controlled way;
- **cell-to-cell recognition**, e.g. some glycoproteins are antigens;
- glycoproteins also act as **receptors** in the same way as glycolipids;
- **making connections with other cells;**

- in **photosynthesis** and **respiration**, proteins in the membranes of chloroplasts and mitochondria, respectively, play a role in energy transfer reactions. The reactions in photosynthesis that are driven by light take place on membranes in the chloroplasts, and the formation of ATP, a chemical which acts as an energy carrier, takes place here as well as on the membranes inside mitochondria by a similar mechanism.

Transport across the cell surface membrane

A phospholipid bilayer around cells makes a very effective barrier, particularly against the movement of water-soluble molecules and ions. The aqueous contents of the cell are therefore prevented from escaping. However, some exchange between the cell and its environment is essential.

SAQ 5.1

Suggest **three** reasons why exchange between the cell and its environment is essential.

There are four basic mechanisms, diffusion, osmosis, active and bulk transport, by which exchange is achieved, which we shall now consider.

Diffusion

If you open a bottle of perfume in a room, it is not long before molecules of scent spread to all parts of the room (and are detected when they fit into membrane receptors in your nose). This will happen, even in still air, by the process of diffusion. **Diffusion** can be defined as the movement of molecules (or ions) from a region of their higher concentration to a region of their lower concentration. It happens because of the natural kinetic energy (energy of movement) possessed by molecules or ions, which makes them move about at random. As a result of diffusion, molecules tend to reach an equilibrium situation where they are evenly spread within a given volume of space.

The respiratory gases, oxygen and carbon dioxide, cross membranes by diffusion. Both can cross through the phospholipid bilayer directly between the phospholipid molecules. Oxygen is uncharged and non-polar, so crosses quickly. Carbon dioxide is a polar molecule but is small enough to pass through rapidly. Water molecules, despite being very polar, can diffuse rapidly across the phospholipid bilayer because they too are small enough. However, charged ions and larger polar molecules, such as sugars, amino acids and nucleotides, cannot diffuse across the bilayer. They pass through special **channel proteins**, such as that shown in *figure 5.3*, or through carrier proteins (see below). Such diffusion is called **facilitated diffusion** because it is facilitated (made possible) by a protein.

Channel proteins form water-filled pores across the bilayer through which specific ions or molecules can diffuse. The proteins have particular shapes and therefore let through only particular molecules. In other words they are *specific*. The disease cystic fibrosis (page 21) is caused by a defect in a membrane protein that regulates the activity of a chloride (Cl^-) channel.

A **carrier protein** is a more sophisticated device. It is a protein that can change its shape to make diffusion possible. It has binding sites for particular solute molecules and these molecules can enter and leave the binding sites at random. When allowing diffusion it works as shown in *figure 5.4*. In the 'ping' state, the binding site for the solute molecule is exposed to the outside of the cell; in the 'pong' state it is exposed to the inside. The molecule changes rapidly from one shape to the other at random (up to 100 cycles per second). If there is a higher concentration of solute molecules on the outside of the cell than on the inside, then it is more likely that molecules on the outside of the membrane will come into contact with a binding site when it is exposed than will molecules on the inside. In a given period of time more molecules will cross the membrane from the high to the low concentration. In other words, diffusion will occur.

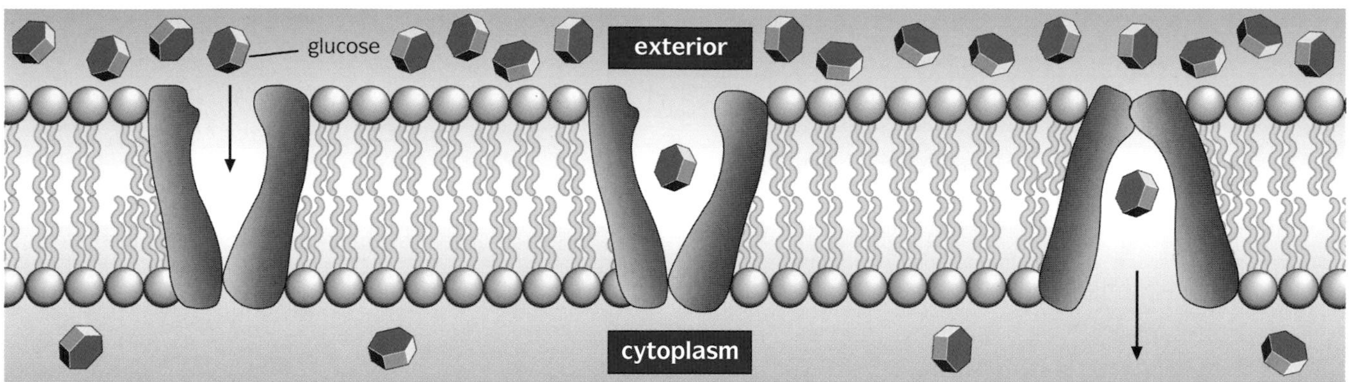

● ***Figure 5.4*** Changes in the shape of a carrier protein during facilitated diffusion.

Osmosis

Osmosis is best regarded as a special type of diffusion involving water molecules only. It is defined as the movement of water molecules from a region of their higher concentration to a region of their lower concentration **through** a **partially permeable membrane**. The latter is a membrane which allows only certain molecules through.

In explanations that follow, remember that solute + solvent = solution. In a sugar **solution**, for example, the **solute** is sugar and the **solvent** is water.

SAQ 5.2

Look at *figure 5.5*.

a Which solution is more dilute and which is more concentrated?

b Which solution has the higher concentration of water molecules?

c In which direction will water molecules move by osmosis?

Since the solute molecules cannot cross the membrane, the two solutions **A** and **B** cannot come into equilibrium by the diffusion of **both** solute and water molecules, as would happen if there were no membrane. Instead, only water molecules can pass through the membrane. They will show a net movement from **A** to **B** because there is a higher concentration of water molecules in **A** than in **B**.

The tendency for water molecules to move from one place to another is measured as the **water potential.** Water moves from a place of higher water potential to a region of lower water potential. Solution **A** therefore has a higher water potential than solution **B**. Solute molecules reduce water potential. The extent of this lowering is called the **solute potential.** Pure water has the highest possible water potential. By convention, this is set at zero. Since solutes make water potential lower, they make water potential less than zero, that is negative. The more solute, the more negative (lower) the solute potential and the water potential become.

SAQ 5.3

In *figure 5.5*, which solution has the higher solute potential?

The symbol for water potential is Ψ (the Greek letter psi). The symbol for solute potential is Ψ_s.

Figure 5.6 shows the effect of osmosis on an animal cell. The experiment shows how important it is to maintain a constant Ψ inside the bodies of animals.

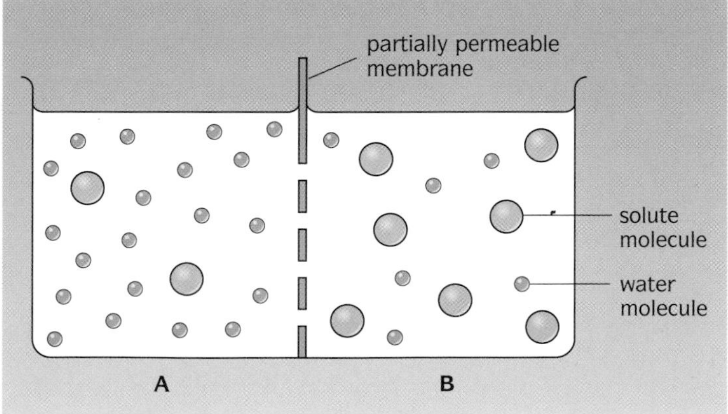

● ***Figure 5.5*** Two solutions separated by a partially permeable membrane. The solute molecules are too large to pass through the pores in the membrane.

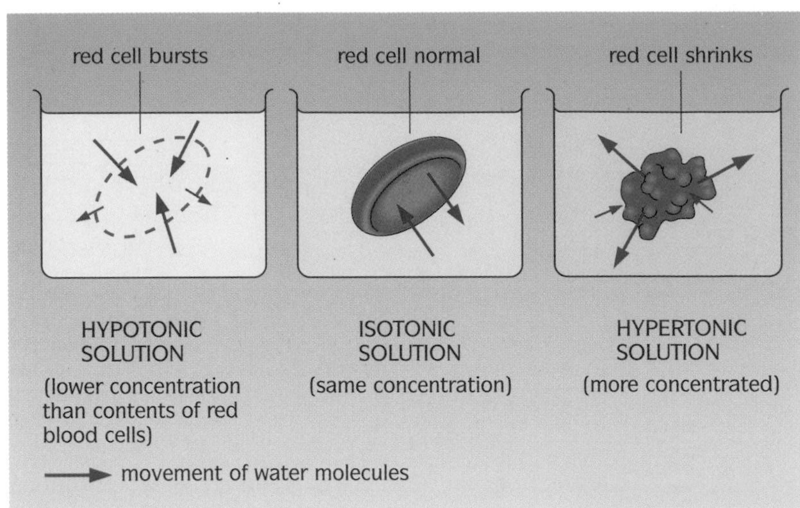

● ***Figure 5.6*** Movement of water into or out of red blood cells by osmosis in solutions of different concentration.

SAQ 5.4

In the experiment shown in *figure 5.6*:

a which solution has the highest water potential?

b which solution has the lowest solute potential?

c in which solution is the water potential of the red cell the same as that of the solution?

For a solution or for an animal cell, water potential equals solute potential. However, in plant cells another factor comes into play. If a plant cell is placed in pure water or in a very dilute solution, it does not swell until it bursts like an animal cell would. It is prevented from bursting by its cell wall which is very strong and inelastic. As water enters the cell, pressure builds up which is soon so great that it stops further water entering the cell. (*Figure 5.7* shows a simplified model of this.) In fact, pressure builds up so quickly that very little dilution of the cell contents takes place (almost no change in Ψ_s). At this point, equilibrium is reached and water potential inside the cell equals that outside (water *always* moves from higher to lower Ψ, so at equilibrium there can be no difference in water potentials).

Pressure increases tendency of water molecules to move from **B** to **A**, and so increases water potential of **B**. The amount of this increase is the pressure potential and can balance the effect of solute potential.

partially permeable membrane
solute molecule
water molecule
A
B

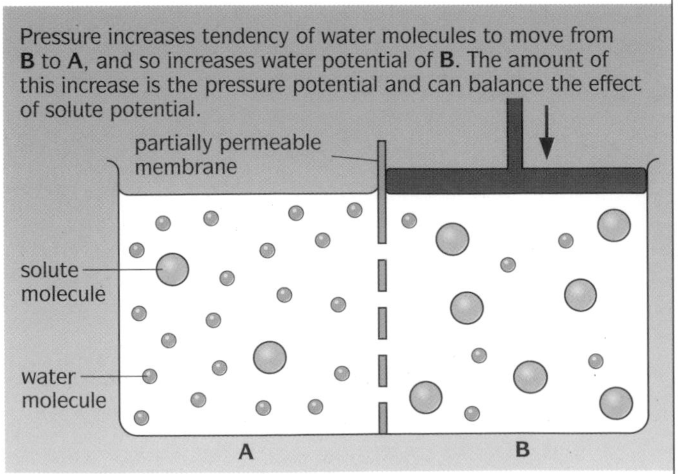

● ***Figure 5.7*** Two solutions separated by a partially permeable membrane. A piston is added to side **B**, enabling pressure to be applied to solution **B**.

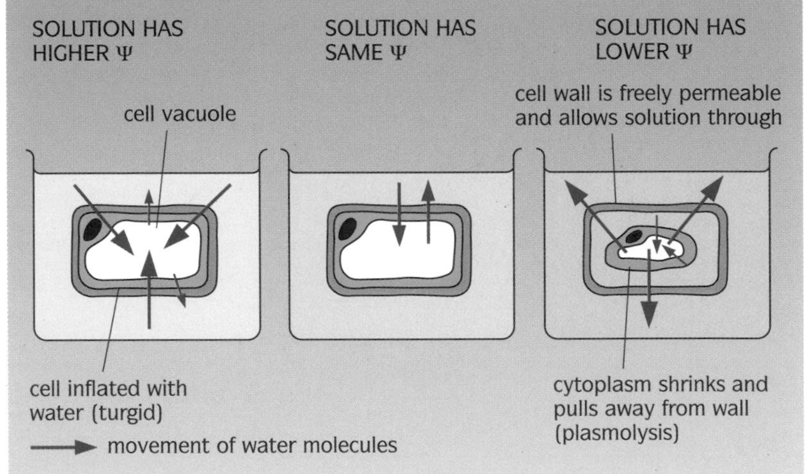

● ***Figure 5.8*** Osmotic changes in a plant cell in solutions of different water potential.

The pressure that develops inside the cell is called the **pressure potential** (Ψ_p) or turgor pressure and, like solute potential, it contributes to water potential. As pressure builds up, there is a greater tendency for water to leave the cell; in other words water potential increases inside the cell as pressure potential increases. For plant cells then, $\Psi = \Psi_s + \Psi_p$. Solute potential is negative, pressure potential is positive.

Figure 5.8 shows possible osmotic changes in a plant cell in different solutions. These can easily be observed with a light microscope using strips of epidermis peeled from rhubarb petioles or from the swollen storage leaves of onion bulbs placed in sucrose solutions of varying concentration.

SAQ 5.5

Figure 5.8 shows a phenomenon called plasmolysis. Why can plasmolysis not take place in an animal cell?

Active transport

If the concentration of particular ions, such as potassium and chloride, inside cells is measured, it is often found that they are 10–20 times more concentrated inside than outside. Cells cannot manufacture inorganic ions, so they must be able to accumulate them against a concentration gradient. This requires energy.

Active transport is the **energy-consuming transport** of molecules or ions across a membrane **against** a concentration gradient (from **lower** to **higher** concentration) made possible by transferring energy from respiration. Energy is needed because the molecules or ions are being moved **against** the normal diffusion gradient. Like facilitated diffusion, it is achieved by **carrier proteins**, each of which is specific for a particular type of molecule or ion. However, unlike facilitated diffusion, active transport transfers energy from respiration. The energy is supplied by the molecule ATP which is produced during respiration inside the cell. The ATP supplies the energy needed to make the carrier protein change shape as illustrated in *figure 5.4*.

An important example of such a carrier protein is the **calcium pump**. Calcium pumps are common in membranes but they have a special role in muscle cells. Muscle cells contain an extensive form of ER known as **sarcoplasmic reticulum** *(figure 5.9)*. This stores calcium ions as a result of the activity of a calcium pump in its membrane. The pump forms 90% of the membrane protein. It pumps calcium in from the surrounding cytoplasm, using energy from ATP. When a nerve impulse stimulates the muscle cell, it causes a sudden release of this calcium which triggers off muscle contraction.

Active transport is also important in reabsorption in the kidneys where certain useful molecules and ions have to be reabsorbed into the blood after filtration into the kidney tubules (nephrons). It is also involved in the absorption of some products of digestion from the gut. In plants, active transport is used to load sugar from the photosynthesising cells of leaves into the phloem tissue for transport around the plant.

● ***Figure 5.9*** A false-colour, freeze-fracture TEM of a section through skeletal muscle to show the sarcoplasmic reticulum. The muscle fibrils can be seen as faint parallel lines in the purple region, running from upper left to lower right. The sarcoplasmic reticulum runs between them and appears orange and bubble-like. It stores calcium ions which are collected by active transport and when released in response to a nerve impulse, cause contraction of the muscle fibrils.

Bulk transport

So far we have been looking at ways in which individual molecules or ions cross membranes. Mechanisms also exist for the bulk transport of large quantities of materials into cells (endocytosis) or out of cells (exocytosis).

Endocytosis involves the engulfing of the material by the cell surface membrane to form a small sac, or 'endocytotic vacuole'. It takes two forms:

- **phagocytosis** or 'cell eating' – this is the bulk uptake of solid material. Cells specialising in this are called **phagocytes.** The process is called **phagocytosis** and the vacuoles **phagocytic vacuoles.** An example is the engulfing of bacteria by certain white blood cells *(figure 5.10a)*.
- **pinocytosis** or 'cell drinking' – this is the bulk uptake of liquid. The small vacuoles (vesicles) formed are often extremely small, in which case the process is called **micropinocytosis.** The human egg cell takes up nutrients from cells that surround it (the follicle) by pinocytosis.

Exocytosis is the reverse of endocytosis and is the process by which materials are removed from cells (*figure 5.10b*). It happens, for example, in the secretion of digestive enzymes from cells of the pancreas. Secretory vesicles carry the enzymes to the cell surface and release their contents. Plant cells use exocytosis to get their cell wall building materials to the outside of the cell surface membrane.

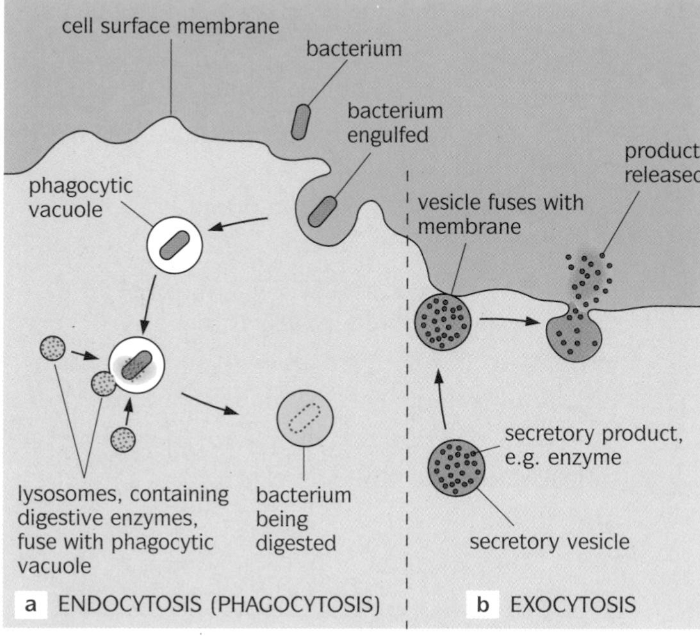

● ***Figure 5.10*** Stages in **a** endocytosis (phagocytosis) and **b** exocytosis.

Questions

1 Explain how the properties of phospholipids are important in the formation of membranes.

2 Discuss the roles played by proteins in membranes.

3 Explain, with reference to suitable examples, what is meant by **a** facilitated diffusion and **b** active transport.

4 Certain cells of the pancreas make and secrete digestive enzymes. The following sequence of organelles is involved: ribosomes, ER, Golgi apparatus, Golgi vesicles. Summarise the role of these organelles and describe the process of exocytosis by which the enzymes are released.

SUMMARY

- The cell surface membrane controls exchange between the cell and its environment. Special carrier proteins and channel proteins are sometimes involved.
- Within cells, membranes allow compartmentation and division of labour to occur, within membrane-bound organelles, such as the nucleus, ER and Golgi apparatus.
- Some metabolic pathways take place on membranes. Membranes also contain receptor sites for hormones and neurotransmitters; possess cell recognition markers, such as antigens; allow cell-to-cell signalling to take place, and may contain enzymes, such as microvilli on epithelial cells in the gut.
- Diffusion is the movement of molecules or ions from a region of their higher concentration to one of lower concentration. Oxygen and carbon dioxide cross membranes by diffusion through the phospholipid bilayer. Diffusion of ions and larger polar molecules through membranes is allowed by channel or carrier proteins.
- Water moves from regions of higher water potential to regions of lower water potential. When this takes place through a partially permeable membrane this diffusion is called osmosis. Pure water has a water potential of 0. Adding solute reduces the water potential by an amount known as the solute potential, which has a negative value. Adding pressure to a solution increases the water potential by an amount known as the pressure potential.
- In dilute solutions, animal cells burst as water moves into the cytoplasm from the solution. In dilute solutions, a plant cell does not burst because the cell wall provides resistance to prevent it expanding. The pressure that builds up is the pressure potential. A plant cell in this state is turgid.
- Some ions and molecules move across membranes by active transport, against the concentration gradient. This needs a carrier protein and ATP to provide energy.
- Exocytosis and endocytosis involve the formation of vacuoles to move larger quantities of materials respectively out of, or into, cells.

Control and coordination

By the end of this chapter you should be able to:

1 explain that control systems involve receptors, effectors and communication methods, and that regulatory control mechanisms involve negative feedback;

2 explain the importance of homeostasis in mammals;

3 explain what is meant by the term endocrine gland;

4 describe the structure of the pancreas, and state the precise source of secretion of insulin and glucagon;

5 describe and explain the roles of glucagon and insulin in the control of blood glucose concentration and how they affect the activities of cells;

6 describe the structure of motor and sensory neurones and relate their structure to their functions;

7 describe the positions and roles of motor neurones, sensory neurones and intermediate neurones in a spinal reflex arc;

8 explain what is meant by resting potential, and how it is maintained;

9 explain what is meant by action potential, and how action potentials are transmitted along neurones and how they carry information;

10 describe how myelinated and unmyelinated axons differ in structure and in speed of conduction;

11 explain how action potentials are generated in receptors;

12 explain how synapses function and describe their roles.

Most animals are complex organisms, made up of many millions of cells. Different parts of the organism perform different functions. It is essential that information can pass between these different parts, so that their activities can be coordinated. Sometimes, the purpose of this information transfer is to regulate the levels of some substance within the organism, such as the control of blood sugar levels in mammals. Sometimes, the purpose may be to change the activity of some part of the organism in response to some external stimulus, such as moving away from an unpleasant stimulus.

One method of achieving coordination between cells in different places is by transferring information in the form of chemicals from one part to another. Another method of information transfer uses nerve cells. This chapter deals first with coordination and control by means of chemical messengers, and then with information transfer through the mammalian nervous sytem.

Homeostasis

A vital function of control systems in mammals is to maintain a stable internal environment. This is called **homeostasis.** 'Internal environment' means the conditions inside the body, in which cells function. For a cell, its immediate environment is the tissue fluid which surrounds it. Many features of this environment affect the functioning of the cell. Three such features are:

- **temperature** – low temperatures slow metabolic reactions, while high temperatures cause denaturation of proteins, including enzymes;
- **amount of water** – lack of water in the tissue fluid causes water to be drawn out of cells by osmosis, causing metabolic reactions in the cell to slow or stop, while too much water entering the cell may cause it to swell and burst;
- **amount of glucose** – glucose is the fuel for respiration, so lack of it causes respiration to slow or stop, depriving the cell of an energy source, while too much glucose may draw water out of the cell by osmosis.

In this chapter, we shall look at the way in which the concentration of glucose in the blood is controlled.

Hormonal communication

Exocrine and endocrine glands

The chemicals which are used to carry information from one part of a mammal's body to another part are called **hormones**. They are made in **endocrine glands** (*figure 6.1*).

A **gland** is a group of cells which produces and releases one or more substances, a process known as **secretion**. Endocrine glands contain secretory cells which pass their secretions directly into the blood. 'Endocrine' means 'secreting to the inside', a reference to the fact that endocrine glands secrete hormones into blood capillaries inside the gland.

Endocrine glands are not the only type of gland. We have many glands in our digestive system, for example, such as the salivary glands which secrete saliva. These glands are **exocrine** glands (*figure 6.1*). 'Exocrine' means 'secreting to the outside'. The secretory cells of exocrine glands secrete their substances, which are *not* hormones, into a tube or **duct**, along which the secretion flows. Salivary glands secrete saliva into salivary ducts, which carry the saliva into the mouth.

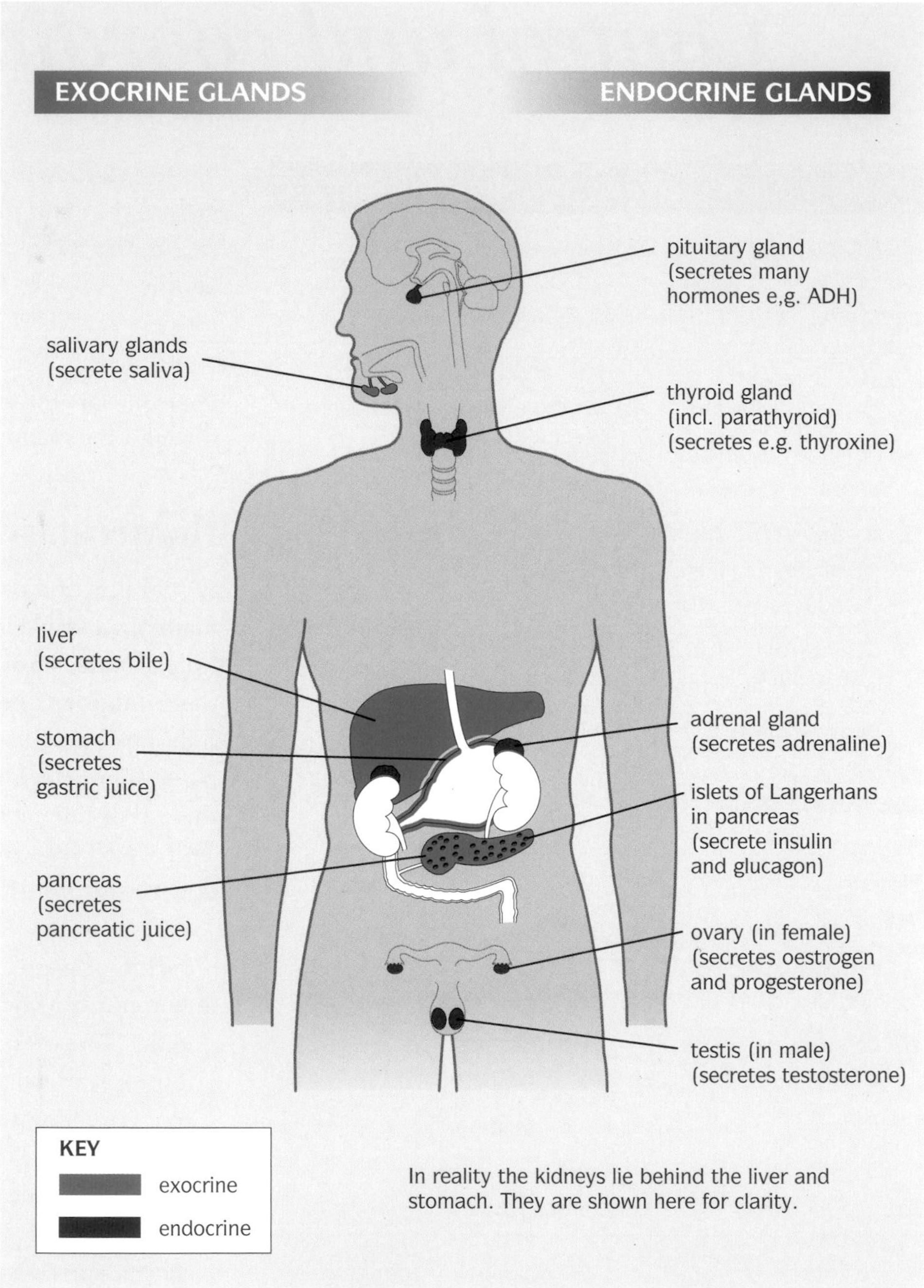

● ***Figure 6.1*** The positions of some exocrine and endocrine glands in the human body.

Hormones

Mammalian hormones have many features in common. They are usually relatively small molecules. Many hormones, such as insulin, are proteins whereas others, such as testosterone, are steroids.

After they have been secreted from an endocrine gland, hormones are transported around the body in the blood plasma. The concentrations of hormones in human blood are very small. For any one hormone, the concentration is rarely more than a few micrograms of hormone per cm^3 of blood. Their rate of secretion from endocrine glands is also low, usually of the order of a few micrograms or milligrams a day. These small quantities of hormone can, however, have very large effects on the body.

Most endocrine glands can secrete hormones very quickly when an appropriate stimulus arrives. For example, adrenaline, the 'fight or flight' hormone secreted in response to a frightening stimulus, is secreted from the adrenal glands within one second of the stimulus being perceived. This means that the effects of hormones can be 'turned on' quite quickly.

Many hormones have a very short life in the body. They are broken down by enzymes in the blood or in cells, or are lost in the urine. Insulin, for example, lasts for only around 10–15 minutes, while adrenaline lasts for between 1 and 3 minutes. This means that the effects of hormones can also be 'turned off' quite quickly.

SAQ 6.1

If you are in a frightening situation, adrenaline will be secreted and cause your heart rate to increase. This can go on for several hours. If adrenaline has such a short life-span in the body, how can its effect continue for so long?

Hormones are transported all through the body in the blood. However, each hormone has a particular group of cells which it affects, called **target cells.** These cells, and only these cells, are affected by the hormone because they contain **receptors** specific to the hormone. The receptors for protein hormones, such as insulin, are on the cell surface membrane. These hormones bind with the receptors on the outer surface of the membrane, causing a response by the cell without actually entering it. Steroid hormones, however, are lipid-soluble, and so can pass easily through the cell surface membrane into the cytoplasm. The receptors for steroid hormones are *inside* the cell, in the cytoplasm.

SAQ 6.2

Explain why steroid hormones can pass easily through the cell surface membrane, while protein hormones cannot.

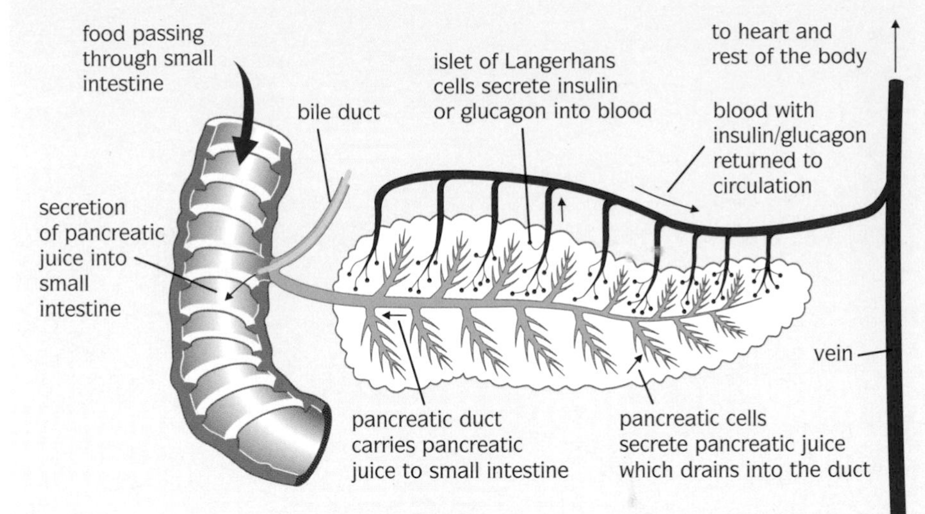

● ***Figure 6.2*** The pancreas is both an exocrine and endocrine gland.

The pancreas

Figures 6.2 and *6.3* show the structure of the pancreas. The pancreas is a very unusual gland, because parts of it function as an exocrine gland, while other parts function as an endocrine gland. The exocrine function is the secretion of pancreatic juice, which flows along the pancreatic duct into the duodenum, where it helps in digestion. The endocrine function is carried out by groups of cells called **islets of Langerhans**, which are scattered throughout the pancreas.

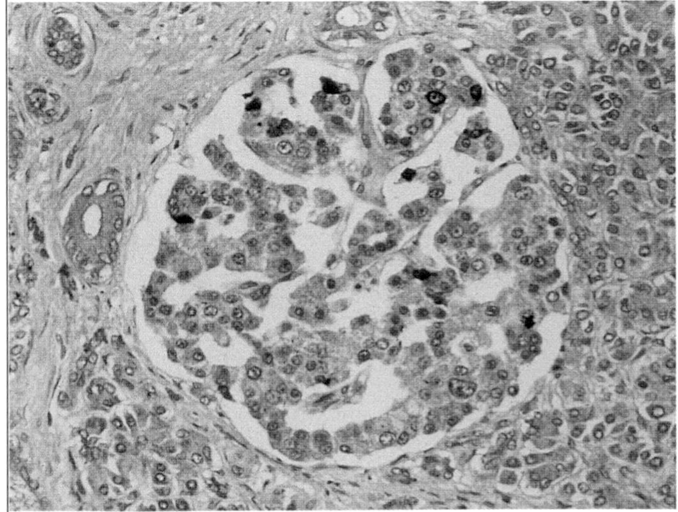

● ***Figure 6.3*** Light micrograph of pancreas (×650). In the centre of the picture is an islet of Langerhans, containing α and β cells, and many blood capillaries.

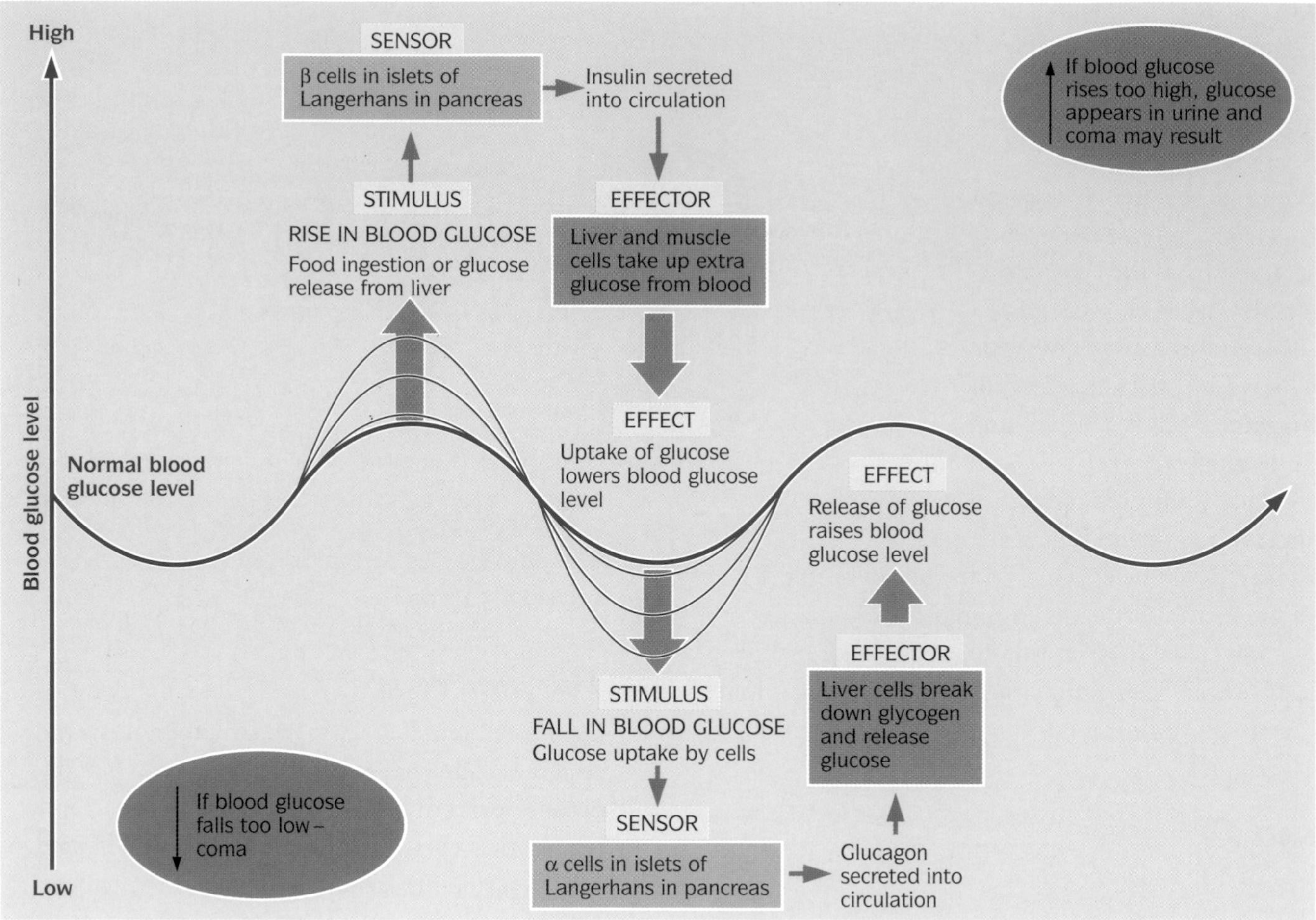

High

SENSOR

β cells in islets of Langerhans in pancreas

Insulin secreted into circulation

If blood glucose rises too high, glucose appears in urine and coma may result

STIMULUS

RISE IN BLOOD GLUCOSE

Food ingestion or glucose release from liver

EFFECTOR

Liver and muscle cells take up extra glucose from blood

EFFECT

Uptake of glucose lowers blood glucose level

Blood glucose level

Normal blood glucose level

EFFECT

Release of glucose raises blood glucose level

EFFECTOR

STIMULUS

FALL IN BLOOD GLUCOSE

Glucose uptake by cells

Liver cells break down glycogen and release glucose

If blood glucose falls too low – coma

SENSOR

α cells in islets of Langerhans in pancreas

Glucagon secreted into circulation

Low

● ***Figure 6.4*** The control mechanism for blood glucose levels.

The islets contain two types of cells. α **cells** secrete **glucagon**, while β **cells** secrete **insulin**. These two hormones, both small proteins, are involved in the control of blood glucose levels *(figure 6.4)*.

The control of blood glucose

Carbohydrate is transported through the human bloodstream in the form of glucose, in solution in the blood plasma. For storage, glucose can be converted into the polysaccharide **glycogen**, a large, insoluble molecule made up of many glucose units linked together *(figure 3.7*, page 38*)*, which can be stored inside cells, especially liver and muscle cells *(figure 6.5)*.

In a healthy human, each 100 cm^3 of blood normally contains between 80 and 120 mg of glucose. If blood glucose level drops below this, then cells may run short of glucose for respiration, and be unable to carry out their normal activities. Very high

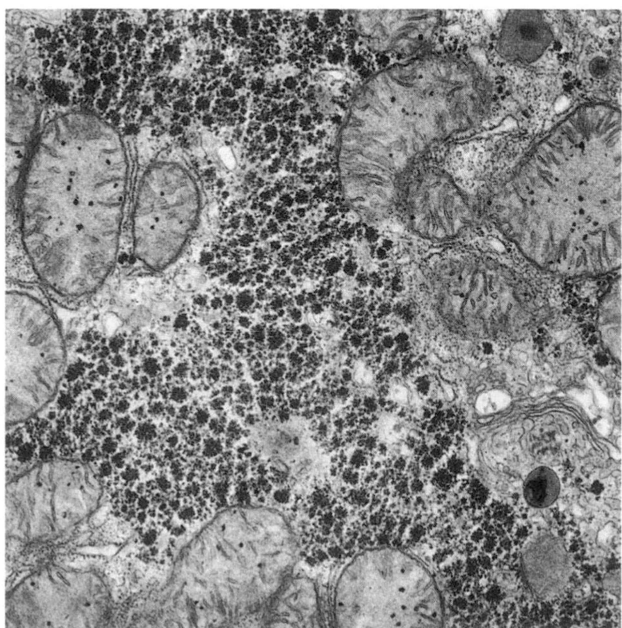

● ***Figure 6.5*** Electron micrograph of part of a liver cell (×20 000). The dark spots are glycogen granules in the cytoplasm. Numerous mitochondria can also be seen.

blood glucose levels can also cause major problems, again upsetting the normal behaviour of cells.

After a meal containing carbohydrate, glucose from the digested food is absorbed from the small intestine and passes into the blood. As this blood flows through the pancreas, the α cells and β cells detect the raised glucose levels. The α cells respond by stopping the secretion of glucagon, while the β cells respond by secreting insulin into the blood plasma. The insulin is carried to all parts of the body, in the blood.

Insulin affects many cells, especially those in the liver and muscles. The effects on these cells include:

- an increased absorption of glucose from the blood into the cells;
- an increase in the rate of use of glucose in respiration;
- an increase in the rate at which glucose is converted into the storage polysaccharide glycogen.

All of these processes take glucose out of the blood, so lowering the blood glucose levels. A drop in blood glucose concentration is detected by the α cells and β cells in the pancreas. The α cells respond by secreting glucagon, while the β cells respond by stopping the secretion of insulin.

The lack of insulin puts a stop to the increased uptake and usage of glucose by liver and muscle cells, although uptake still continues at a more 'normal' rate. The presence of glucagon affects the activities of the liver cells. (Muscle cells are not responsive to glucagon.) These effects include:

- the breakdown of glycogen to glucose;
- the use of fatty acids instead of glucose as the main fuel in respiration;
- the production of glucose from other compounds, such as fats.

As a result, the liver releases glucose into the blood. This blood flows around the body, passing through the pancreas. Here, the α cells and β cells sense the raised glucose levels, switching off glucagon secretion and perhaps switching on insulin secretion if the glucose levels are higher than normal.

Negative feedback

The control of blood sugar levels by insulin and glucagon illustrates several features which are found in virtually all control systems in living organisms. (Indeed, these features are also found in non-living control systems. If you have an interest in these, perhaps in electronic control circuits, you may like to consider the similarities between them.)

Firstly, such a control system must have a **receptor** or **sensor**. This receives information, that is the **input**, concerning the parameter which is to be controlled. In this case, the receptors are the α cells and β cells, which sense the blood glucose levels. The information received by the receptor switches on a **control** mechanism. In this case this is also provided by the α and β cells, which respond by secreting, or not secreting, glucagon and insulin respectively. The control mechanism causes action by an **effector**, to produce an **output**. In this case, the effectors are the liver and muscle cells which act to raise or lower blood glucose levels.

In a control system such as this, whose function is to keep a potentially varying parameter from varying too much, there must be **feedback** of information to the receptors, telling them the results of their actions and causing them to adjust these actions to bring things back to normal. In the control of blood glucose levels, information about this is 'fed back' to the α cells and β cells as the blood flows through them. This feedback causes

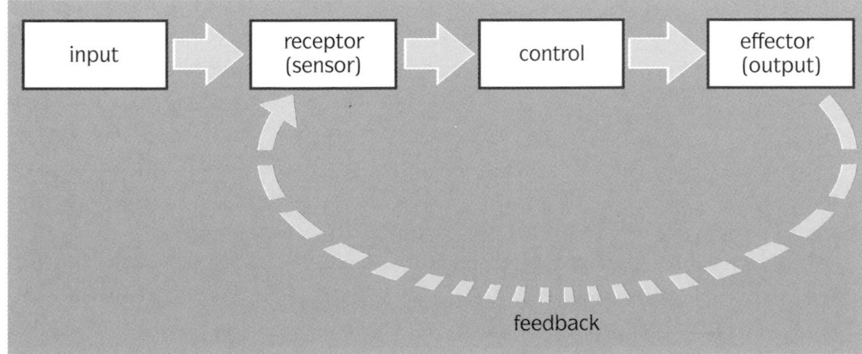

● ***Figure 6.6*** A closed loop control system has feedback to the sensor, allowing it to respond to the changes it has brought about. In most control systems in living organisms the feedback is negative.

them to adjust their output. If blood sugar levels are high, for example, and insulin is secreted by the β cells and brings the blood sugar level down, then the lower blood sugar level will switch off the β cells and switch on the α cells. This is called **negative feedback** *(figure 6.6)*.

Blood sugar levels never remain constant, even in the healthiest person. One reason for this is the inevitable time delay between a change in the blood glucose level and the onset of actions to correct it. Time delays in control systems result in **oscillation**, where things do not stay absolutely constant, but sometimes rise slightly above and sometimes drop slightly below the 'required' level. Continuous monitoring of levels is essential if these oscillations are not to become so large that they are dangerous.

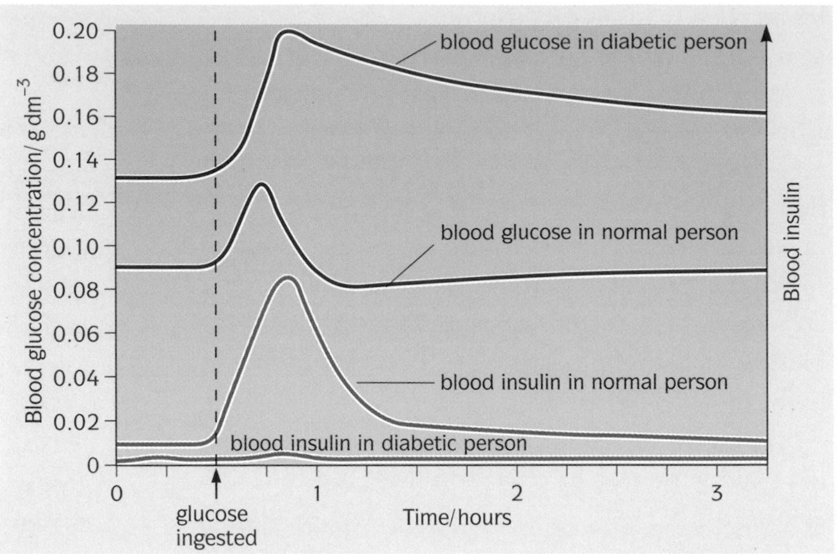

● ***Figure 6.7*** Blood glucose and insulin levels following intake of glucose in a normal person and a person with insulin-dependent diabetes.

Diabetes mellitus

Sugar diabetes, or diabetes mellitus, is one of the commonest metabolic diseases in humans. In developed countries, approximately 1% of people suffer from diabetes mellitus. The incidence is lower in developing countries, for reasons which are not yet fully understood.

There are two forms of sugar diabetes. In **juvenile-onset diabetes**, sometimes called **insulin-dependent diabetes**, the pancreas seems to be incapable of secreting sufficient insulin. It is thought that this might be due to a deficiency in the gene which codes for the production of insulin, or because of an attack on the β cells by the person's own immune system. This form of diabetes, as suggested by its name, usually begins very early in life.

The second form of diabetes is called **non-insulin-dependent diabetes**. In this form, the pancreas secretes insulin as normal, but the liver and muscle cells do not respond to it. It frequently begins relatively late in life.

The symptoms of both types of diabetes mellitus are the same. After a carbohydrate meal, blood glucose levels rise and stay high *(figure 6.7)*. Normally the kidney does not allow any glucose to enter the urine which it produces, but if blood glucose levels become very high, the kidney cannot reabsorb all the glucose so that some passes out in the urine. Extra water and salts accompany this glucose, and the person consequently feels very hungry and thirsty.

In a diabetic, uptake of glucose into cells is slow, even when blood glucose levels are high. Thus cells lack glucose, and metabolise fats and proteins as an alternative energy source. This can lead to a build-up of substances called keto-acids in the blood, which lowers the blood pH. The combination of dehydration, salt loss and low blood pH can cause coma in extreme situations.

Between meals, when blood glucose levels would normally be kept up by mobilisation of glycogen reserves, the blood glucose levels of a person with untreated diabetes may plummet. This is because there is no glycogen to be mobilised. Once again, coma may result, this time because of a lack of glucose for respiration.

SAQ 6.3

Explain why people with diabetes mellitus have virtually no glycogen to be mobilised.

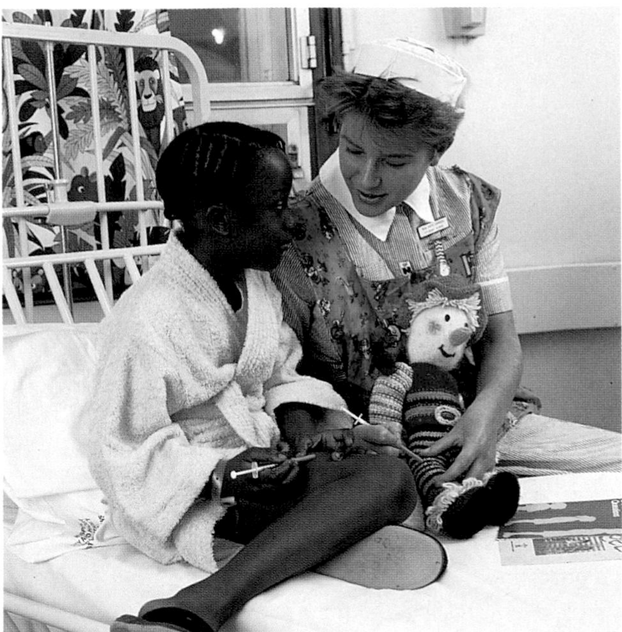

● ***Figure 6.8*** A nurse teaches a girl with insulin-dependent diabetes to inject insulin. She will have to do this daily, all her life.

In insulin-dependent diabetes, regular injections of insulin, together with a carefully controlled diet, are used to keep blood glucose levels near normal (*figure 6.8*). The person must monitor their own blood glucose level, taking a blood sample several times a day. In non-insulin-dependent diabetes, insulin injections would be useless. Control is by diet alone.

SAQ 6.4

a Insulin cannot effectively be taken by mouth. Why is this so?

b Suggest how people with non-insulin-dependent diabetes can control their blood glucose level.

How hormones affect cells

You saw earlier that hormones act on cells by combining with specific receptors, either on the cell surface membrane or in the cytoplasm of cells. All hormone receptors that have so far been analysed are large protein or glycoprotein molecules. Only cells with the appropriate receptors will bind these hormones, and thus only these target cells will be affected.

Insulin and glucagon both affect their target cells by binding to receptors on their cell surface membranes. Neither of these hormones actually enters the cells; their attachment to the membrane starts off a chain of reactions inside the cell which affects the uptake, use or production of glucose by the cells.

One effect of insulin is to speed up the rate at which cells absorb glucose. Glucose can only get into a cell through special carrier proteins in the cell surface membrane (*figure 6.9*). The more carrier proteins there are in the membrane, the faster glucose can be absorbed. Cells keep 'spare' glucose carriers within vesicles in their cytoplasm. When insulin binds to its receptor on the cell surface membrane, it triggers the cell to send these spare glucose carriers out to the membrane. Once these are in place, which takes less than 10 minutes, the rate at which the cell absorbs glucose rises dramatically.

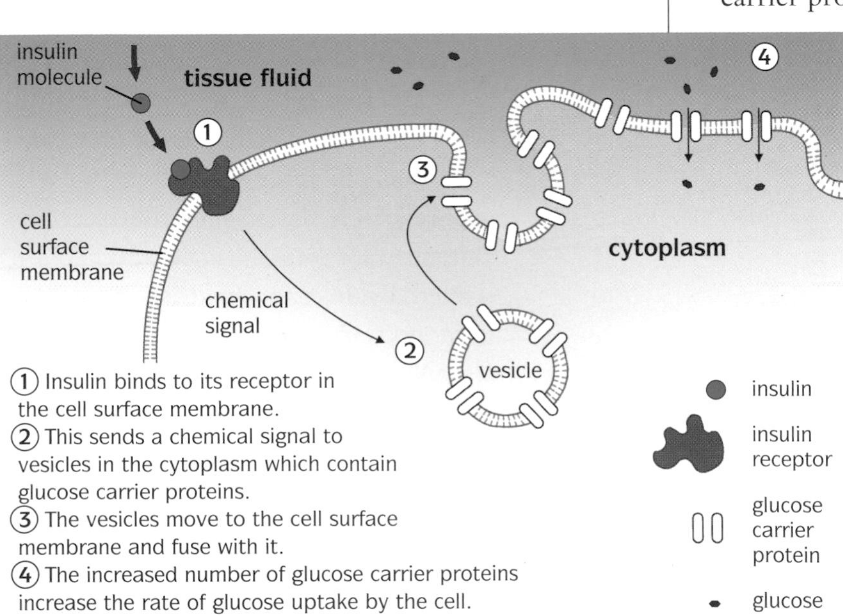

● ***Figure 6.9*** How insulin increases the uptake of glucose by a cell.

One effect of glucagon is to speed up the rate of breakdown of glycogen inside cells. The way it does this is shown in *figure 6.10*. When glucagon binds with its receptor on the cell surface membrane, it triggers a change in the structure of this receptor, which

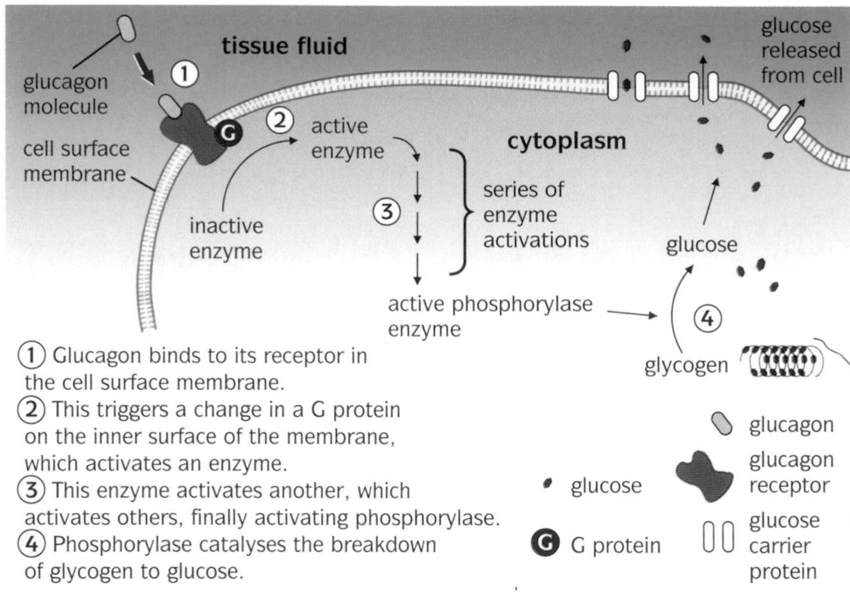

● ***Figure 6.10*** How glucagon speeds up glycogen breakdown in a cell.

in turn affects a protein on the inner surface of the membrane, called a G-protein. The G-protein activates an enzyme which activates other enzymes, resulting in the activation of an enzyme called **phosphorylase**, which converts glycogen into glucose.

Just a few glucagon molecules can have a very large effect on the cell. This is because each activated enzyme molecule can convert many substrate molecules into product molecules, acting over and over again. At each step in the chain of reactions which involves an enzyme, the effect is therefore amplified. This is called **cascade amplification.**

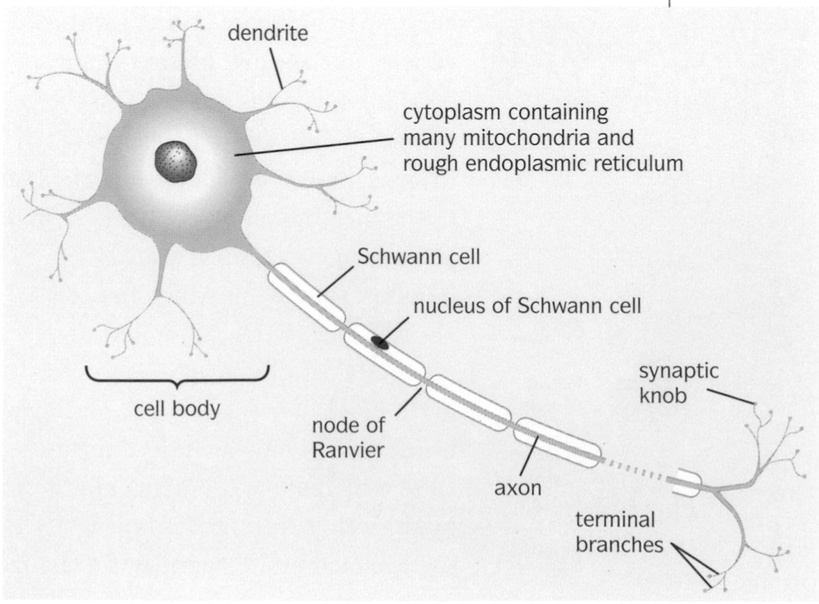

● ***Figure 6.11*** A motor neurone. The axon may be over a metre long.

Nervous communication

Neurones

So far in this chapter we have looked at the way in which hormones are used by mammals to send messages from one part of the body to another. The hormones are carried in the blood, and so spread all through the body. Mammals also have another method of communication within their bodies. This method is faster and more precise and involves the transmission of electrical signals or impulses along precisely constructed pathways. The cells which carry these signals are called **neurones.**

Figure 6.11 shows the structure of a mammalian neurone. This is a **motor neurone** which transmits messages from the brain or spinal cord to a muscle or gland.

The cell body of a motor neurone lies within the spinal cord or brain. The nucleus of a neurone is always in its cell body. Often, dark specks can be seen in the cytoplasm. These are groups of ribosomes involved in protein synthesis.

Many thin cytoplasmic processes extend from the cell body. In a motor neurone, all but one of these processes are relatively short. They conduct impulses *towards* the cell body, and are called **dendrons** or **dendrites**. One process is much longer, and conducts impulses *away* from the cell body. This is called the **axon.** A motor neurone with its cell body in your spinal cord might have its axon running all the way to one of your toes, so axons may be extremely long. Within the cytoplasm of an axon, all of the usual organelles such as endoplasmic reticulum, Golgi

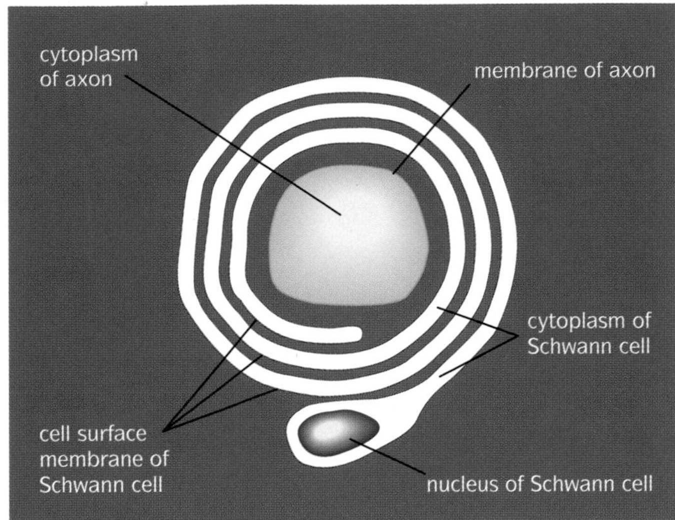

● ***Figure 6.12*** Transverse section across the axon of a myelinated neurone.

apparatus and mitochondria, are present. Particularly large numbers of mitochondria are found at the tips of the terminal branches of the axon, together with many vesicles containing chemicals called transmitter substances. Their function will be explained later (page 83).

In some neurones, cells called **Schwann cells** wrap themselves around the axon all along its length. *Figure 6.12* shows one such cell, viewed as the axon is cut transversely. The Schwann cell spirals around, enclosing the axon in many layers of its cell surface membrane. This enclosing sheath, called the **myelin sheath**, is made largely of lipid, together with some proteins. Not all axons have myelin sheaths. Some non-vertebrate animals, such as earthworms, have no myelin sheaths around their neurones. In humans, about one-third of our motor and sensory neurones are myelinated. The sheath affects the speed of conduction of the nerve impulse (page 80). The small, uncovered areas of axon between Schwann cells are called **nodes of Ranvier**. They occur about every 1–3 mm in human neurones. The nodes themselves are very small, around 2–3 μm long.

Figure 6.13 shows how the shapes of neurones with different functions differ. The basic structure of a **sensory neurone** is the same as that of a motor neurone, but it has one long dendron and an axon which is often shorter than the dendron. Sensory neurones bring impulses from receptors (cells which pick up stimuli, such as touch or light) to the brain or spinal cord. There they pass them on to other neurones.

A reflex arc

In the human body, a sensory neurone and a motor neurone may form a reflex arc. A **reflex arc** is the pathway along which impulses are carried from a receptor to an effector, without involving 'conscious' regions of the brain. *Figure 6.14* shows the structure of a spinal reflex arc in which the impulse is passed from neurone to neurone inside the spinal cord. Some spinal reflex arcs have a third neurone between the sensory and motor neurones, called an intermediate neurone *(figure 6.13)*. Others have no intermediate neurone, and the impulse passes directly from the sensory neurone to the motor neurone.

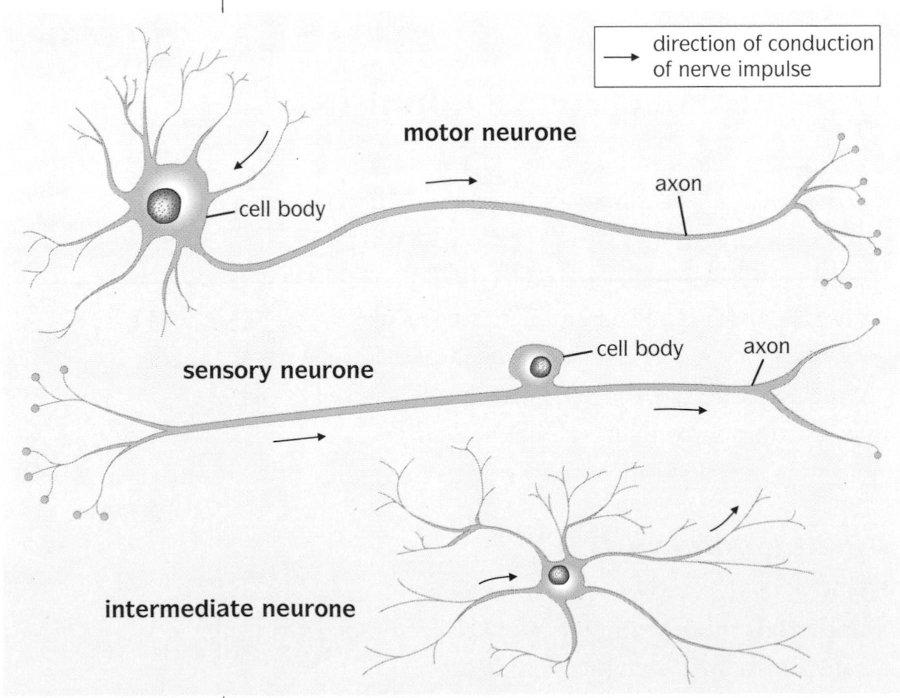

● ***Figure 6.13*** Motor, sensory and intermediate neurones.

Within the spinal cord, the impulse will also be passed on to other neurones which take the message up the cord to the brain. This happens at the same time as the message is travelling along the motor neurone to the effector. The effector therefore responds to the stimulus before there is any voluntary response, involving conscious regions of the brain. This type of reaction to a stimulus is called a **reflex action.** It is a fast, automatic response to a stimulus. Reflex actions are a very useful way of responding to danger signals, such as the touch of a very hot object on your skin or the sight of an object flying towards your eye.

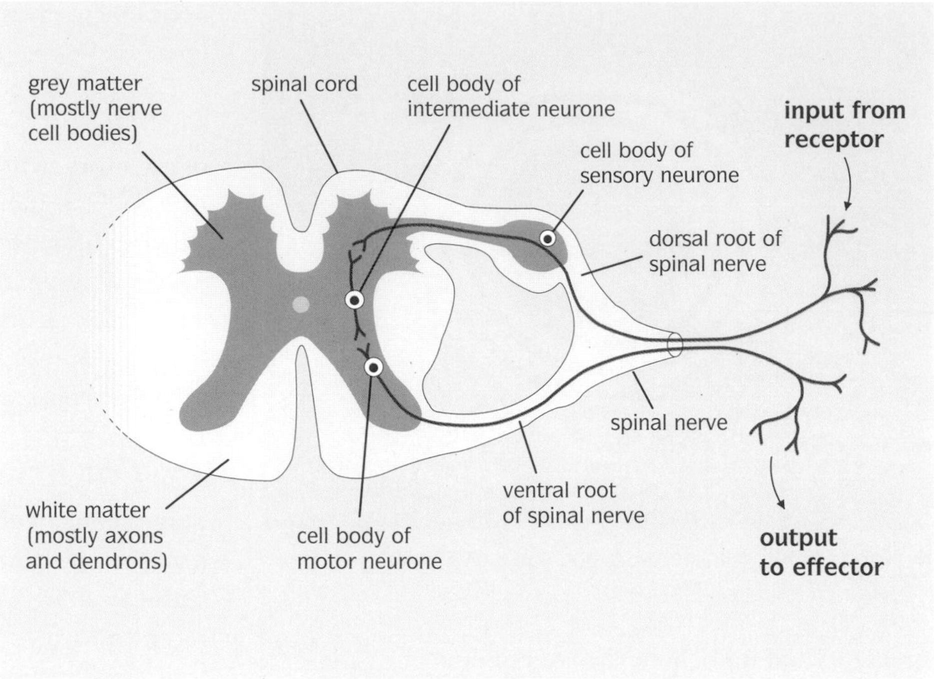

● ***Figure 6.14*** A reflex arc. The spinal cord is shown in transverse section.

SAQ 6.5

Think of three reflex actions other than the two already mentioned. For each action, state the precise stimulus, name the receptor which first detects this stimulus, name the effector which responds to it, and describe the way in which this effector responds.

Transmission of nerve impulses

Neurones transmit impulses as electrical signals. These signals travel very rapidly along their cell surface membranes from one end of the cell to the other. These signals are not a flow of electrons like an electric current. The signals are very brief changes in the distribution of electrical charge across the cell surface membrane, caused by very rapid movement of sodium and potassium ions into and out of the axon.

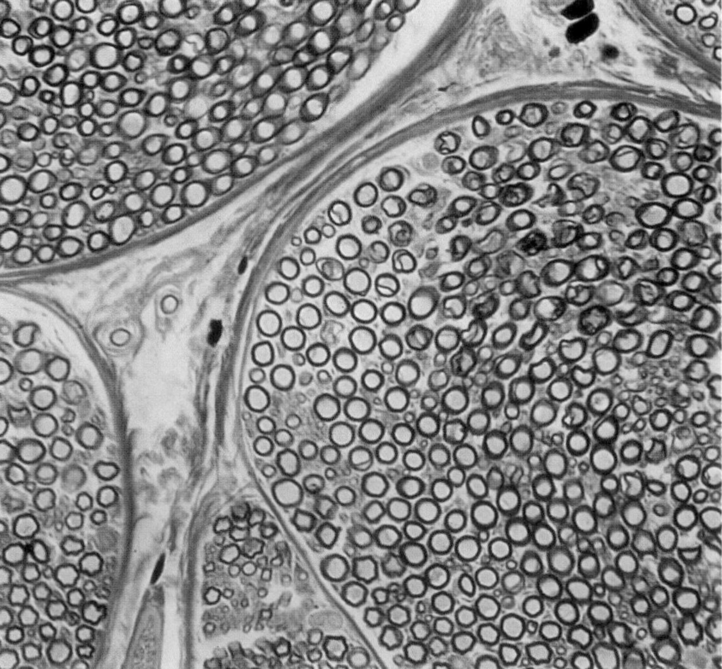

● ***Figure 6.15*** A light micrograph of a transverse section of a nerve tissue (×300). The circles are axons and dendrons in cross-section. Some of these are myelinated (the ones with thick dark lines around) and some are not. Each group of axons and dendrons is surrounded by a perineurium (red lines). Several such groups make a complete nerve.

Resting potential

Figure 6.16 shows part of an unmyelinated axon. Some axons in some organisms, such as squids and earthworms, are very wide, and it is possible to insert tiny electrodes into their cytoplasm to measure these changes in electrical charge.

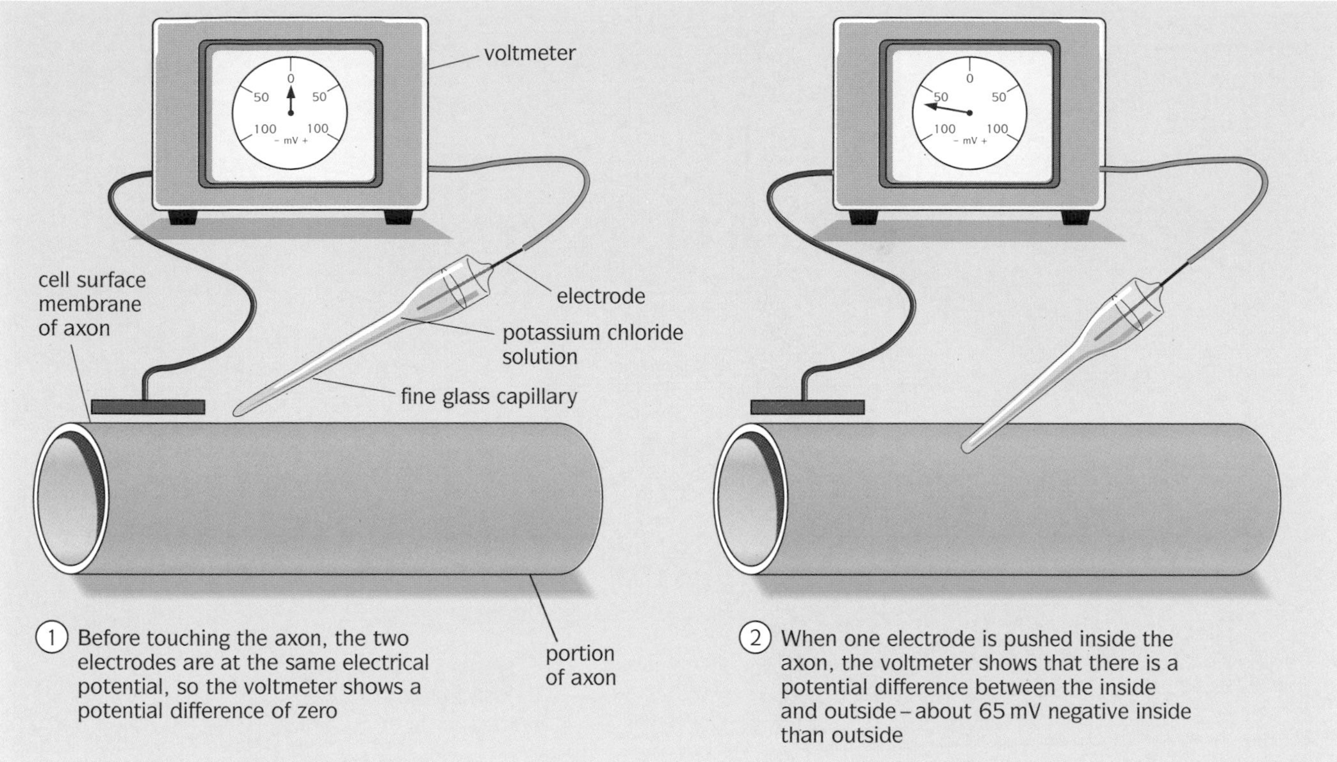

● ***Figure 6.16*** Measuring the resting potential of an axon.

In a resting axon, it is found that the inside of the axon always has a slightly negative electrical potential compared with the outside *(figure 6.17a)*. The difference between these potentials, called the **potential difference**, is often around −65 mV. In other words, the electrical potential of the inside of the axon is 65 mV lower than the outside.

The resting potential is produced and maintained by the **sodium–potassium pump** in the cell surface membrane of the axon *(figure 6.17b)*. Sodium ions, Na^+, are picked up from the cytoplasm by a carrier protein in the membrane and carried to the outside. At the same time, potassium ions, K^+, are brought into the cytoplasm from the external fluids. Both of these processes involve moving the ions against their concentration gradients, and so use energy from the hydrolysis of ATP.

The sodium–potassium pump removes three sodium ions from the cell for every two potassium ions it brings into the cell. Moreover, K^+ diffuses back out again much faster than Na^+ diffuses back in. The end-result is an overall excess of positive ions outside the membrane compared with the inside.

Action potentials

With a small addition to the apparatus shown in *figure 6.16*, it is possible to stimulate the axon with a very brief, small electric current *(figure 6.18)*. If this is done, the steady trace on the oscilloscope suddenly changes. The potential difference across the cell surface membrane of the axon suddenly switches from −65 mV to +40 mV. It swiftly returns to normal after a brief 'overshoot' *(figure 6.19)*. The whole process takes about 3 ms (milliseconds).

This rapid, fleeting change in potential difference across the membrane is called an **action potential.** It is caused by changes in the permeability of the cell surface membrane to Na^+ and K^+.

First, the electric current used to stimulate the axon causes the opening of channels in the cell surface membrane which allow sodium ions to pass through. As there is a much greater concentration of sodium ions outside the axon than inside, they flood in through the open channels. The now relatively high concentration of positively charged sodium ions *inside* the axon makes it less negative

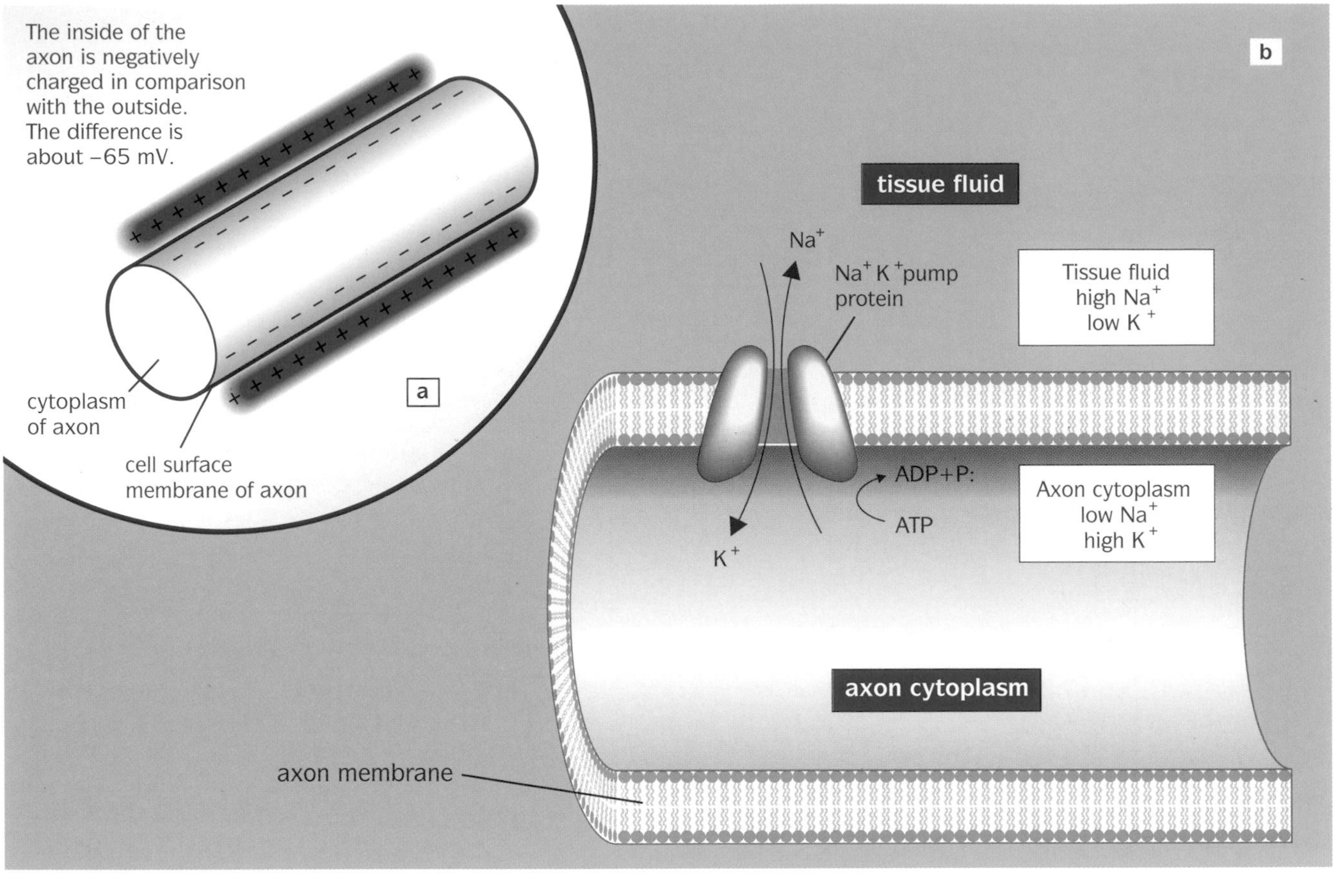

● ***Figure 6.17*** **a** At rest, an axon has negative electrical potential inside. **b** The sodium–potassium pump maintains the resting potential by keeping more sodium ions outside than there are potassium ions inside.

inside than it was before. The membrane is said to be **depolarised.** As sodium ions continue to flood in, the inside of the axon swiftly continues to build up positive charge, until it reaches a potential of +40 mV compared with the outside.

At this point, the sodium channels close, so sodium ions stop diffusing into the axon. At the same time potassium channels open. Potassium ions therefore diffuse *out* of the axon, down their concentration gradient. The outward movement of potassium ions removes positive charge from inside the axon to outside, thus beginning to return the potential difference to normal. This is called **repolarisation.** So many potassium ions leave the axon that the potential difference across the membrane briefly becomes even more negative than the normal resting potential. The potassium channels then close, and the sodium–potassium pump begins to act again, restoring the normal distribution of sodium and potassium ions across the membrane, and therefore restoring the resting potential.

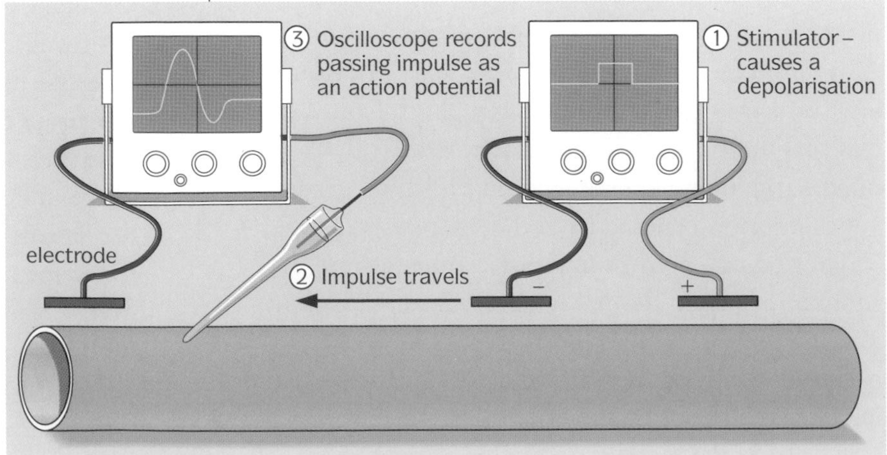

● ***Figure 6.18*** Recording an action potential.

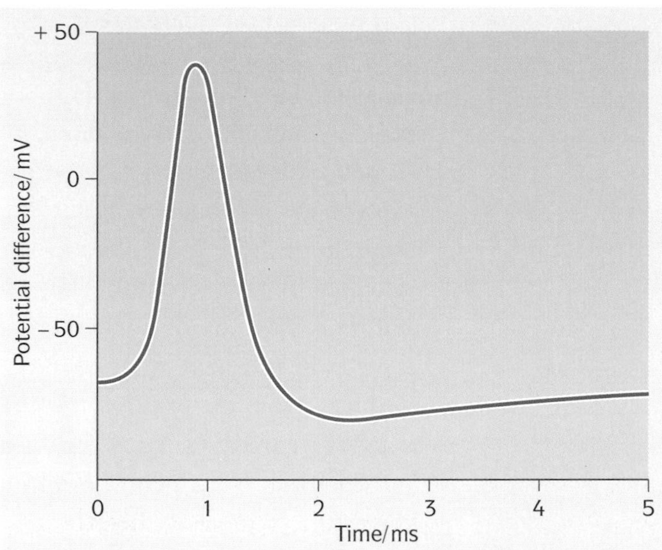

● ***Figure 6.19*** An action potential.

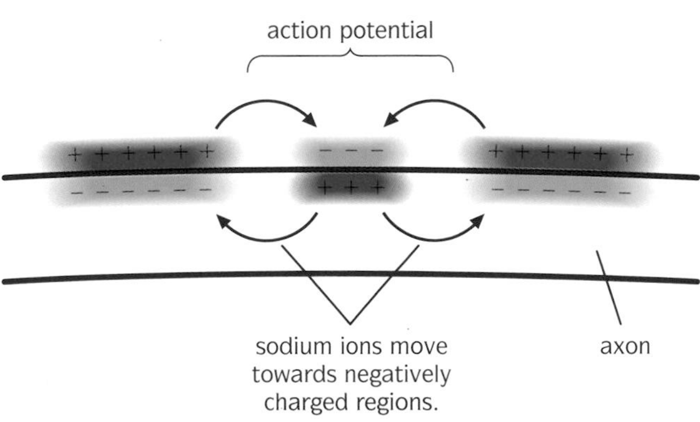

● ***Figure 6.20*** How action potentials are transmitted along an axon. Local circuits are set up between the region where there is an action potential and the resting regions. This causes the resting regions to depolarise.

Transmission of action potentials

The description of an action potential above concerns events at one particular point in an axon membrane. However, the function of a neurone is to transmit information *along* itself. How do action potentials transmit information along a neurone?

An action potential at any point in an axon's cell surface membrane triggers the production of an action potential in the membrane on either side of it. *Figure 6.20* shows how it does this. The temporary depolarisation of the membrane where the action potential is causes a 'local circuit' to be set up between the depolarised region and the resting regions on either side of it. Sodium ions flow sideways inside the axon, away from the positively charged region towards the negatively charged regions on either side. This depolarises these adjoining regions and so generates an action potential in them.

In practice, if an action potential has been travelling in one direction from a point of stimulation, a 'new' action potential is only generated *ahead* of, and not behind, it. This is because the region behind it will still be recovering from the action potential it has just had and its distribution of sodium and potassium ions will not yet be back to normal. It is therefore incapable of producing a new action potential for a short time. This is known as the **refractory period.**

How action potentials carry information

Action potentials do not change in size as they travel. However long an axon is, the action potential will continue to reach a value of +40 mV inside all the way along. Moreover, the intensity of the stimulus which originally generated the action potential has absolutely no effect on the size of the action potential. A very strong light shining in your eyes will produce action potentials of precisely the same size as a dim light. Nor does the speed at which the action potentials travel vary according to the size of the stimulus. In any one axon, the speed of axon potential transmission is always the same.

What *is* different about the action potentials resulting from a strong and a weak stimulus is their **frequency**. A strong stimulus produces a rapid succession of action potentials, each one following along the axon just behind its predecessor. A weak stimulus results in fewer action potentials per second *(figure 6.21)*.

Moreover, a strong stimulus is likely to stimulate more neurones than a weak stimulus. While a weak stimulus might result in action potentials passing along just one or two neurones, a strong stimulus could produce action potentials in many more.

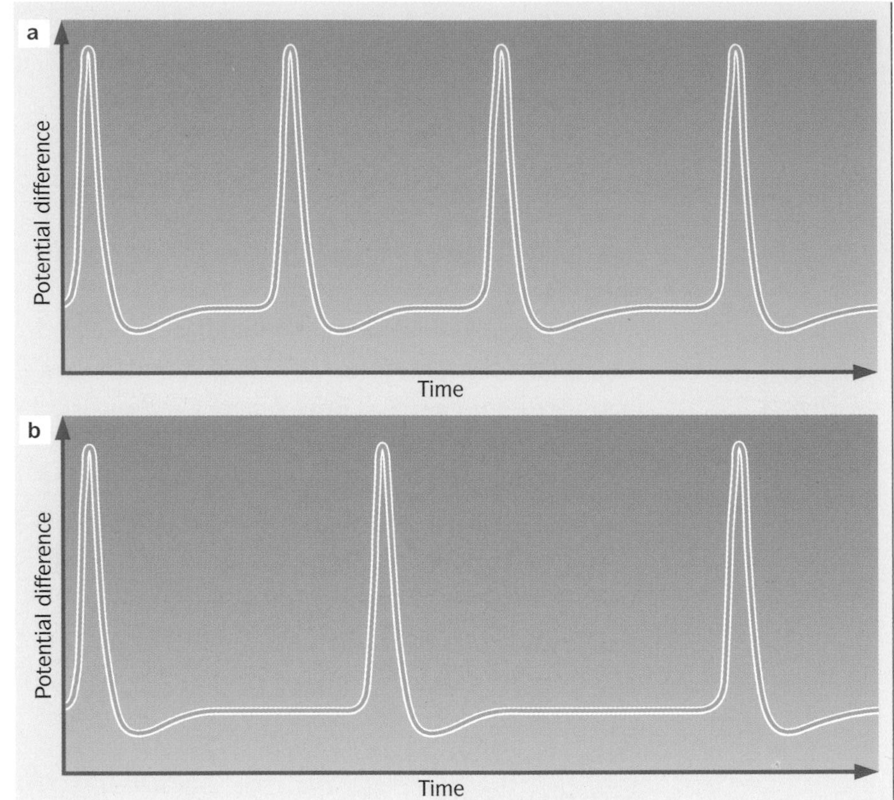

● ***Figure 6.21*** Action potentials resulting from **a** a strong stimulus and **b** a weak stimulus. Note that the size of each action potential remains the same, only their frequency changes.
a A high frequency of impulses is produced when a receptor is given a strong stimulus. This high frequency carries the message 'strong stimulus'.
b A lower frequency of impulses is produced when a receptor is given a weaker stimulus. This lower frequency carries the message 'weak stimulus'.

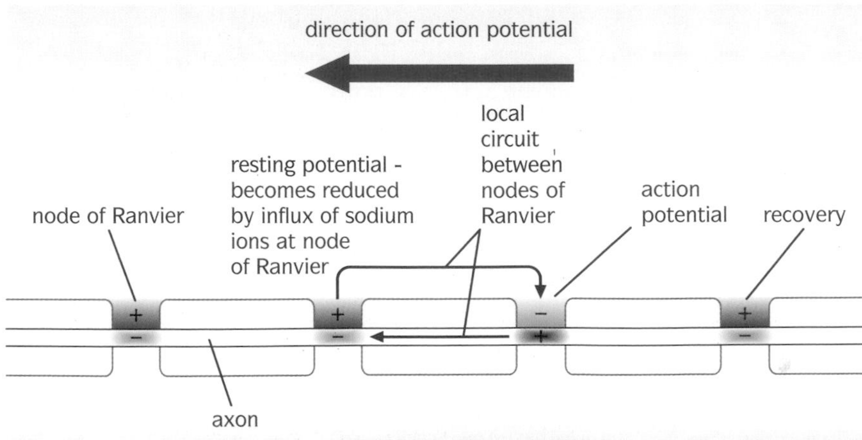

● ***Figure 6.22*** Transmission of an action potential in a myelinated axon. The myelin sheath acts as an insulator, preventing differences in potential across the parts of the axon membrane surrounded by this sheath. Potential differences can only occur at the nodes of Ranvier. The action potential therefore 'jumps' from one node to the next, travelling much more swiftly than in a non-myelinated axon.

The brain can therefore interpret the *frequency* of action potentials arriving along the axon of a sensory neurone, and the *number* of neurones carrying action potentials, to get information about the *strength* of the stimulus being detected by that receptor. The **nature** of the stimulus, whether it is light, heat, touch or so on, is deduced from the *position* of the sensory neurone bringing the information. If the neurone is from the retina of the eye, then the brain will interpret the information as meaning 'light'. If for some reason a different stimulus, such as pressure, stimulates a receptor cell in the retina, the brain will still interpret the action potentials from this receptor as meaning 'light'. This is why rubbing your eyes when they are shut can cause you to 'see' patterns of light.

Speed of conduction

In a myelinated human neurone, action potentials travel at up to $100\,\mathrm{m\,s^{-1}}$. In unmyelinated neurones, the speed of conduction is much slower, being as low as $0.5\,\mathrm{m\,s^{-1}}$ in some cases. Myelin speeds up the rate at which action potentials travel by insulating the axon membrane. Sodium and potassium ions cannot flow through the myelin sheath, so it is not possible for depolarisation or action potentials to occur in parts of the axon which are surrounded by it. They can only occur at the nodes of Ranvier.

Figure 6.22 shows how an action potential is transmitted along a myelinated axon. The local circuits that are set up stretch

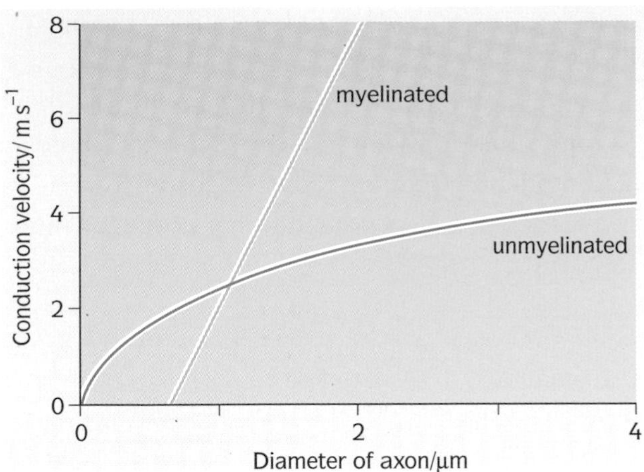

● ***Figure 6.23*** Speed of transmission in myelinated and non-myelinated axons of different diameters.

from one node to the next. Thus action potentials 'jump' from one node to the next, a distance of 1–3 mm. This can increase the speed of transmission by up to 50 times that of an unmyelinated axon of the same diameter.

Diameter also affects the speed of transmission *(figure 6.23)*. Thick axons transmit action potentials faster than thin ones. Earthworms, which have no myelinated axons, have a few very thick unmyelinated ones which run all along their body from head to tail. A bird peck at an earthworm's head sets up action potentials in these giant axons, which sweep along the length of the body, stimulating muscles to contract. The rapid response which results may enable the earthworm to escape.

What starts off an action potential?

In the description of the generation of an action potential on page 77, the initial stimulus was a small electric current. In normal life, however, action potentials are generated by a wide variety of stimuli, such as light, touch, sound, temperature or chemicals.

A cell which responds to such stimuli by initiating an action potential is called a **receptor cell**. Receptor cells are often found in sense organs. For example, light receptor cells are found in the eye and sound receptor cells are found in the ear. Some receptors, such as light receptors, are special cells which generate an action potential and send it on to a sensory neurone, while others, such as some kinds of touch receptors, are simply the ends of the sensory neurones themselves.

One type of receptor found in the dermis of the skin is a **Pacinian corpuscle** *(figure 6.25)*. Pacinian corpuscles contain an ending of a sensory neurone, surrounded by several layers of connective tissue, called a **capsule**. The ending of the sensory neurone inside the capsule has no myelin.

When pressure is applied to a Pacinian corpuscle, the capsule is pressed out of shape, and deforms the nerve ending inside it. This deformation causes sodium and potassium channels to open in the cell membrane, allowing sodium ions to flood in and potassium ions to flow out. This depolarises the membrane. The increased positive charge inside the axon is called a **receptor potential**. The harder the pressure applied to the Pacinian corpuscle, the more channels open and the greater the receptor potential becomes. If the pressure is great enough, then the receptor potential becomes large enough to trigger an action potential *(figure 6.26)*.

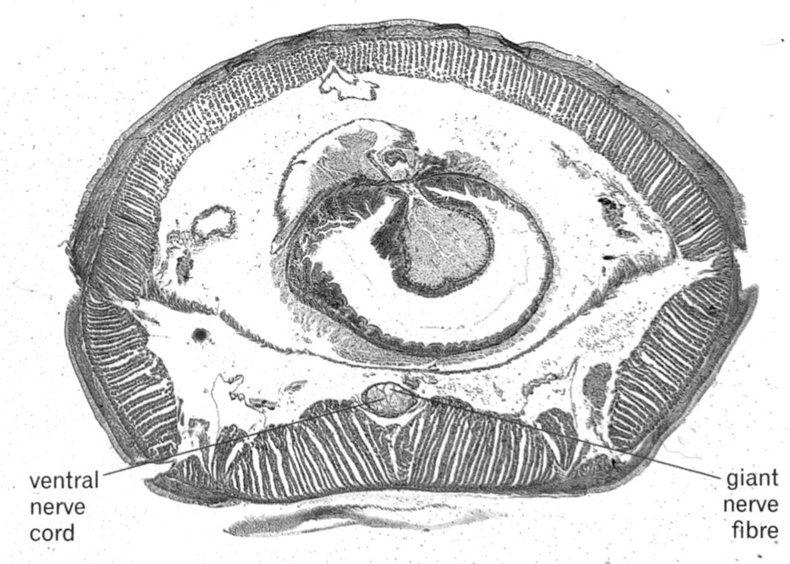

● ***Figure 6.24*** Transverse section of an earthworm (×20). The ventral nerve cord contains three giant nerve fibres. What is the diameter of the largest one?

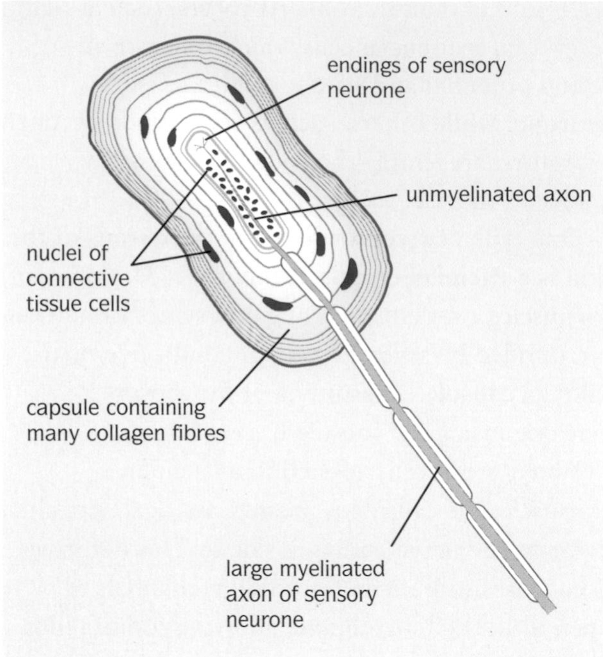

● ***Figure 6.25*** A Pacinian corpuscle. These corpuscles are found in the dermis, and are sensitive to pressure.

Below a certain threshold, therefore, the pressure stimulus only causes local depolarisation, not an action potential, and therefore no information is transmitted to the brain. Above this threshold, action potentials are initiated. As the pressure increases, the action potentials are produced more frequently.

SAQ 6.6

Use *figure 6.26* to answer these questions.

a What is a *receptor potential*?

b Describe the relationship between the pressure applied to a Pacinian corpuscle and the size of the receptor potential which is generated.

c What is the *threshold receptor potential*?

d Describe the relationship between the strength of the stimulus applied and the frequency of action potentials generated.

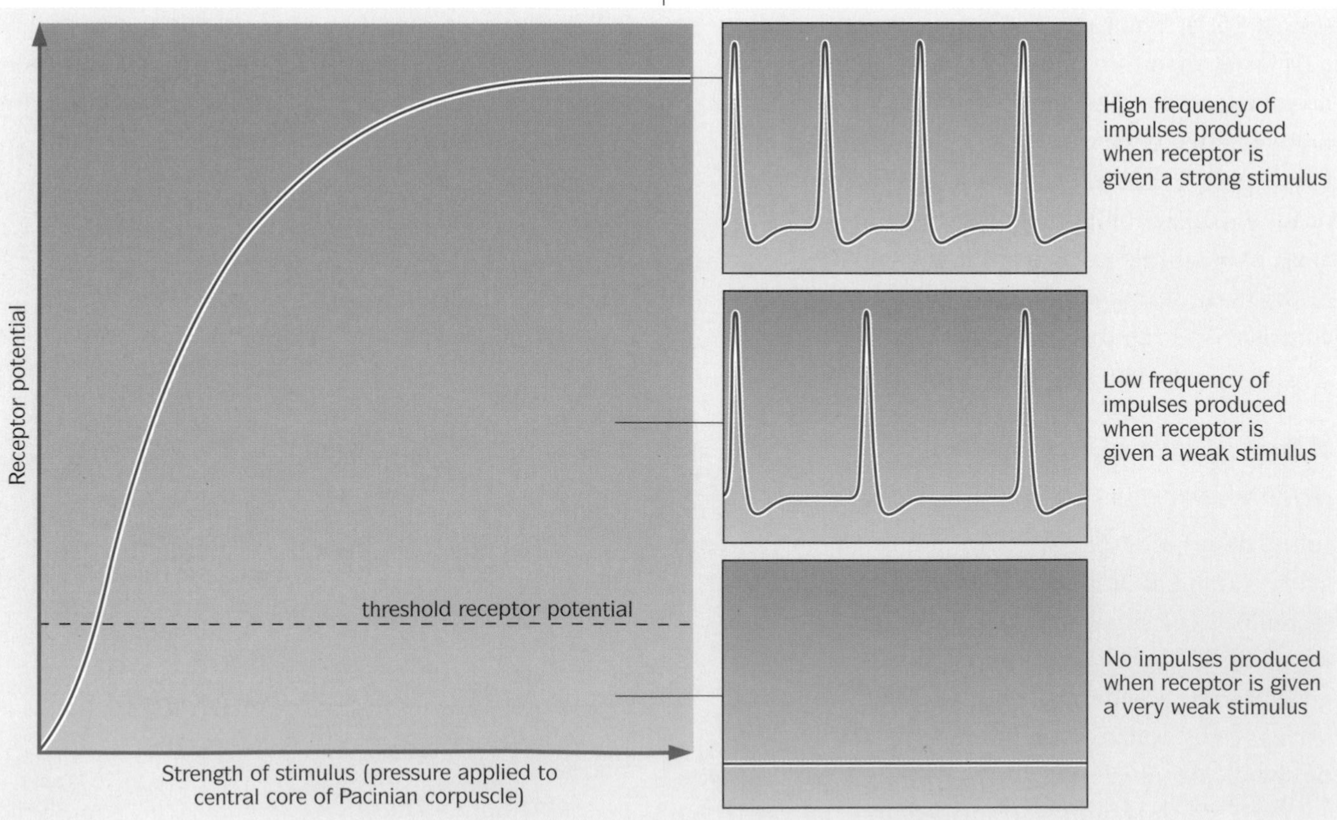

● ***Figure 6.26*** As pressure is applied to the inner bulb of a Pacinian corpuscle, it produces a depolarisation of the membrane of the sensory nerve ending. This is called the receptor potential. Greater pressures produce greater receptor potentials. If the receptor potential reaches a particular size, called the threshold, then an action potential is triggered.

Synapses

Where two neurones meet, they do not quite touch. There is a very small gap, about 20 nm wide, between them. This gap is called the **synaptic cleft.** The parts of the two neurones near to the cleft, plus the cleft itself, make up a **synapse** *(figure 6.27)*.

The mechanism of synaptic transmission

Action potentials cannot jump across synapses. Instead, the signal is passed across by a chemical, known as a **transmitter substance.** In outline, an action potential arriving along the cell surface membrane of the first, or **presynaptic**, neurone, causes it to release transmitter substance into the cleft. The transmitter substance molecules diffuse across the cleft, which takes less than a millisecond as the distance is so small. This may set up an action potential in the cell surface membrane of the second, or **postsynaptic**, neurone.

Let us look at these processes in more detail. The cytoplasm of the presynaptic neurone contains vesicles of transmitter substance *(figure 6.28)*. More than 40 different transmitter substances are known; **noradrenaline** and **acetylcholine** are found throughout the nervous system, while others such as **dopamine** and **glutamic acid** occur only in the brain. For the moment, we will concentrate on synapses which use acetylcholine (ACh) as the transmitter substance. These are known as **cholinergic synapses.**

You will remember that, as an action potential sweeps along the cell surface membrane of a neurone, local circuits depolarise the next piece of membrane, opening sodium channels and so propagating the action potential. In the part of the membrane of the presynaptic neurone which is next to the synaptic cleft, the arrival of the action potential also causes **calcium channels** to open. Thus, the action potential causes not only sodium ions but also calcium ions to rush in to the cytoplasm of the presynaptic neurone.

This influx of calcium ions causes vesicles of ACh to move to the presynaptic membrane and

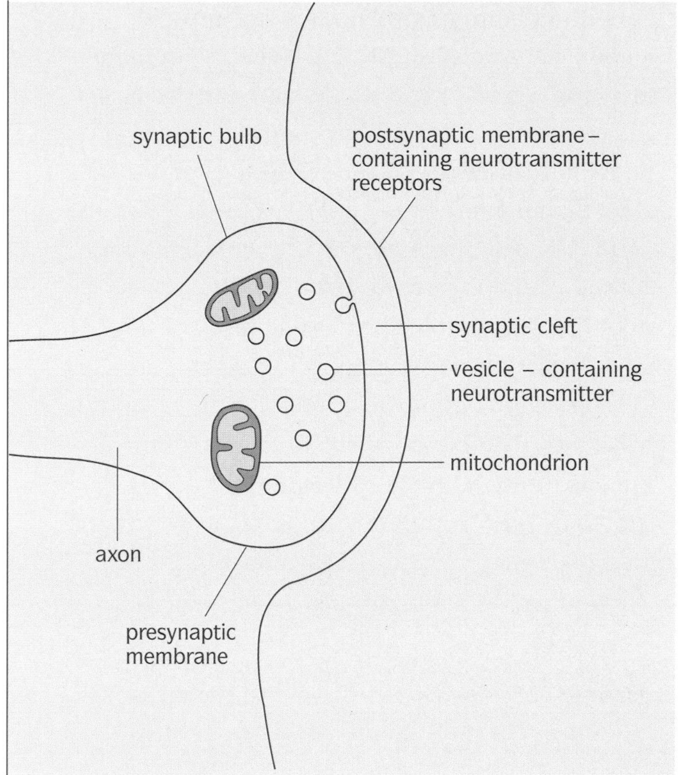

● ***Figure 6.27*** A synapse.

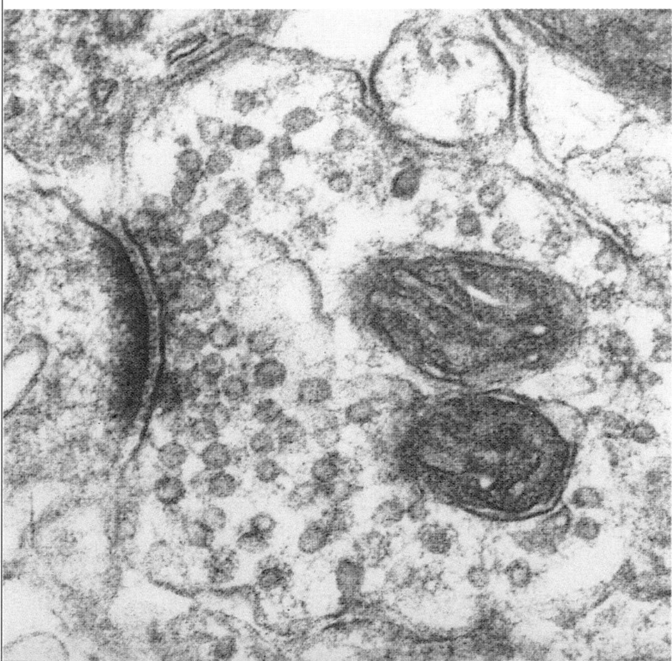

● ***Figure 6.28*** Electron micrograph of a synapse (×9000). The presynaptic neurone is to the right of the picture. Two mitochondria and numerous vesicles, which contain transmitter substance, can be seen. The postsynaptic neurone is darkly stained near the cell surface membrane close to the synaptic cleft.

fuse with it, emptying their contents into the synaptic cleft *(figure 6.29)*. Each action potential causes just a few vesicles to do this, and each vesicle contains up to 10 000 molecules of ACh. The ACh diffuses across the synaptic cleft, usually in less than 0.5 ms.

The cell surface membrane of the postsynaptic neurone contains **receptor proteins.** Part of the receptor protein molecule has a complementary shape to part of the ACh molecule, so that the ACh molecules can temporarily bind with the receptors. This changes the shape of the protein, opening channels through which sodium ions can pass *(figure 6.30)*. Sodium ions rush into the cytoplasm of the postsynaptic neurone, depolarising the membrane and starting off an action potential.

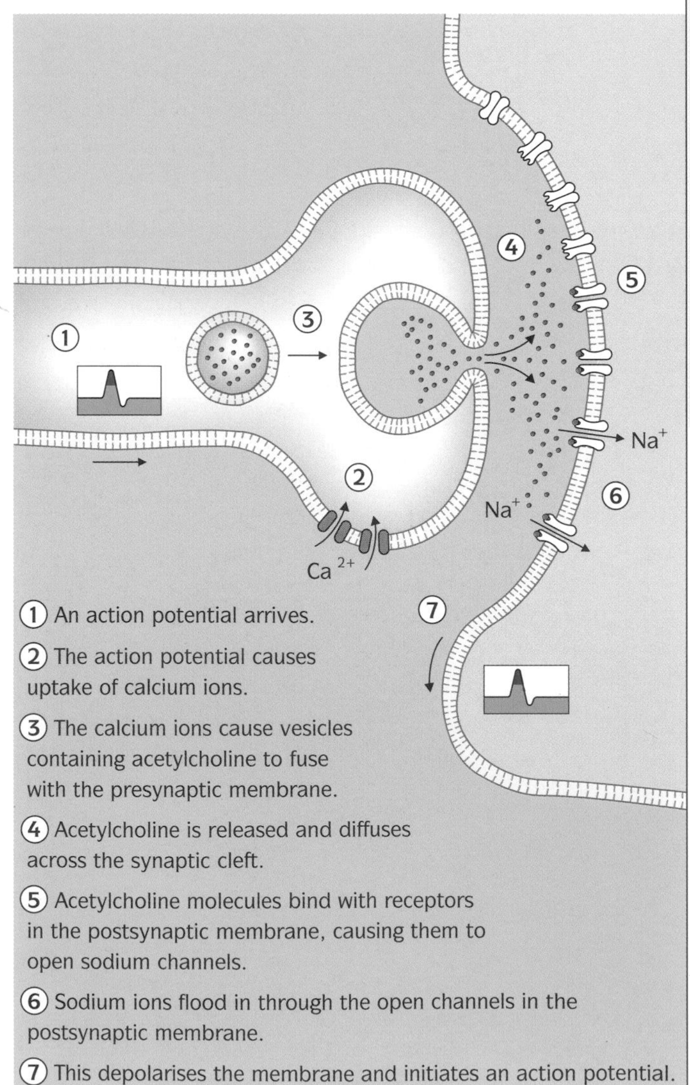

● ***Figure 6.29*** Synaptic transmission.

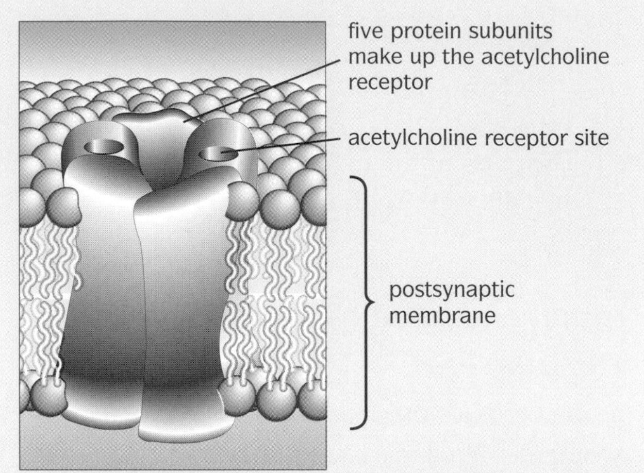

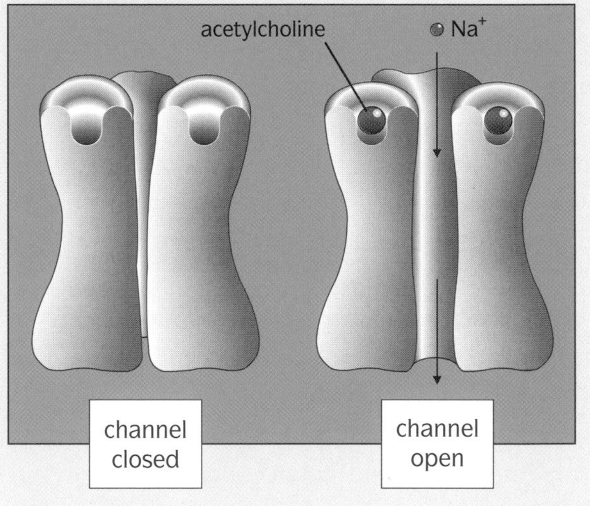

● ***Figure 6.30*** Detail of how the acetylcholine receptor works. The receptor is made of five protein subunits spanning the membranes arranged to form a cylinder. Two of these subunits contain acetylcholine receptor sites. When acetylcholine molecules bind with both of these receptor sites the proteins change shape, opening the channel between the units. Parts of the protein molecules around this channel contain negatively charged amino acids, which attract positively charged sodium ions and pull them through the channel.

If the ACh remained bound to the postsynaptic receptors, the sodium channels would remain open, and action potentials would fire continuously. To prevent this from happening, and also to avoid wasting the ACh, it is recycled. The synaptic cleft contains an enzyme, **acetylcholinesterase,** which splits each ACh molecule into acetate and choline.

The choline is taken back into the presynaptic neurone, where it is combined with acetyl coenzyme A to form ACh once more. The ACh is then transported into the presynaptic vesicles, ready for the next action potential. The entire sequence of events, from initial arrival of the action potential to the re-formation of ACh, takes about 5–10 ms.

At synapses using the transmitter substance noradrenaline, the recycling is done rather differently. Here, there is no enzyme to break down the noradrenaline molecules. Instead, they are actively absorbed back into the presynaptic neurone just as they are, and can be packed into vesicles again ready for reuse.

Much of the research on synapses has been done not at synapses between two neurones, but between a motor neurone and a muscle. These synapses are called **neuromuscular junctions** *(figure 6.31)*. They function in the same way as described above. An action potential is produced in the muscle, which may cause it to contract.

SAQ 6.7

Suggest why:

a impulses travel in only one direction at synapses;

b if action potentials arrive repeatedly at a synapse, the synapse eventually becomes unable to transmit the impulse to the next neurone.

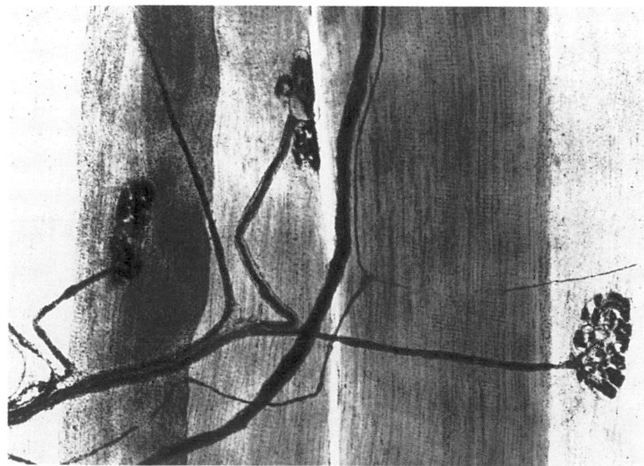

● ***Figure 6.31*** Light micrograph of neuromuscular junctions (×320). You can see how three of the axons terminate in a number of branches on the surface of the muscle fibre, forming motor end plates. Action potentials are passed from the axon to the muscle, across a synaptic cleft, at these end-plates.

The effects of other chemicals at synapses

Many drugs and other chemicals act by affecting the events at synapses.

Part of the **nicotine** molecule is similar in shape to ACh molecules, and will fit into the ACh receptors on postsynaptic membranes *(figure 6.32)*. This produces similar effects to ACh, initiating action potentials in the postsynaptic neurone or muscle fibre. Unlike ACh, however, nicotine is not rapidly broken down by enzymes, and so remains in the receptors for longer than ACh. A large dose of nicotine can be fatal.

The **botulinum toxin** is produced by an anaerobic bacterium which occasionally breeds in contaminated canned food. It acts at the presynaptic membrane where it prevents the release of ACh. Eating food that contains this bacterium is frequently fatal. However, the toxin does have important medical uses. In some people, for example, the muscles of the eyelids contract permanently, so that they cannot open their eyes. Injections of tiny amounts of the botulinum toxin into these muscles can cause them to relax, so allowing the lids to be raised.

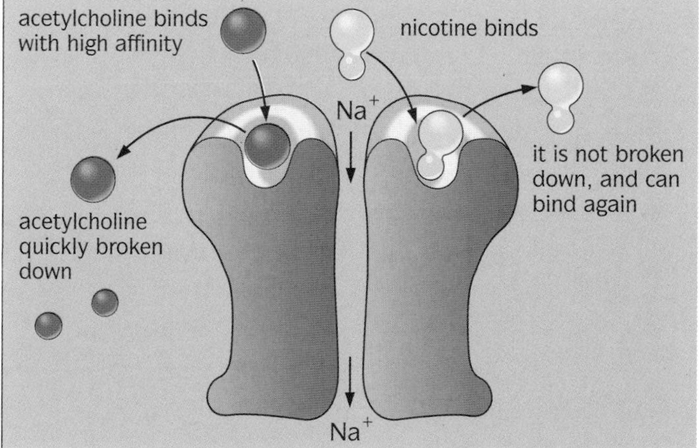

● ***Figure 6.32*** Nicotine molecules have similarities in shape to acetylcholine molecules, and will fit into some acetylcholine receptor sites causing sodium channels to open. So nicotine can generate action potentials in postsynaptic neurones. Not all acetylcholine receptors are equally responsive to nicotine; those at neuromuscular junctions have only a low affinity for nicotine.

Organophosphorous insecticides inhibit the action of acetylcholinesterase, thus allowing ACh to cause continuous production of action potentials in the postsynaptic membrane. Many flea sprays for cats and dogs contain organophosphorous insecticides. Several **nerve gases** also act in this way.

The roles of synapses

Synapses slow down the rate of transmission of a nervous impulse. Responses to a stimulus would be much quicker if action potentials generated in a receptor travelled along an unbroken neuronal pathway from receptor to effector, rather than having to cross synapses on the way. So why have synapses?

- *Synapses ensure one-way transmission*
  Signals can only pass in one direction at synapses. This allows signals to be directed towards specific goals, rather than spreading at random through the nervous system.
- *Synapses increase the possible range of actions in response to a stimulus*
  Synapses allow a wider range of behaviour than could be generated in a nervous system in which neurones were directly 'wired up' to each other. Think for a moment of your possible behaviour when you see someone you know across the street. You can call out to them and walk to meet them, or you can pretend not to see them and hurry away. What decides which of these two responses, or any number of others, you will make?

  Your nervous system will receive information from various sources about the situation. Receptors in your eyes will provide details about who the person is, and whether they have seen you or not. Stored away in your brain will be memories about the person – good friend? something you want to talk about with them? boring?

  Your brain will also have other information to consider – are you in a hurry? have you time to kill?

  All of these pieces of information will produce action potentials in many neurones in your nervous system. As a result of this, action potentials may or may not be sent to the muscles of your legs to make them turn and carry you across the street.

  The way in which the 'turn' and 'not turn' decision is reached in your nervous system depends on what happens at synapses. Each neurone within the brain has many, often several thousand, synapses with other neurones. Action potentials arriving at some of these synapses will **stimulate** an action potential in the neurone, as described on page 84. Action potentials arriving at others will cause the release of transmitter substances which, far from producing an action potential in the neurone, will actually make it *more* difficult to depolarise its cell surface membrane, and so **inhibit** the production of an action potential. Whether or not an action potential is produced depends on the summed effect of the number and frequency of action potentials arriving at all the stimulatory and inhibitory synapses on that particular neurone. In very simple terms, if the action potentials carrying 'good friend' information outweigh those carrying 'in a hurry' information, you will probably decide to turn towards the person even if it may make you late for your appointment.

  The loss of *speed* in this response is more than compensated for in the possible *variety* of responses which can be made. We *do* have, however, some very rapid and very stereotyped responses. These are called **reflex actions**, and involve quick, automated responses to stimuli. Two examples are blinking when an object speeds towards your eye, or jumping when you hear an unexpected noise. In a reflex action, there are normally only two or three neurones involved: a sensory neurone and a motor neurone, with perhaps an intermediate neurone in between (*figure 6.14*). These actions are ones where the survival value of a very rapid response is greater than the value of a carefully considered one.

- *Synapses are involved in memory and learning* Despite much research, little is yet known about how memory operates. However, there is much evidence that it involves synapses. For example, if your brain frequently receives information about two things at the same time, say a sound of a particular voice and a sight of a particular face, then new synapses are thought to form in your brain which link the neurones involved in the passing of information along the particular pathways from your ears and eyes. In future, when you hear the voice, information flowing from your ears along this pathway automatically flows into the other pathway too, so that your brain 'pictures' the face which goes with the voice.

SUMMARY

- Control systems involve receptors, a communication method, and effectors. Regulatory control systems also involve negative feedback.
- Animals use both hormones and neurones to communicate between receptors and effectors. Hormones are made in endocrine glands and transported in blood plasma to their target cells, where they bind to specific receptors and so affect the behaviour of the cells.
- Blood glucose levels are controlled by the action of insulin and glucagon, which are secreted by the islets of Langerhans in the pancreas and affect liver and muscle cells. Negative feedback keeps the blood glucose level from varying too much from the norm.
- Neurones are cells adapted for the rapid transmission of electrical signals. Sensory neurones transmit signals from receptors to the central nervous system (brain and spinal cord); motor neurones transmit signals from the central nervous system to effectors; intermediate neurones transmit signals within the central nervous system. In vertebrates, the axons of many neurones are insulated by a myelin sheath which speeds up transmission.
- Signals are transmitted as action potentials. A resting neurone has a negative potential inside compared with outside. An action potential is a fleeting reversal of this potential, caused by changes in permeability of the cell surface membrane to potassium and sodium ions. Action potentials are always the same size. Information about the strength of a stimulus is given by the frequency of action potentials produced.
- Action potentials may be initiated within the brain or at a receptor. Receptors respond to information from the environment. Environmental changes result in permeability changes in the membranes of receptor cells, which in turn produce changes in potential difference across the membrane. If sufficiently great, this will trigger an action potential.
- Neurones do not make direct contact with one another, but are separated by a very small gap called a synaptic cleft. Impulses pass across this gap as bursts of transmitter substance, released by the presynaptic neurone when an action potential arrives. Any one neurone within the central nervous system is likely to have at least several hundred synapses with other neurones, some of which will be stimulatory and some inhibitory. This allows integration within the nervous system, resulting in complex and variable patterns of behaviour, and in learning and memory.

Questions

1 Discuss the ways in which the structure of a motor neurone is related to its function.

2 Compare and contrast the ways in which the nervous system and the endocrine system bring about communication between different parts of the body.

Appendix Formulae of the naturally occurring amino acids

The general formula for an amino acid is shown in figure 3.15. In the list below, only the R groups are shown; the rest of the amino acid molecule is represented by a block.

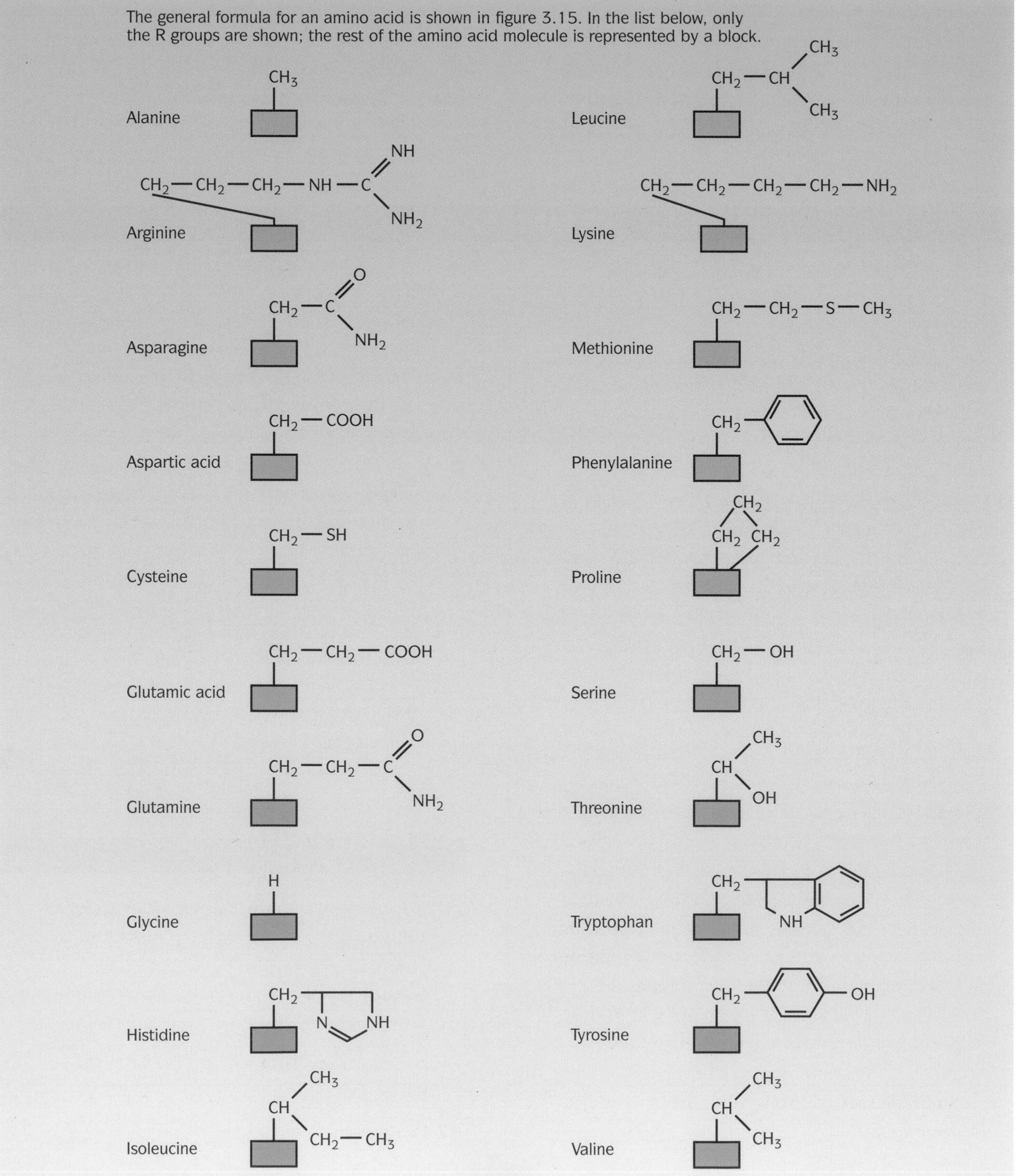

Answers to self-assessment questions

Chapter 1

1.1 *Structures found in both animal and plant cells*: nucleus with nucleolus and chromatin; cytoplasm containing mitochondria, Golgi apparatus and other small structures; cell surface membrane.
Structure found only in animal cells: centriole.
Structures found only in plant cells: chloroplasts, large central vacuole, cell wall with middle lamella and plasmodesmata.

1.2 *Detail seen with electron microscope*: in the **nucleus**, chromatin can be distinguished; the nucleus is seen to be surrounded by a double membrane with **pores** in it; **mitochondria** have surrounding double membrane, the inner layer forming folds pointing inwards; **endoplasmic reticulum** is extensive throughout cell, some with **ribosomes** and some without; small structures seen under the light microscope can be distinguished as **lysosomes** and **vesicles**; free **ribosomes** seen throughout cell; **centriole** consists of two structures. (The microvilli seen on *figure 1.11* are not characteristic of all cells.)

1.3 *Details seen with electron microscope*: in the **nucleus**, chromatin can be distinguished; **nuclear membrane** can be seen as a double structure, continuous with rough endoplasmic reticulum, and with **pores** in it; there is extensive **rough** and **smooth endoplasmic reticulum** throughout cell; free **ribosomes** in cytoplasm; **mitochondria** have double membrane, the inner layer having folds into matrix in middle; **chloroplasts** have double outer membrane; **grana** can be seen as stacks of double membrane sacs connected to other grana by longer sacs.

Chapter 2

2.1 The chromosomes are arranged in order of size in the karyotype.

2.2 See *figure*.

There are eight possible different gametes:

parent nucleus

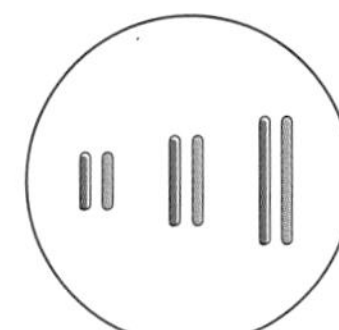

assuming short, medium, and long homologous pairs (total of 6 chromosomes, 2 sets of 3)

possible types of gamete:

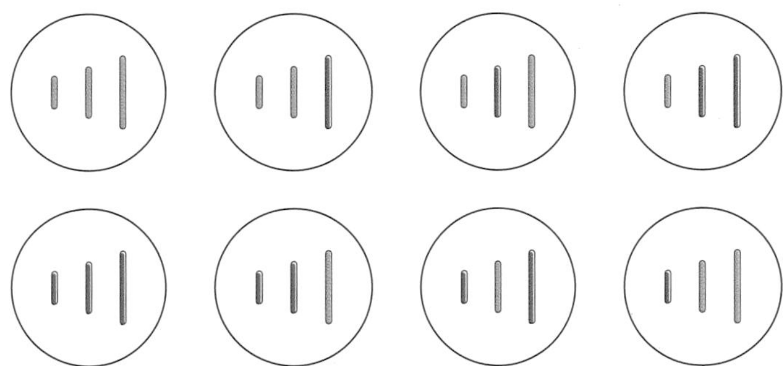

Rules: must be three chromosomes, one from each homologous pair

● ***Answer for*** SAQ 2.2

2.3 2^n where n = haploid number. In SAQ 2.2, $2^n = 2^3 = 8$ possible types of gametes.

2.4 $2^n = 2^{23} = 8\ 388\ 608$ (about 8 million).

2.5 $2^{23} \times 2^{23} = 2^{46}$ = about 64 million million.

Chapter 3

3.1 **a** $C_3H_6O_3$ or $(CH_2O)_3$ **b** $C_5H_{10}O_5$ or $(CH_2O)_5$

3.2 Hydrolysis

Chapter 4

4.1 In case of inaccuracy of measurement at 30 seconds. The shape of the curve is more likely to give an accurate value.

4.2 See *figure*.

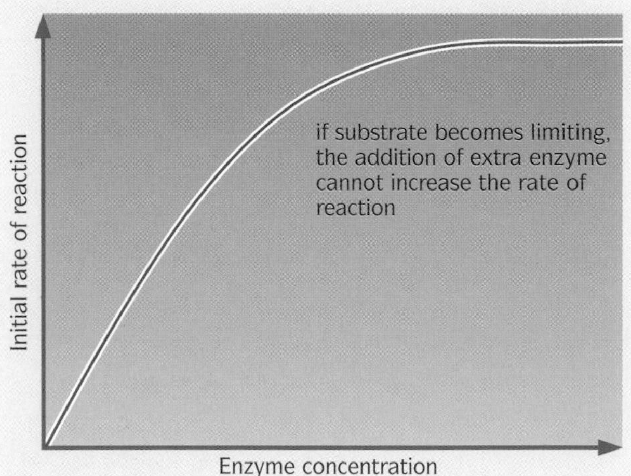

● ***Answer for*** SAQ 4.2

4.3 **a** See *figure*.

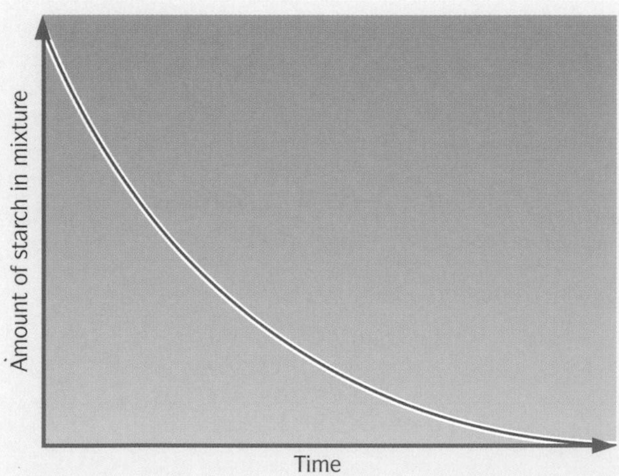

● ***Answer for*** SAQ 4.3a

b Calculate the slope of the curve right at the beginning of the reaction.

4.4 Measure the volume of oxygen given off over time for several hydrogen peroxide–catalase reactions at different temperatures. In each case, all conditions other than temperature must remain constant. In particular, the same volume of hydrogen peroxide and of catalase solutions should be used each time. Plot total volume of oxygen against time for each reaction. Calculate the slope of the line at the beginning of the reaction in each case to give the initial reaction rate. Then plot initial reaction rate against time.

4.5 **a** Haemoglobin colours blood stains. Protein-digesting enzymes hydrolyse haemoglobin to amino acids, which are colourless. They are also soluble, so will wash away in water.

b Many protein-digesting enzymes have an optimum temperature of around 40 °C.

c Other components of washing powders, such as the oil-removing detergents, work best at high temperatures.

4.6 One possible answer is as follows; other answers might be equally acceptable.

Set up two sets of five tubes containing equal volumes of the same concentration of milk suspension. Make up five buffer solutions of varying pH. Add equal volumes of buffer solution to the milk suspension, two of each pH. To one set of tubes, add equal volumes of trypsin solution. To the other set of tubes, add the same volume of water; these act as controls. Time the disappearance of cloudiness in each tube. Plot rate of reaction (1/time taken) against pH.

Chapter 5

5.1 Large number of possible reasons, e.g. gain nutrients, remove waste products, gain oxygen for respiration, secrete hormones, secrete enzymes, maintain constant pH and ionic concentration.

5.2 **a** Solution **A** is more dilute and solution **B** is more concentrated.

b **A** has the higher concentration of water molecules.

c Water will move from solution **A** to solution **B** by osmosis.

5.3 Solution **A**. The solute potential is less negative and therefore higher than **B**.

5.4 **a** Hypotonic **b** Hypertonic **c** Isotonic

5.5 The animal cell does not have a cell wall. Plasmolysis is the pulling away of cytoplasm from the cell wall.

Chapter 6

6.1 The adrenal glands may continue to secrete adrenaline over a long period, for as long as the stimulus to do so continues.

6.2 The cell surface membrane is a bilayer of phospholipids. Steroids can dissolve in these lipids, and so pass through.

6.3 The lack of insulin, or the lack of response to insulin, means that cells either do not take up extra glucose when it is in excess, or they do not convert it to glycogen stores.

6.4 **a** Insulin is a protein. Its molecules would be hydrolysed to amino acids in the digestive system.

b People with non-insulin-dependent diabetes are encouraged to test their urine regularly for glucose. They can adjust their diet accordingly. They should eat small amounts of carbohydrate fairly regularly, rather than large quantities at any one time. High-sugar foods, such as confectionery, should be avoided, as these may result in a rapid and dangerous rise in blood glucose levels.

6.5 A wide variety of answers are possible, some of which are suggested below:

Stimulus	*Receptor*	*Effector*	*Response*
sudden loud sound	hair cells in cochlea of ear	various muscles especially in legs	rapid contraction producing movement
smell of food cooking	chemoreceptors in nose	salivary glands	secretion of saliva
sharp tap on knee	stretch receptors	thigh muscle	contraction, causing lower leg to be raised

6.6 **a** A receptor potential is an electrical potential generated in a receptor when a stimulus is applied. In a receptor such as a Pacinian corpuscle, it is produced by the opening of sodium channels which results in a depolarisation of the nerve ending (that is, a less negative potential inside the axon than when it is at rest).

b Increasing pressure produces an increasing receptor potential. At low levels of pressure, a small increase in pressure results in a relatively large increase in receptor potential. At higher levels of pressure, the increase in receptor potential is less. (The functional significance of this pattern, which is found in most receptors, could be discussed; it results in a relatively high level of sensitivity to low-level stimuli as long as they are above the critical threshold.)

c The threshold receptor potential is the smallest receptor potential at which an action potential is generated.

d The greater the strength of the stimulus applied, the greater the frequency of action potentials generated.

6.7 **a** Vesicles of transmitter substance are only present in the presynaptic neurone, not in the postsynaptic neurone.

b Repeated action potentials may cause the release of transmitter substance into the cleft at a greater rate than it can be replaced in the presynaptic neurone.

Index (Numbers in italics refer to figures.)